FCE
buster

152

Practice
Book

with Answer Key

with
2
Audio CDs

Contents map

	Topic	Reading	Grammar and Vocabulary	Use of English	Listening	Speaking
Unit 1 Our Society 8 – 13	Social Issues	Part 1 Multiple choice	Phrasal Verbs Revision of Tenses Word Formation	Part 4 Key word transformations	Part 2 Sentence completion	Part 1 Interview
Unit 2 Food for Thought! 14 – 19	Food and Nutrition	Part 2 Gapped text	Quantifiers Prefixes and Suffixes Food and Drink	Part 2 Open cloze	Part 3 Multiple matching	Part 3 Collaborative task
Unit 3 Be a Sport! 20 – 25	Sports Activities	Part 3 Multiple matching	Comparatives and Superlatives Extreme Sports	Part 3 Word formation	Part 1 Multiple choice	
Unit 4 Music and the Internet Revolution 26 – 31	Music and Technology	Part 1 Multiple choice	*the, a / an,* zero article Music and the Internet	Part 1 Multiple-choice cloze	Part 2 Sentence completion	Part 2 Long turn
Unit 5 Read on... 32 – 37	Reading Genres	Part 3 Multiple matching	Conjunctions Narrative Tenses Books	Part 2 Open cloze	Part 3 Multiple matching	Part 3 Collaborative task
Unit 6 Tomorrow's World 38 – 43	Jobs and Professions	Part 1 Multiple choice	Future Tenses Jobs	Part 3 Word formation	Part 4 Multiple choice	
Unit 7 What a Brainwave! 44 – 49	Inventions	Part 2 Gapped text	Passive Forms Phrasal Verbs	Part 4 Key word transformations	Part 2 Sentence completion	Part 4 Discussion
Unit 8 Happy Holidays! 50 – 55	Transport and Travel	Part 1 Multiple choice	*Wh-* questions Question Tags Holidays	Part 3 Word formation	Part 1 Multiple choice	
Unit 9 Man's Best Friend 56 – 61	The Animal Kingdom	Part 2 Gapped text	Determiners Animal Idioms	Part 1 Multiple-choice cloze	Part 4 Multiple choice	
Unit 10 Are you a Fashion Fanatic? 62 – 67	Fashion and Trends	Part 3 Multiple matching	Emphatic structures with *what* Past Habits Phrasal Verbs Fashion and Clothes	Part 2 Open cloze	Part 3 Multiple matching	Part 4 Discussion

	Topic	Reading	Grammar and Vocabulary	Use of English	Listening	Speaking
Unit 11 Keep up Appearances 68 – 73	Feelings	Part 1 Multiple choice	Suffixes Personality Adjectives	Part 1 Multiple-choice cloze	Part 2 Sentence completion	Part 2 Long turn
Unit 12 It all Ads up! 74 – 79	Advertising	Part 2 Gapped text	Relative Pronouns and Clauses Advertising and the Media	Part 4 Key word transformations	Part 2 Sentence completion	Part 2 Long turn
Unit 13 Break a Leg! 80 – 85	Entertainment	Part 1 Multiple choice	Gerund and Infinitives Entertainment	Part 3 Word formation	Part 3 Multiple matching	Part 1 Interview
Unit 14 Get yourself an Education! 86 – 91	Education	Part 2 Gapped text	Modal Verbs Education	Part 4 Key word transformations	Part 4 Multiple choice	
Unit 15 Sweet Dreams! 92 – 97	Sleep and Dreams	Part 2 Gapped text	Obligation, Necessity and Permission Dreams and Sleep	Part 4 Key word transformations	Part 2 Sentence completion	Part 2 Long turn
Unit 16 The Sounds of Music 98 – 103	Music	Part 3 Multiple matching	Phrasal Verbs Musical Instruments	Part 4 Key word transformations	Part 1 Multiple choice	
Unit 17 Big Spender! 104 – 109	Money and Shopping	Part 1 Multiple choice	Zero, First and Second Conditionals Money and Shopping	Part 1 Multiple-choice cloze	Part 4 Multiple choice	
Unit 18 City Life 110 – 115	Places and People	Part 3 Multiple matching	Conditionals Places we live in	Part 2 Open cloze	Part 3 Multiple matching	Part 2 Long turn
Unit 19 Man and Nature 116 – 121	Environment	Part 2 Gapped text	*Wish, If only, I'd rather* Natural Disasters and the Environment	Part 3 Word formation	Part 2 Sentence completion	Part 2 Long turn
Unit 20 Myths and Legends the World over 122 – 127	Mysteries	Part 3 Multiple matching	Say, tell, ask Myths and Legends	Part 1 Multiple-choice cloze	Part 4 Multiple choice	

Introduction

How FCE Buster Practice Book works

Reading

Step-by-step Practical Tips offer guidance with the strategies students need to use to pass all the Papers of the FCE Examination.

Each unit focuses on an individual part of the FCE Reading Paper with attractive, authentic, up-to-date magazine and newspaper articles, as well as literary texts, which make the task more meaningful for the students.

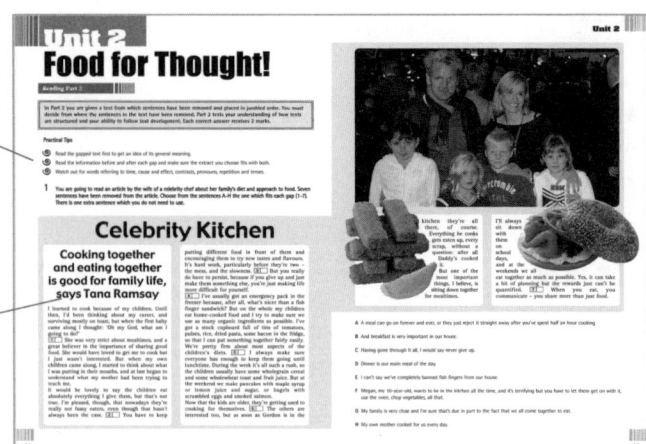

Vocabulary and Grammar

The Reading part is followed by a section dedicated to Vocabulary and Grammar. The lexis relates to the topic or theme of the unit and the grammar is that required by the FCE syllabus. Several exam-style tasks are provided as well as opportunities to practise the Vocabulary and Grammar through various fun activities.

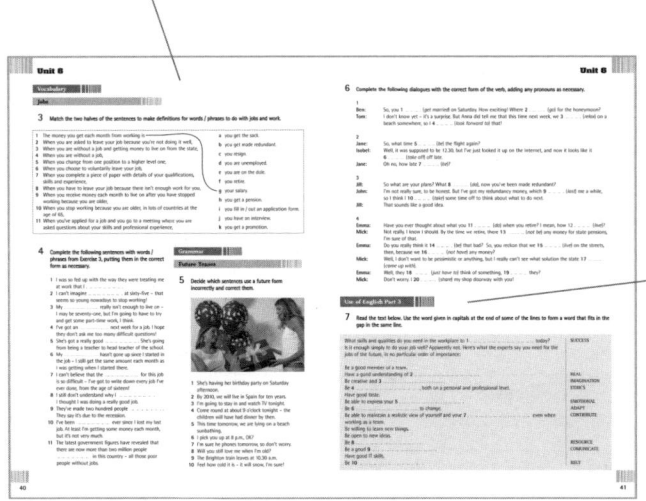

Use of English

Each unit includes one of the tasks from the FCE Use of English Paper:
Part 1: multiple-choice cloze
Part 2: open cloze
Part 3: word formation
Part 4: key word transformations.
There are five tasks for each part across the twenty units of the book, thereby providing equal practice of each task type. The texts for Parts 1-3 are linked thematically to the topic of the unit.

Listening

Each unit focuses on a different Part of the FCE Listening Paper. Students are introduced to the topic and lexis dealt with in the listening activity via pre-listening tasks.

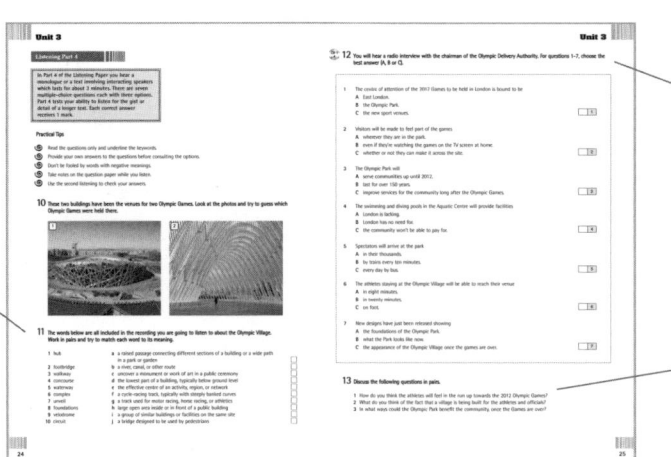

The listening texts are made up of authentic adapted material and are of the same level and length as those found in the FCE Examination.

Each listening task is followed by post-listening activities which give the students the opportunity to exchange opinions and ideas.

Speaking

Each unit covers a different part of the FCE Speaking Paper. Students are invited to describe photos or drawings or carry out problem-solving activities which are typically found in the FCE Examination.

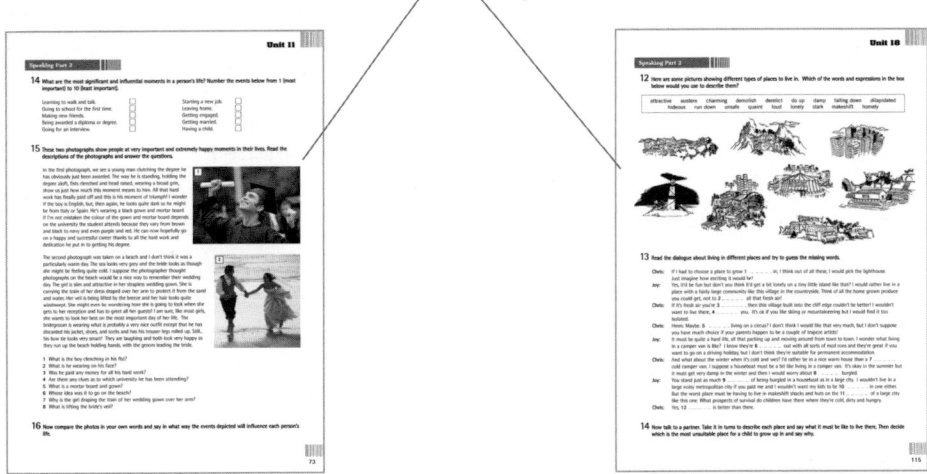

Writing Reference

At the end of the book there is an extensive Writing Reference which offers guidance and examples of the type of writing tasks the students are expected to produce at FCE level: informal letter, article, essay, letter of application, report, story, review, set text.

Each type of writing task is clearly presented and carefully explained, with the help of a model answer and follow-up activities of analysis and development.

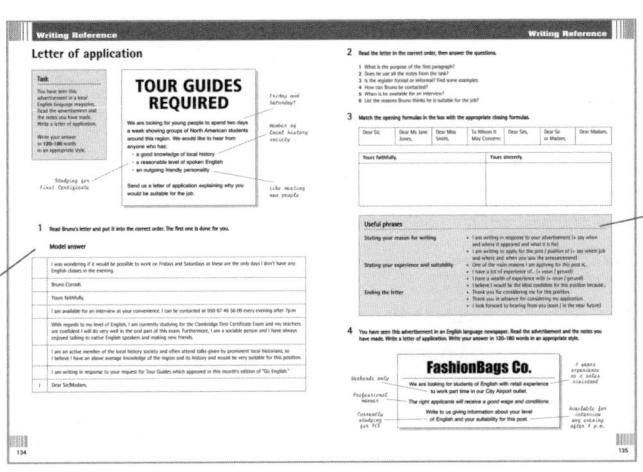

Useful phrases help students organise their writing and represent an efficient database of functional language.

FCE Practice Test

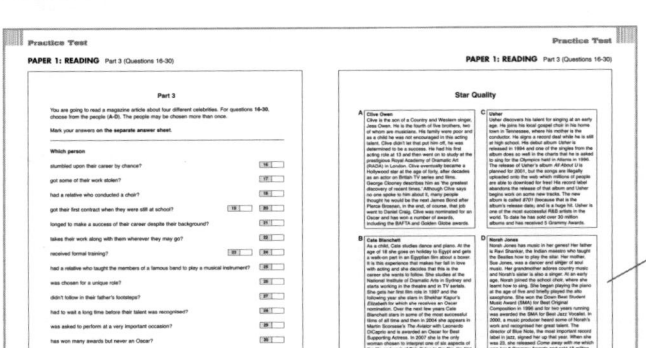

Further practice of the FCE Examination is offered in the FCE Practice Test which is provided at the end of the book. The recordings of the four parts of the Listening Paper are available on the CDs.

FCE Exam Overview

There are five Papers in the **Cambridge ESOL FCE** examination: **Reading, Writing, Use of English, Listening, Speaking.**
Each part is worth 20% of the total marks which are added together to determine the final grade.
Passing Grades: Grade A (80% and above)   Grade B (75% to 79%)   Grade C (60% to 74%)
Failing Grades: Grade D (55% to 59%)   Grade E (54% and below)

PAPER 1	READING		1 hour
Part	Task type and focus	Format	Number of questions
1	Multiple choice. Detail, opinion, gist, attitude, tone, purpose, main idea, meaning from context, text organisation features (exemplification, comparison, reference).	A text followed by four-option multiple-choice questions.	8
2	Gapped text. Text structure, cohesion and coherence.	A text from which sentences have been removed and placed in jumbled order after the text. Candidates must decide from where in the text the sentences have been removed.	7
3	Multiple matching. Specific information, detail, opinion and attitude.	A text or several short texts preceded by multiple-matching questions. Candidates must match prompts to elements in the text.	15

PAPER 2	WRITING		80 minutes
Part	Task type and focus	Format	Number of tasks and length
1	Question 1 Writing a letter or e-mail. Focus on advising, apologising, comparing, describing, explaining, expressing opinions, justifying, persuading, recommending and suggesting.	Candidates are required to deal with input material of up to 160 words. This may include material taken from advertisements, extracts from letters, e-mails, schedules, etc.	1 compulsory task 120-150 words
2	Question 2-4 Writing one of the following: an article, an essay, a letter, a report, a review, a story. Question 5 (Question 5 has two options) Writing one of the following, based on one of two prescribed reading texts: an article, an essay, a letter, a report, a review. Various focuses according to the task, including: advising, comparing, describing, explaining, expressing opinions, justifying, recommending.	A situationally based writing task specified in no more than 70 words.	One task to be selected from a choice of five. 120-180 words

PAPER 3	USE OF ENGLISH		45 minutes
Part	Task type and focus	Format	Number of questions
1	Multiple-choice cloze. Lexical / lexico-grammatical.	A modified cloze test containing 12 gaps and followed by 12 four-option multiple-choice items.	12
2	Open cloze. Grammatical / lexico-grammatical.	A modified cloze text containing 12 gaps.	12

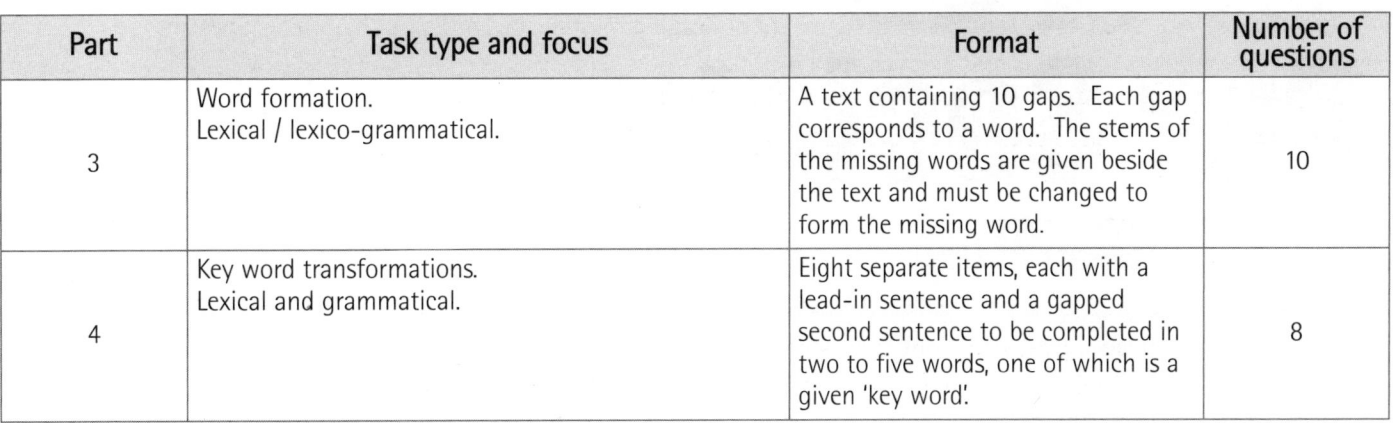

Part	Task type and focus	Format	Number of questions
3	Word formation. Lexical / lexico-grammatical.	A text containing 10 gaps. Each gap corresponds to a word. The stems of the missing words are given beside the text and must be changed to form the missing word.	10
4	Key word transformations. Lexical and grammatical.	Eight separate items, each with a lead-in sentence and a gapped second sentence to be completed in two to five words, one of which is a given 'key word'.	8

PAPER 4	LISTENING		40 minutes
Part	Task type and focus	Format	Number of questions
1	Multiple choice. General gist, detail, function, purpose, attitude, opinion, relationship, topic, place, situation, genre, agreement, etc.	A series of short unrelated extracts, of approximately 30 seconds each, from monologues or exchanges between interacting speakers. There is one multiple-choice question per text, each with three options.	8
2	Sentence completion. Detail, specific information, stated opinion.	A monologue or text involving interacting speakers and lasting approximately 3 minutes. Candidates are required to complete the sentences with information heard on the recording.	10
3	Multiple matching. General gist, detail, function, purpose, attitude, opinion, relationship, topic, place, situation, genre, agreement, etc.	Five short related monologues, of approximately 30 seconds each. The multiple-matching questions require selection of the correct option from a list of six.	5
4	Multiple choice. Opinion, attitude, gist, main idea, specific information.	A monologue or text involving interacting speakers and lasting approximately 3 minutes. There are seven multiple-choice questions, each with three options.	7

PAPER 5	SPEAKING		14 minutes
Part	Task type and focus	Format	Timing
1	A conversation between the interlocutor and each candidate (spoken questions).	General interactional and social language.	3 minutes
2	An individual 'long turn' for each candidate with a brief response from the second candidate. In turn, the candidates are given a pair of photographs to talk about.	Organising a larger unit of discourse; comparing, describing, expressing opinions.	4 minutes
3	A two-way conversation between the candidates. The candidates are given spoken instructions with written and visual stimuli, which are used in a decision-making task.	Sustaining an interaction; exchanging ideas, expressing and justifying opinions, agreeing and / or disagreeing, suggesting, speculating, evaluating, reaching a decision through negotiation, etc.	3 minutes
4	A discussion on topics related to the collaborative task (spoken questions).	Expressing and justifying opinions, agreeing and / or disagreeing.	4 minutes

Our Society

In Part 1 you are given a text with eight four-option multiple choice questions. Part 1 tests detailed understanding of a text, including the opinions and attitudes expressed in it. Each correct answer receives 2 marks.

Practical Tips

◎ Do not assume that an option is correct simply because it contains a word that is also in the text.

◎ Follow the order of the questions as they are in the same order as the information in the text.

◎ When dealing with incomplete sentences, make sure that the whole sentence matches what is written in the text and not just the phrase in option A, B, C or D.

1 Read the article about the introduction of ID cards in the UK and decide which of the following (1–3) best summarises the article.

1 In support of ID cards ☐
2 Some pros and cons of ID cards ☐
3 The case against ID cards ☐

The Great ID Card Debate

The UK does not currently have ID cards, but all that is about to change. From 2008, foreign nationals will get biometric identity cards, and the first ID cards will be issued to British citizens from 2009. The British Government says the cards 'will provide people with an easy and secure way of proving who they are.' Twenty-one out of twenty-five European Union member states already have them, but many British people don't want them. So what's the problem?

According to the British Government website, 'each ID card will be unique and will combine the cardholder's biometric data with their identity details called a 'biographical footprint'. These identity details and the biometrics will be stored on the National Identity Register (NIR). Basic identity information will also be held in a chip on the ID card itself. The government continues: 'This technology brings many benefits, including increased protection against identity theft or fraud'. These crimes are a growing problem in the UK – using ID cards with unique biometric data should make such crimes more difficult. The government also hopes that the cards will be a useful weapon in the fight against other major crime and terrorism.

Whilst there are clearly some benefits to it, the ID scheme does have its problems. It is going to be extremely expensive to introduce and maintain; the technology involved is new and the amount of information that needs to be stored is enormous. For the individual, too, ID cards could be expensive: if you are found not carrying your card, you will be fined up to £1000; and you will have to pay every time a change is made to your details, for example, if you move or get married – something that will hit the poorest members of society the hardest.

Many groups of people, including some MPs, are worried about the amount of information that the government will be able to hold about everyone in the UK. The new ID card law allows DNA information on every citizen to be stored. No one is yet sure how that information will be kept secret and who will have access to that information. A committee of MPs looking into human rights are also worried that certain ethnic groups, particularly Black and Asian, will have to show their cards much more than a white person.

There are convincing arguments for and against the use of ID cards and British people are divided about whether or not they are a good idea. What is certain is that over the next decade ID cards will be introduced, but it is not yet certain whether there will be a rebellion by people opposed to the cards. When an unpopular tax was introduced by the then Prime Minister Margaret Thatcher in the 1980s, it had to be scrapped because so many people were against it. Will the same happen with ID cards?

2 Read the article again. For questions 1-8, choose the answer (A, B, C or D) which you think fits best according to the text.

1 ID cards in the UK will be issued
A first to British citizens.
B first to foreigners living in Britain.
C to British citizens and foreigners at the same time.
D only to British citizens.

2 The new UK ID cards will include
A an individual's biography.
B a fingerprint and a footprint.
C information about an individual's identity.
D biological information about an individual.

3 The British government believes that ID cards will
A help prevent certain crimes.
B stop terrorism.
C be useful for people wrongly accused of committing a crime.
D stop rising crime in the UK.

4 One problem associated with the new ID scheme is the
A new technology needed for its introduction.
B high cost of its introduction and upkeep.
C enormous amount of space needed to keep all the information.
D practical difficulties of implementing it.

5 If citizens are found without their ID card, they
A will have to pay a penalty of £1000.
B will be arrested.
C will have to change their card.
D may have to pay a penalty of £1000.

6 In relation to the ID card scheme, some people in the UK are worried about
A having information about DNA stored.
B the government having the wrong information.
C privacy and access issues.
D MPs having access to personal information.

7 Another concern is that ID cards
A will lead to discrimination against certain groups of people.
B are a violation of human rights.
C will lead to discrimination against all ethnic groups.
D will cause inconvenience to people.

8 A government measure introduced in the UK in the 1980's
A was not as unpopular as the ID card scheme.
B caused a revolution in the UK.
C was abolished due to opposition from the public.
D had to be altered due to public pressure.

Vocabulary

Word Formation

3 Complete the table with the correct form of the word.

verb	noun	person noun	adjective	adverb
	1 *poverty*		poor	
	harmony		2	3
	refuge	4		
immigrate	5	6	7	
	8	citizen		
conflict	9		10	11
tolerate	12		13	14
negotiate	15	16	17	
	culture		18	19
integrate	20		21	
22	emigration	23	24	

4 Choose the correct word from the table in Exercise 3 to complete what the speakers say about different social issues.

Shirin
I came to live in the UK in 2001, with my family. It can be difficult to a *integrate* when you move to a new country, because, at first, everything is so different, so unfamiliar to you.

Rachel
I spent three months working at a health clinic in Uganda. I saw people who have almost nothing – I mean, living in complete b .... You can really understand why people that c .... would want to d .... to another country – they're looking for a better life for themselves and their children.

Mehmet
I had to escape from my country because of the e .... there. It was too dangerous to stay. Life is much better in the UK, but being an f .... in London is not always easy. Sometimes, people are really not very g ....

Grammar

Phrasal Verbs

5 Choose the correct particle/s to add to *make* to form a phrasal verb to match the definition.

after	for	into	off	off with
out	over to	up	up	

1 leave in a hurry, usually to escape
make ...*off*...
2 transfer sth to sb so that they own it
make sth ....:..*to*. sb
3 pursue sb
make .... sb
4 move in the direction of
make .... sth/sb/sw
5 see, hear or understand with difficulty
make sth/sb ....
6 transform
make sth .... sth
7 invent
make sth ....
8 run away with sth
make .... sth
9 form a number or amount
make .... sth

sth = something
sb = somebody
sw = somewhere

6 Match the two halves of the sentences.

1 The speaking part of the exam is just as important as the other parts;
2 Julie's boyfriend's accent is so strong
3 He regretted asking for a divorce
4 They broke into the shop in the middle of the night
5 After the argument with her parents,
6 When my bag was stolen,

a when the judge ordered him to make the family home over to his ex-wife. ☐
b it makes up 20% of the total score. ☐
c she made off as quickly as she could. ☐
d my friend made after the thief to try and get it back. ☐
e and made off with thousands of pounds worth of electrical equipment. ☐
f that I often can't make out what he's saying. ☐

Grammar

Revision of Tenses

7 Match each sentence to its function.

1 I went there in 1994.
2 He believes in God.
3 Have you ever been to London?
4 I'm writing a book, which has to be finished by Christmas!
5 I've been working all day – I'm exhausted!
6 I've had my cat for three years, now.
7 She lives in France.
8 Take this umbrella – it's raining.
9 The last train leaves at 11pm.
10 There has been an earthquake in China.

a an experience in the past, without mentioning an exact time ☐
b something that happened a short time ago, e.g. a news item ☐
c something that happened at a specific time in the past ☐
d something that started in the past which continues up to now ☐
e something that started in the past and continues up to now, with the emphasis on the continuation of the activity and/or the result of the action ☐
f a permanent state ☐
g a stative verb (be, like, prefer, believe, know, hear, etc.) ☐
h a timetabled event ☐
i an action happening now ☐
j a temporary situation in progress now ☐

8 Complete the sentences with the correct verb form – A, B, or C.

1 Britain .... a multicultural society.
A was always   B has always been   C was always being
2 The class .... at 4pm. Don't be late!
A starts   B has started   C started
3 She .... in the UK for a year, now.
A lived   B lives   C 's been living
4 My daughter .... Russian at the moment. Next term, it's Chinese!
A is studying   B studies   C has studied
5 The government .... its plans to introduce identity cards.
A has been announcing   B was announcing
C has announced
6 .... really terrified? I mean, so scared you couldn't move?
A Are you ever   B Have you ever been   C Are you
7 Wait a moment – I .... my emails.
A 've checked   B checked   C 'm just checking
8 How much .... about Britain?
A has she been knowing   B does she know
C is she knowing

Use of English Part 4

> In Part 4 there are eight questions, each with a lead–in sentence, a keyword in bold, and a gapped sentence. You have to complete the second sentence in two to five words, including the keyword, so that it has a similar meaning to the lead–in sentence. Do not change the form of the keyword.

Practical Tips

⊚ Try to deduce the meaning of the first sentence from its context.

⊚ Think of the transformation required in the second sentence; of the part of speech which is needed.

9 Complete the second sentence so that it has a similar meaning to the first sentence, using the word given.

1 The children are eager to listen to their mother reading them a story at bedtime.
LOOK
The children .... their mother reading them a story at bedtime.

2 There was so much noise that he had difficulty hearing what they were saying.
OUT
There was so much noise that he .... what they were saying.

3 I moved to this house a year ago.
LIVED
I .... in this house for a year.

4 Tom is in Spain on holiday.
HAS
Tom .... to Spain on holiday.

5 Britain is composed of four countries - England, Scotland, Wales and Northern Ireland.
UP
Britain is .... four countries - England, Scotland, Wales and Northern Ireland.

6 I started writing this report five hours ago and I'm still writing it now.
WRITING
I .... this report for five hours.

7 She was transformed into a celebrity, after winning a TV talent contest.
MADE
She was .... a celebrity, after winning a TV talent contest.

8 The last time I went to Paris was in 1985.
BEEN
I have .... 1985.

In Part 2 of the Listening Paper you hear a monologue or a dialogue involving different speakers which lasts for about three minutes. There are ten questions which take the form of notes with gaps in them, table completion or incomplete sentences. Part 2 tests your ability to listen for specific words or phrases and produce written answers in response to the sentences or note prompts. Each correct answer receives 1 mark.

Practical Tips

- Read the questions carefully, paying attention to the text both before and after the gap.

- Make sure you complete the gap with the words you hear. Do not paraphrase.

- Don't get stuck on one gap! If you can't fill it in, move on to the next and come back to it the second time you listen to the recording.

- Pay attention to your spelling, especially words which are spelt out in the recording.

- Go over your numbers, dates and times as they often correspond to the answers you are expected to fill in.

- Write clearly and don't leave any sentences incomplete.

10 This photograph shows a group of friends which come from different ethnic communities.

a Describe the people in the photograph and discuss the qualities you think people need in order to get on in a multicultural society.

b Are you familiar with the term *Asylum Seeker*? Do you think countries should provide these people with food and shelter? Does this provoke intolerance and resentment within the community? What is the situation in your country? Share your opinions with your partner.

 CD 1 2

11 You will hear an interview with a man from a voluntary organisation about a competition to promote equality and human rights. For questions 1–10, complete the sentences.

THE *ONE BIRMINGHAM* COMPETITION

According to Simon [**1**] of the population will be made up of ethnic minorities by 2020.

He visited schools and youth clubs to find out about young people's understanding of [**2**] relationships.

He found out that the positive opinions some people appear to have on the [**3**] are quite different when explored further afield.

One complaint was that Asylum seekers get whatever they want, while people born in the UK are obliged to go on a [**4**].

One boy declared that if forced to, he would safeguard the area against [**5**].

The *One Birmingham* competition seeks to strengthen [**6**] within the area.

The competitors have to come up with ideas to bring people from contrasting environments [**7**].

They have to choose a [**8**] to show their ideas with.

By *medium*, Simon means [**9**], photography, an article, or a film.

The winning prize is £500, which can be used to [**10**] the project they presented.

12 Now listen to the interview again and match the figures in the left-hand column to the facts in the right-hand column.

1 50
2 14–19
3 31
4 500

a the prize money. ☐
b the competition's closing date. ☐
c the age range of the competitors. ☐
d the percentage of ethnic communities in the future. ☐

Speaking Part 1

> In Speaking Part 1 the examiner asks you several questions and encourages you to give information about yourself, to talk about past experiences, present circumstances and future plans.
> Speaking Part 1 assesses your ability to provide basic personal information and opinions on a range of topics.

Practical Tips

- Try to give complete, spontaneous answers to the questions.

- Avoid rehearsing answers which will sound unnatural and might not be suitable for the questions asked.

- Practise social language by role-playing social occasions where you meet people such as parties or sports centres.

- Revise your past, present and future tenses in order to answer the questions accurately.

13 In pairs, work with a partner and ask each other the questions from each topic.

Homelife

Candidate A
1 Do you live in the town or the country? What's it like?
2 Are there a lot of green areas where you live?
3 Were you born in the town you live in?
4 Do you get on well with your neighbours?

Candidate B
1 Would you rather live in a small country village or a large chaotic city? Why?
2 What facilities does your town provide for the public?
3 Does your town ever become unbearable to live in? When and why?
4 If you could move house, where would you move to? Why?

Personal Experiences

Candidate A
1 Who has influenced you most in your life?
2 Do you have a lot in common with your friends?
3 What's the most interesting place you've ever visited?
4 Do you have any dreams for the future?

Candidate B
1 Who is the most important person in your life?
2 What is your best friend like?
3 What's the most exciting thing that's ever happened to you?
4 What are your plans for the future?

Leisure and Entertainment

Candidate A
1 What kind of books do you enjoy reading most?
2 What do you enjoy watching on TV?
3 Where's the best place to go in the evening in your town?
4 Tell me about your favourite actor or actress.

Candidate B
1 Tell me about a book you've read recently.
2 Where can you meet new people in your area?
3 How expensive is it to go out in the evening where you live?
4 How often do you go to the cinema?

Routines

Candidate A
1 Do you have a favourite day of the week? Which one? Why?
2 Did you go anywhere interesting last weekend?
3 How often do you go out in the evening?
4 Do you have too much time on your hands or not enough?

Candidate B
1 Do you usually do the same things every day?
2 What are you going to do this weekend?
3 Who do you normally go out with at weekends?
4 Do you have enough free time for a hobby?

Sport

Candidate A
1 What sports do you enjoy watching? Why?
2 Do you prefer individual or team sports?
3 What's the most popular sport in your country? Why is it so popular?
4 Which sports are the most dangerous in your opinion?

Candidate B
1 Would you rather watch or play sport? Why?
2 Are there plenty of places to do sports in your town?
3 If you could try a new sport, which would you choose? Why?
4 Do you think sportsmen earn too much? Why? Why not?

Unit 2
Food for Thought!

In Part 2 you are given a text from which sentences have been removed and placed in jumbled order. You must decide from where the sentences in the text have been removed. Part 2 tests your understanding of how texts are structured and your ability to follow text development. Each correct answer receives 2 marks.

Practical Tips

- Read the gapped text first to get an idea of its general meaning.
- Read the information before and after each gap and make sure the extract you choose fits with both.
- Watch out for words referring to time, cause and effect, contrasts, pronouns, repetition and tenses.

1 You are going to read an article by the wife of a celebrity chef about her family's diet and approach to food. Seven sentences have been removed from the article. Choose from the sentences A-H the one which fits each gap (1-7). There is one extra sentence which you do not need to use.

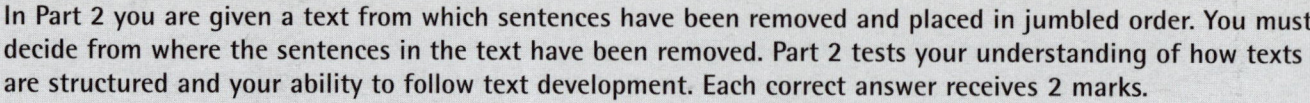

Celebrity Kitchen

Cooking together and eating together is good for family life, says Tana Ramsay

I learned to cook because of my children. Until then, I'd been thinking about my career, and surviving mostly on toast, but when the first baby came along I thought: 'Oh my God, what am I going to do?'
1 [ ] She was very strict about mealtimes, and a great believer in the importance of sharing good food. She would have loved to get me to cook but I just wasn't interested. But when my own children came along, I started to think about what I was putting in their mouths, and at last began to understand what my mother had been trying to teach me.

It would be lovely to say the children eat absolutely everything I give them, but that's not true. I'm pleased, though, that nowadays they're really not fussy eaters, even though that hasn't always been the case. **2** [ ] You have to keep putting different food in front of them and encouraging them to try new tastes and flavours. It's hard work, particularly before they're two – the mess, and the slowness. **3** [ ] But you really do have to persist, because if you give up and just make them something else, you're just making life more difficult for yourself.

4 [ ] I've usually got an emergency pack in the freezer because, after all, what's nicer than a fish finger sandwich? But on the whole my children eat home-cooked food and I try to make sure we use as many organic ingredients as possible. I've got a stock cupboard full of tins of tomatoes, pulses, rice, dried pasta, some bacon in the fridge, so that I can put something together fairly easily. We're pretty firm about most aspects of the children's diets. **5** [ ] I always make sure everyone has enough to keep them going until lunchtime. During the week it's all such a rush, so the children usually have some wholegrain cereal and some wholewheat toast and fruit juice. But at the weekend we make pancakes with maple syrup or lemon juice and sugar, or bagels with scrambled eggs and smoked salmon.

Now that the kids are older, they're getting used to cooking for themselves. **6** [ ] The others are interested too, but as soon as Gordon is in the kitchen they're all there, of course. Everything he cooks gets eaten up, every scrap, without a question: after all Daddy's cooked it.

But one of the most important things, I believe, is sitting down together for mealtimes.

I'll always sit down with them on school days, and at the weekends we all eat together as much as possible. Yes, it can take a bit of planning but the rewards just can't be quantified. **7** When you eat, you communicate – you share more than just food.

A A meal can go on forever and ever, or they just reject it straight away after you've spent half an hour cooking.

B And breakfast is very important in our house.

C Having gone through it all, I would say never give up.

D Dinner is our main meal of the day.

E I can't say we've completely banned fish fingers from our house.

F Megan, my 10-year-old, wants to be in the kitchen all the time, and it's terrifying but you have to let them get on with it, use the oven, chop vegetables, all that.

G My family is very close and I'm sure that's due in part to the fact that we all come together to eat.

H My own mother cooked for us every day.

Food and Drink

2 Match the phrases for quantities of food to the pictures.

1 a packet of pasta ☐
2 a can of soft drink ☐
3 a slice of bread ☐
4 a box of cereal ☐
5 a bottle of milk ☐
6 a piece of cake ☐
7 a tin of tuna ☐
8 a carton of juice ☐
9 a bar of chocolate ☐
10 a cup of coffee ☐
11 a bowl of cereal ☐
12 a packet of crisps ☐
13 a carton of milk ☐
14 a glass of juice ☐

3 Put the food from the pictures in Exercise 2 into the groups below according to their health rating, then add the following food items to the groups below.

| red meat   fruit   vegetables |
| butter   olive oil   low-fat cheese |
| rice   eggs   biscuits |

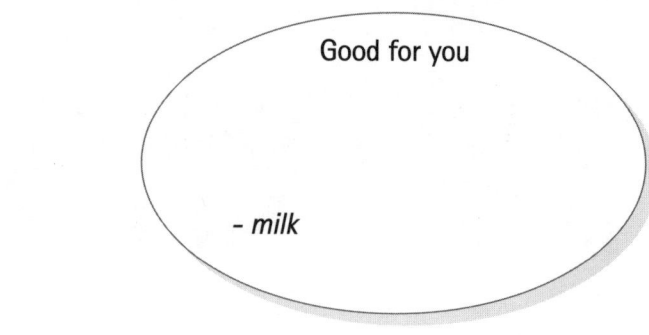

Good for you

- milk

Bad for you

A little bit's OK

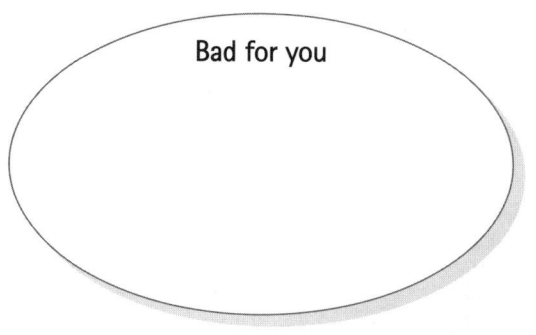
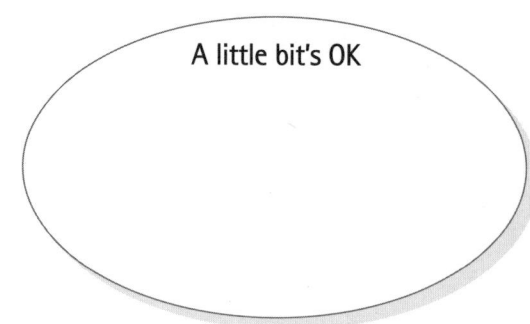

Quantifiers

4 Choose the correct quantifier/s in the sentences below.

1 He eats *a lot of / many* sandwiches and drinks *a lot of / much* coffee – I don't know how he stays so healthy!
2 We haven't got *some / any* coffee, but there's *lots of / much* tea in the cupboard over there.
3 Were there many / much people at the restaurant?
4 Is there *much / many* cereal left? If not, I could get *some / any* more on my way home.

5 I eat *a few / a little* things that aren't really very healthy, like crisps and chocolate, but not *too many / too much*, I don't think.

6 There aren't *much / many* types of breakfast cereal that are healthy, as far as I'm concerned. They've all got so *much / many* sugar in them.

7 There are *a large number of / a large amount of* calories in just one slice of chocolate cake.

8 Athletes who are training hard need to eat *a great deal of / much* high-calorie food to enable them to perform well.

Vocabulary

Prefixes and Suffixes

5 Complete the sentences below by forming a word from the root word that is given and a prefix and / or suffix from the list.

-able	dis-	-ful	-less
mis-	-ness	re-	un-	pre-

1 He does things without thinking about how other people feel. He's so ....
THINK

2 They .... the directions I gave them to get to my house and got completely lost.
UNDERSTAND

3 Honestly, she seems to .... with everything I say. I didn't realise teenagers could be so difficult!
AGREE

4 It's ....! She eats so much, yet manages to stay so thin – I don't know how she does it.
BELIEVE

5 In some countries, ... is not that easy, because the local councils don't provide separate bins for different kinds of rubbish.
CYCLE

6 Isn't it .... news that Peter and Carmen are getting married? They make a great couple.
WONDER

7 When I was in hospital for six weeks, she visited me every day and brought me lots of presents to cheer me up – without her .... , I'd have got really depressed.
KIND

8 Jane's a really .... person – she's always doing things to help other people.
THINK

9 My aunt"s a film critic, so I got to see a .... of Tarantino's new film.
VIEW

10 If my students don't do very well in a piece of written work, I give them the chance to .... it.
WRITE

Use of English Part 2

> In Part 2 you are given a modified open cloze text containing 12 gaps. You have to think of a word which will fill the gap correctly. This part focuses on grammar and vocabulary. Each correct answer receives 1 mark.

Practical Tips

 Read the title and the gapped text first to get an idea of its overall meaning.

 Think whether a *verb, preposition, article, adjective, adverb, determiner, pronoun* or *noun* is needed to fill the gap. Pay attention to spelling!

6 Read the text and think of the word which best fits each gap. Use only one word.

An Olympic Diet

What did you have for breakfast? A cup of tea and a bowl of cereal? Or a **0** *glass* of orange juice and a **1** .... of toast? Compare that with what US swimming champion Michael Phelps eats in the morning, and you could be left feeling a bit hungry. To start the day, Phelps has three fried egg sandwiches with cheese, lettuce, tomatoes, fried onions and mayonnaise; one five-egg omelette; a bowl of cereal; three slices of French toast with sugar on top; three chocolate-chip pancakes; and two **2** .... of coffee. Whilst all that would keep most people **3** .... for the rest of the day – if not a **4** .... days – the winner of eight gold medals at the Beijing Olympics, **5** .... exercises for 5 hours a day, 6 days a week, tucks into a lunch consisting of half a kilogram of pasta and two large ham and cheese sandwiches with mayonnaise, all washed down by high-calorie energy drinks. And no, he doesn't skip dinner! For his evening **6** .... , he puts away another half a kilogram of pasta, followed by a large pizza and more energy drinks. Phelps's daily calorie intake is an unbelievable 12,000 calories, whereas the amount recommended for the average male is around 2, 500.
Is such a high-calorie diet healthy? Sports doctors, trying to explain the Phelps eating phenomenon, have pointed **7** .... that athletes who exercise vigorously for **8** .... many hours each day have to eat enough to replace all the calories that they've burned **9** .... If they don't, their muscles **10** .... recover and they won't have enough energy stored up to compete at this level. But what about the choice of foods? Can **11** .... a large amount of food like eggs, ham and cheese be good for him? Nutritionists say that, with the calorie demands on his body, he can probably eat **12** .... he wants to.

Listening Part 3

In Part 3 of the Listening Paper you hear five short related monologues with different speakers. Each monologue lasts approximately 30 seconds. There are six options, five of which you have to match to the correct speaker. Part 3 tests your ability to listen for gist and detail. Each correct answer receives 1 mark.

Practical Tips

- Read the rubric in order to find out what the general topic related to the five monologues is.
- Use the 30 seconds provided before the recording to read each option carefully.
- Underline the keywords in each option.
- Listen out for matches to the keywords.

7 Are you allergic to any of these foods? Do you know what happens when you eat something you are allergic to? What precautions should be taken? Discuss your ideas in pairs or small groups.

 8 You will hear five different people talking about food allergies and intolerance. For questions 1-5, choose from the list (A-F) the effects this has had on their lives. Use the letters only once. There is one extra letter which you do not need to use.

A	feels much better since she got medical advice	
	Speaker 1	1
B	has grown up to be shy and awkward	
	Speaker 2	2
C	has to carry a special device on her at all times	
	Speaker 3	3
D	is no longer allergic	
	Speaker 4	4
E	is scrupulous about checking ingredients	
	Speaker 5	5
F	has to avoid foods such as oysters, mussels and clams	

9 Listen again and name the foods each person is allergic or intolerant to.

Speaker 1 ....
Speaker 2 ....
Speaker 3 ....
Speaker 4 ....
Speaker 5 ....

10 Now read the symptoms and name the allergies.

1 mouth swelling and difficulty breathing
....
2 itchy rash
....
3 bloating and stomach ache
....

Speaking Part 3

In Speaking Part 3 the examiner gives you a picture containing several illustrations or photographs which forms the basis for a task which you carry out in pairs. Speaking Part 3 assesses your ability to engage in a discussion and work towards a negotiated outcome of the task set. (Time: 3 minutes)

Practical Tips

- If you don't fully understand what is required, ask the examiner to repeat his or her instructions.

- Move the discussion forward by initiating the discussion and inviting your partner to speak.

- Be careful to turn take. Don't dominate the discussion and make sure your partner gets an equal opportunity to speak.

- Make sure you describe all the situations depicted before making any decisions.

11 Here are some pictures showing people with different allergic reactions. Read the dialogue and number the pictures from 1 to 7.

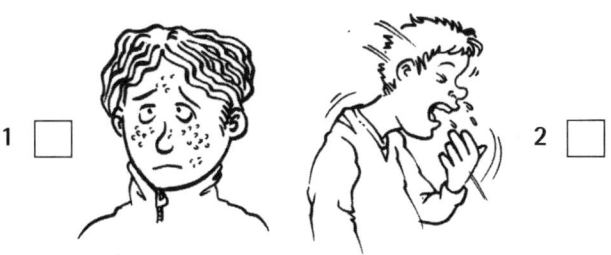

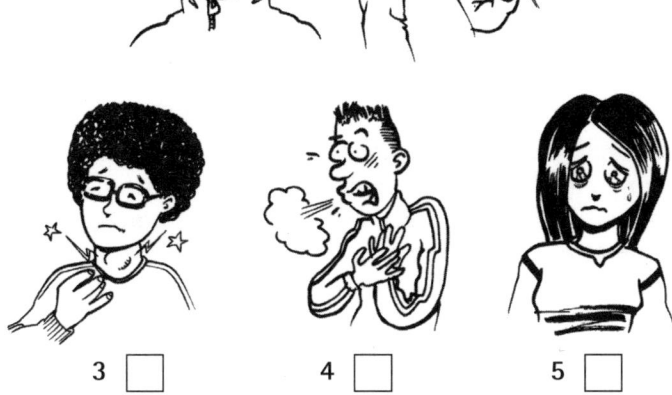

Tom: Shall I start? Well...erm....the boy in the top left hand corner wearing the tracksuit top has a nasty rash on his face. Poor thing! It's all over his face, on his cheeks, his nose and even on his forehead. I wonder what caused it?

Lucy: I suppose anything... it might be something he ate, something he washed his face with or perhaps he's got really delicate skin and the cold weather made it so red and sore.

Tom: Looks more to me like he ate something that didn't agree with him.

Lucy: Hmm... like this person here. Look how he's holding his stomach! He must have some sort of food intolerance, like lactose intolerance. I've heard that can give you terrible bouts of stomach ache.

Tom: What about this man? What do you think he might be allergic to?

Lucy: Well... considering how violently he's sneezing I would say he's got hay fever.

Tom: Me, too. I wonder if this girl suffers from hay fever, too? Look how swollen and bloodshot her eyes are.

Lucy: Hmm... They do look sore.

Tom: What do you think's the matter with this man? He's fainted, hasn't he?

Lucy: Yes. It's a good job his friend was there to catch him. I wonder what made him faint? It could be anything really...

Tom: He might have eaten something that's made him feel bad. I mean, what if he didn't realize he was allergic to shellfish and he had a violent allergic reaction.

Lucy: Hmm... I suppose so. What about the man with the sore throat? It looks pretty swollen, doesn't it?

Tom: Yes, his Adam's apple's really standing out there! Perhaps he was eating some fish and got a bone stuck in his throat...

Lucy: How awful! I'd hate that to happen. He might have eaten some hot chilli peppers in some sort of Mexican dish and they've irritated his throat.

Tom: Possibly. What's this man doing? It looks like he's having difficulty breathing. He must be having the worst allergic reaction of all!

Lucy: Yes, he's gasping for air and holding his chest. I reckon he's having an anaphylactic attack and needs a jab of adrenaline.

Tom: Hmm... So do I. It happened to me once. I was in a restaurant having lunch when I ate some broad beans. Little did I know, I was allergic to them! All of a sudden, my throat started to swell and I couldn't breath. I was rushed to hospital and given a jab of adrenaline and then I was fine.

Lucy: Ugh! Poor you!

12 Talk in pairs. Describe each person's reaction, saying what they might be allergic to.

Be a Sport!

In Part 3 you are given a text or several short texts with fifteen multiple-matching questions. Part 3 tests your ability to locate specific information. Each correct answer receives 1 mark.

Practical Tips

- Skim the text to get an idea of its overall meaning.
- Read the questions and then scan the text to find the part that matches each question.

1 You are going to read some stories from a newspaper article about extraordinary Olympic athletes. For questions 1-14, choose from the stories (A-D). The stories may be chosen more than once.

Great Olympic Moments

A - Michael Johnson breaks the world 200m record, Atlanta, 1996
What Johnson did in this race almost defied belief. At one point the cameraman has to jerk forwards to keep up with him because he's about to run off the screen. Johnson's time of 19.32 broke his own world record by a third of a second. No other man in history has run below 19.6. It was one of the few redeeming points of the '96 Olympics. More importantly, it is a record about which we suspend our disbelief. This was a moment of brilliance that will remain in the memories of everyone who saw it. Watching it felt like the world had stopped to marvel at a passing comet.

B - Luz Long tells Jesse Owens where to go, Berlin, 1936
Long, a 19-year-old German, was Jesse Owens' main rival in the long jump in 1936. Long was tall, blond and well educated. He was a national hero. In the qualifying rounds, Long equalled the Olympic record while Owens was struggling badly. The judges had counted a practice jump as one of his three official efforts. Disconcerted, Owens overstepped his second jump. He fell down dejected on the trackside. Long introduced himself, and suggested Owens placed a towel in front of the take-off board so as to leap from several inches behind the line. Owens did, and managed to qualify. In the final, Owens' sixth jump, which broke Long's Olympic record, won him gold, whereas Long won the silver medal. Long and Owens walked arm-in-arm to the dressing room afterwards, posing for press photos. 'It took a lot of courage for him to befriend me in front of Hitler,' Owens said afterwards, 'Hitler must have gone crazy watching us embrace.'

Which athlete

- was surprised by the format of an event having been changed? `1` ☐
- got a gold medal for jumping without doing any practice jumps? `2` ☐
- helped another to improve his performance? `3` ☐
- was discovered to have talent as an athlete while doing an everyday activity? `4` ☐
- didn't win a gold medal at the Olympic Games described? `5` ☐
- was better at sport than studying? `6` ☐
- ran so fast in a race that it was difficult to film the event? `7` ☐
- rejected an award? `8` ☐
- did something that would have made someone who was watching very angry? `9` ☐
- won two gold medals eight years apart? `10` ☐
- performed so well that it's very difficult to believe? `11` ☐
- was nearly killed? `12` ☐
- didn't get any financial support to compete in the Olympics? `13` ☐
- has their performance compared to an event in space? `14` ☐

C – James B Connolly wins in the triple jump, Athens, 1896

Connolly was the first Olympic champion in the history of the modern Olympics. It was his strength of will that helped him overcome all manner of difficulties and prejudices. A good athlete but a poor scholar, he was refused two months leave from Harvard university to compete in Athens. Told he would have to resign and then reapply for his place next year, Connolly simply walked out of the Dean's office and never came back. Other Harvard athletes had been given the time off, but they were all members of the distinguished Boston Athletic Association. Connolly was too poor to join the Association. While the BAA athletes had their expenses paid, Connolly had to pay for his own trip. He spent his life-savings, $700, on a steamer ticket. On board he was blackballed by other athletes because of his lack of social standing. Connolly arrived in Athens to find that he'd miscalculated the dates and that, rather than having 12 days to train, he would in fact be starting his competition the following day. Worse, the organisers had decided that the competition would be a hop-hop-jump, rather than the hop-step-jump for which he'd been preparing. In front of a 140,000-strong crowd, Connolly watched the first round jumps of his rivals, then contemptuously threw his hat to a point a yard beyond the furthest mark. In the event he went well beyond it, and won the event. In 1949, Harvard tried to apologise for its treatment, and offered him an honorary doctorate. He turned it down.

D – Betty Robinson wins gold in the 100 metres, Amsterdam, 1928

In 1928 the International Olympic Committee (IOC) were forced to include women's athletics in the Games for the first time. Betty Robinson, only 16, became the first female track medallist. She'd been spotted only a year before the final, when a coach had seen her running to catch a train. The 100m final at Amsterdam was only the fifth senior race of her life, the first having been just four months previously. Her run equalled the world record of 12.2 seconds, and she won gold by the narrowest of margins. The result made her a star. The USA wanted to see Betty Robinson run and win in Los Angeles. But in 1931 she was involved in a plane crash. The man who found her body thought she was dead, put her in his car boot and drove her to a mortician – but she was still alive, in a coma. She woke seven months later, and spent six months in a wheelchair. It took her two years to learn to walk normally again. Incredibly, she eventually returned to racing. She was unable to sprint like before, but she could still run the relay, and in 1936 she won her second gold in the 4x100m.

Unit 3

Vocabulary

Extreme Sports

2 Match the pictures with the words for sports.

1 sailing ☐
2 snowboarding ☐
3 climbing ☐
4 hang-gliding ☐
5 downhill mountain biking ☐
6 kite-surfing ☐

3 Complete the sentences with a suitable adjective using the root verb in brackets.

1 The match was .... (amaze). Really great tennis, and it lasted over five hours, with Nadal winning in the end.
2 I find it .... (astonish) how much footballers get paid. I mean, just for kicking a ball around once a week!
3 Lots of Londoners are .... (thrill) to be hosting the Olympics there in 2012, but there are also lots of people who aren't so pleased about how much it's all costing.
4 We were .... (shock) to hear that they'd lost the match. Everyone had expected them to win easily.
5 The first time she tried skysurfing, she was so .... (exhilarate) by it that she never went back to snowboarding after that.
6 She says that she often feels .... (frighten) when she's doing downhill mountain biking, but that that's part of the appeal!

Grammar

Comparatives and Superlatives

4 Complete the table with the rules for forming regular comparatives and superlatives.

Rule	Comparative	Superlative
one-syllable adjectives, e.g. *long*	add *er*	add 1___
one-syllable adjectives ending in 'e', e.g. *nice*	add 2___	add 3___
one syllable adjectives ending in vowel + consonant, e.g. *hot*	4_____ final consonant + add 5__	6_____ final consonant + add 7__
two-syllable adjectives ending in 'y', e.g. *happy*	change the 'y' to 8 '___' + add 9___	change the 'y' to 10 '___' + add 11___
two-syllable adjectives not ending in 'y' and three-syllable or longer adjectives, e.g. *fluent, expensive*	12_____ + adjective	13_____ 14_____ + adjective

5 Now complete this table with the correct forms of these irregular comparatives and superlatives.

Adjective/Determiner/Adverb	Comparative	Superlative
good	a *better*	b
bad	c	d
much/many	e	f
well, e.g. *He plays the guitar well.*	g	h

6 Complete the sentences with the correct form – comparative or superlative – of these adjectives / determiners / adverbs and add any other words that are needed, e.g. prepositions. More than one answer may be possible for some sentences.

well	large	nice
great	important	challenge
hot	happy	

1 Gianluigi Buffon, for many people, is .... goalkeeper .... all time.

2 Who do you think is .... tennis player around today?

3 Doing regular sport is .... for your health .... lots of people realise – in fact, it's essential.

4 After the London Olympic Games, the Olympic area will be transformed into .... urban park created .... Europe for over a century – it's going to be enormous.

5 She's .... skysurfing .... she is snowboarding.

6 I think Madrid's .... Barcelona, but a lot of people would disagree with me.

7 It's the .... event she's .... competed in.

8 She's only ten years old, but she skis .... me.

7 Complete the sentences with the best option.

1 I think both athletes are as good as each other
....

2 I waited to buy all our skiing equipment until the January sales ....

3 She got a far better mark in the exam than she was expecting, ...

4 Do you mind if I drive a bit faster
....

5 On her cycle trip across China, she got emails on her Blackberry ....

6 Eighty percent of athletes at the London Olympics will be able to reach the venues where they are competing ....

7 He hasn't been able to play in a match on more than one occasion ....

8 She's playing a lot better than she was last season
....

a – he must have missed at least four matches due to injury.

b – it was less expensive then than it had been before Christmas.

c – we're late!

d – I mean, there isn't any difference between the two of them in speed.

e from people as far away as Iceland.

f – she's obviously trained a lot in the past few months.

g in no fewer than 20 minutes.

h considering she didn't revise for it at all!

8 Now underline the phrases for making comparisons.

Use of English Part 3

> In Part 3 you are given a text containing 10 gaps. Each gap corresponds to a word. The roots of the missing words are given beside the text and you have to change them to form the missing word. This part focuses on vocabulary. Each correct answer receives 1 mark.

Practical Tips

🌀 Make sure you read the sentence surrounding the gap before you decide what the missing word is.

🌀 Revise your prefixes and suffixes as well as the various forms a root word can take.

9 Use the word given in capitals to form a word that fits in the gap.

Allyson Felix

At only 20 years old, Allyson Felix is already the 1 .... female 2 .... on the planet.
She won gold at the 2005 Helsinki World Athletic 3 .... for the 200 metres, completing the race in 22.16 seconds – a new world junior record. In the 2008 Olympics in Beijing, she finished as silver 4 .... in the 200 metres and won gold as a member of the women's 400 metres relay team.

FAST
ATHLETICS

CHAMPION

MEDAL

Allyson is 1.68cm tall and 5 .... only 57 kilos. Her nickname is 'chicken legs' because of her skinny legs. In spite of her slight frame, she storms round the track. She has continued to improve her personal 6 .... and has broken a number of world records. She has been featured on the front pages of USA Today, the Washington Post and Sports Illustrated. Her website registers one of the highest number of 7 .... of any site on the Internet. Not only that, but her boyfriend is pretty 8 .... too – he's Olympic 100-metre champion, Justin Gatlin. Allyson is a real 'golden girl' in all senses – she recently 9 .... a million-dollar advertising contract for a famous brand of 10 ....

WEIGHT

GOOD

VISIT

ESPECIALLY

SIGNATURE

SPORT

Listening Part 4   4.

> In Part 4 of the Listening Paper you hear a
> monologue or a text involving interacting speakers
> which lasts for about 3 minutes. There are seven
> multiple-choice questions each with three options.
> Part 4 tests your ability to listen for the gist or
> detail of a longer text. Each correct answer
> receives 1 mark.

Practical Tips

- ⟳ Read the questions only and underline the keywords.
- ⟳ Provide your own answers to the questions before consulting the options.
- ⟳ Don't be fooled by words with negative meanings.
- ⟳ Take notes on the question paper while you listen.
- ⟳ Use the second listening to check your answers.

10 These two buildings have been the venues for two Olympic Games. Look at the photos and try to guess which
Olympic Games were held there.

11 The words below are all included in the recording you are going to listen to about the Olympic Village.
Work in pairs and try to match each word to its meaning.

1	hub	**a**	a raised passage connecting different sections of a building or a wide path in a park or garden
2	footbridge	**b**	a river, canal, or other route
3	walkway	**c**	uncover a monument or work of art in a public ceremony
4	concourse	**d**	the lowest part of a building, typically below ground level
5	waterway	**e**	the effective centre of an activity, region, or network
6	complex	**f**	a cycle-racing track, typically with steeply banked curves
7	unveil	**g**	a track used for motor racing, horse racing, or athletics
8	foundations	**h**	large open area inside or in front of a public building
9	velodrome	**i**	a group of similar buildings or facilities on the same site
10	circuit	**j**	a bridge designed to be used by pedestrians

12 You will hear a radio interview with the chairman of the Olympic Delivery Authority. For questions 1-7, choose the best answer (A, B or C).

1   The centre of attention of the 2012 Games to be held in London is bound to be
   A East London.
   B the Olympic Park.
   C the new sport venues.   [1]

2   Visitors will be made to feel part of the games
   A wherever they are in the park.
   B even if they're watching the games on the TV screen at home.
   C whether or not they can make it across the site.   [2]

3   The Olympic Park will
   A serve communities up until 2012.
   B last for over 150 years.
   C improve services for the community long after the Olympic Games.   [3]

4   The swimming and diving pools in the Aquatic Centre will provide facilities
   A London is lacking.
   B London has no need for.
   C the community won't be able to pay for.   [4]

5   Spectators will arrive at the park
   A in their thousands.
   B by trains every ten minutes.
   C every day by bus.   [5]

6   The athletes staying at the Olympic Village will be able to reach their venue
   A in eight minutes.
   B in twenty minutes.
   C on foot.   [6]

7   New designs have just been released showing
   A the foundations of the Olympic Park.
   B what the Park looks like now.
   C the appearance of the Olympic Village once the games are over.   [7]

13 Discuss the following questions in pairs.

1 How do you think the athletes will feel in the run up towards the 2012 Olympic Games?
2 What do you think of the fact that a village is being built for the athletes and officials?
3 In what ways could the Olympic Park benefit the community, once the Games are over?

Music and the Internet Revolution

1 Read the article below about email. Decide which sentence best summarises the article.

1 There are other ways of communicating, apart from email. ☐
2 The unpredictable way that useful emails arrive makes checking for them addictive, but you can regain control. ☐
3 Since email began in the early 1990s, we've all been wasting a lot of time. ☐

Internet Revolution or Internet Addiction?

Downloading music, watching YouTube videos, shopping on eBay, reading online news, playing video games, checking private emails... people do anything in the office but work. According to an American survey, some employees spend an incredible two hours of company time per day on the Internet, which mounts up to an entire working day per week. A drop in productivity isn't the only consequence of free internet use in workplaces. Apart from viruses and bugs, which may be downloaded via apparently harmless websites, research shows that one in four employees is likely to have a serious web addiction. Things get even worse when it comes to emails.

In the early 1990s, email was a privilege given only to those who could prove they needed it. Now, it has turned into a nuisance that's costing companies millions. We may feel that we have it under control, but not only do we check email more often than we realise, but the interruptions caused are more damaging than was previously thought. One research study in this area found that it takes an average of 64 seconds to recover your train of thought after interruption by email. So people who check their email every five minutes waste 8.5 hours a week figuring out what they were doing moments before. People tend to respond to emails as they arrive, taking an average of only one minute and 44 seconds to react to a new email notification; 70% of alerts get a reaction within six seconds. That's faster than letting the phone ring three times.

Added to this is the time people spend with their inbox. A survey conducted in 2006 upon 250 users showed that 56% spent more than two hours a day in their inbox. Most felt they got too much email – 38% of respondents received more than 100 emails a day – and that it stopped them from doing other things.

A study carried out at universities in Scotland concluded that email users fall into three categories: relaxed, driven and stressed. The relaxed group don't let email influence their lives. They treat it exactly the way that one would treat the mail. They'll deal with it in their own time. The second group feel driven to keep on top of emails, but also feel that they could cope with them. The third group, however, react negatively to the pressure of emails and admit they can cause stress, and stress causes all sorts of health problems.

Researchers discovered that although 64% of employees claimed to check their emails once an hour, and 35% said they checked them every 15 minutes, they were actually checking it much more frequently – about every five minutes. For some people, checking email is no longer a conscious and deliberate act, but a compulsion they are barely aware of.

Another key sign of a user being addicted to email is their relationship to a palmtop gadget, like a Blackberry or iPhone. If they focus on their Blackberry ignoring those around them, it means that they've become hooked on them, and this could be seriously damaging to their mental health. Employers provide programmes to help workers with chemical or substance addictions. But addiction to technology can be equally damaging to a worker's mental condition.

Dr Karol Szlichcinski, a business psychologist, recommends providing guidelines and training to give people 'ways of reducing the disruption caused by email, ways of managing email so that it doesn't ruin your day. Organisational norms build up, and people come to expect others to answer emails within a given timeframe, whether that email is important or not.'

We may think email is simple, but its ease of use is deceptive. For many, it's an advantage, but for an increasing majority it's the tail that wags the dog.

2 Read the article again. For questions 1–8, choose the answer (A, B, C or D) which you think fits best according to the text.

1 The widely-spread use of the Internet in workplaces
A has consistently improved employees' working conditions. ☐
B has contributed to an increase in the hours worked per week. ☐
C allows employees to take one entire day off each week. ☐
D make employees work less than they used to. ☐

2 A research study on email use showed that:
A people spend eight and a half hours a week checking their email. ☐
B that people answer email more quickly than they answer the phone. ☐
C that emails don't cause interruptions. ☐
D people who check their email frequently waste more than eight hours a week regaining their concentration. ☐

3 A study in July 2006 found that email users felt that
A dealing with email prevented them from doing other work. ☐
B they spent too many hours a day dealing with email. ☐
C their managers should control their email for them. ☐
D they should be given more time by their managers to deal with emails. ☐

4 Of the three different types of email user identified by Universities in Scotland
A all three types manage to deal with email without problems. ☐
B two types manage to deal with email without problems, but one doesn't. ☐
C one manages to deal with email without problems, but the other two don't. ☐
D all three have problems dealing with email. ☐

5 According to the research in Scotland, some email users
A deliberately lie about how often they check their email. ☐
B start to feel ill if they don't check their email frequently. ☐
C spent 35% of each day checking emails. ☐
D don't necessarily realise that they check their email as often as they do. ☐

6 An additional indicator of email addiction is where a user
A has mental health problems. ☐
B needs to have the latest gadgets, like a Blackberry or iPhone. ☐
C focuses on a portable email-receiving device in a social situation in preference to people. ☐
D asks their employer for help with their addiction. ☐

7 Dr Karol Szlichcinski says that people need help with email in order to
A organise their working days better. ☐
B help them manage and deal with it better. ☐
C be able to answer emails more quickly. ☐
D make businesses more profitable. ☐

8 In the last line of the article, the phrase 'it's the tail that wags the dog' is used here to mean that many people
A are having their lives controlled by email. ☐
B are in control of their email. ☐
C are against all use of email. ☐
D find email easy to use. ☐

Vocabulary

Music and the Internet

3 Complete the crossword using the clues below.

Across

1 To record music onto a CD.
3 An informal way of saying 'concert'.
4 A contract with a record label.
7 The transfer of data to a larger computer system, or the Internet.
8 A short section of a video, e.g. from a film.
10 A group or system of interconnected people or things.
11 To record music from a CD onto a computer.
12 The illegal copying of a computer program, music, films, etc.
13 An example of a product, produced to try and get people to buy it.

Down

2 When a band doesn't have a contract with a record label.
5 A small computer that is easy to transport and use anywhere.
6 Alternative, different to the majority.
9 The transfer of data from a larger computer system, or the Internet.

4 Read the interview questions and match them to the answers below. Then complete the sentences with words from the crossword in Exercise 3.

1 Is piracy a problem for you?
2 How would you describe your music?
3 How did you go from being 'bedroom musicians' to being the famous band you are today?
4 How do you see the future for pop music?
5 When was your first public performance?
6 How did you first get known? I mean, first get some fans!

a ☐

When we were still **1** .... , we used to make video **2** .... of ourselves performing in my bedroom, just using my Mum's **3** .... , actually, and a camera, as I didn't have my own computer at the time. Then we'd **4** .... them on to different websites – you know, like YouTube and MySpace. And, amazingly, we started to build up a fan base like that, just through the Internet!

b ☐

It's hard to believe, but we got a **5** .... through the Internet, too! Someone from a record label was looking online for new talent, saw us on YouTube and got in touch.

c ☐

We played our first **6** .... last year at the university in town. Loads of our fans that knew us from the websites came along, and of course they knew all the words of the songs, so it was great!

d ☐

Well, it's hard to say, really. A bit indie, with some techno, touches of rock and reggae, too at times – definitely **7** .... anyway!

e ☐

Well, I wouldn't call it a problem, really. I know that people **8** .... our music on to their computers, then **9** .... it on to CDs, or put it on their MP3 players. And I bet that their friends then **10** .... it from the CDs on to their computers! But, hey, we've got to be realistic – it's going to happen and we have to go with it rather than fight it. And it's not like I've never done it myself! Maybe the answer is for musicians today not to expect to be millionaires!

Grammar

Articles: *the, a / an,* zero article

5 Fill in the gaps with *the* or x (zero article).

1 What did you think of .... film? I hated it!
2 In .... north of Europe, ... sun sets early in winter.
3 Can you play .... guitar?
4 I went to .... U.S.A. on .... holiday last year.
5 .... Mp3 players are great for long train journeys.
6 I can't remember what life was like before .... Internet!
7 .... Italy is a beautiful country.
8 Millions of .... young people in .... UK still listen to .... radio.
9 .... Chinese are encouraged by .... state to have only one child.
10 On .... Monday, I have .... English lessons.

6 Read the sentences in exercise 5 again and complete the rules below: *the* or zero article?

1 collective nouns (x3) ....
2 countries ....
3 countries which are groups of states (x2) ....
4 days ....
5 musical instruments ....
6 something definite or already mentioned ....
7 something unique (x5) ....
8 things in general ....
9 with certain expressions ....

7 Reorder the words to make sentences.

1 a / challenge / facing / industry / is / music / new / the
.... challenge.
2 1990's / a / early / email / In / new / phenomenon / still / the / was
In ....
3 a / are / clips / day / Every / hundred / million / on / site / the / video /viewed
Every ....
4 a / access / Anyone / band / can / decide / good / if / Internet / is / the / to / with
Anyone .... good.
5 a / amplifier / home-made / of / One / recorded / songs / the / using / was
One ....
6 addicted / an / are / business / email / In / increasing / number / of / people / the / to / world
In .... email.

Use of English Part 1

In Part 1 you are given a modified cloze test containing 12 gaps, followed by 12 four-option multiple-choise items to choose from. Part 1 focuses on vocabulary and different types of words are tested. Each correct answer receives 1 mark.

Practical Tips

◎ Use the example to help you understand what you have to do.

◎ Learn the grammatical patterns and collocations of words and phrases

◎ Look out for prepositions or adverbs after the gap

8 Read the text below about the future of radio and decide which answer (A, B, C or D) best fits each gap.

Digital Killed the Radio Star?

With so many other **1** ....B.... of listening to music **2** .... nowadays, have young people given up listening to the radio? Not completely, it seems. Around 90% of the UK population above the age of 15 still listens to the radio. MP3 players are hugely popular and they may be a serious **3** .... to radio. The MP3/iPod revolution allows us to be our own **4** .... Early music download sites such as iTunes **5** .... it all off, then the Amazingtunes site was launched in 2007 and it has a fair trade policy where new, unsigned artists can **6** .... their music for free and will receive up to 70% of the money charged for **7** .... as a royalty payment. By the time 'new music' **8** .... on the Radio it may not be so new... and only a few bands ever **9** .... it that far. With Amazingtunes you choose and the variety of music available is amazing. However, it **10** .... less effort to switch on a radio than it does to download and organise MP3 **11** .... , and researchers say that people enjoy the shared experience of listening to a radio programme they know many other people are listening to. If **12** .... for this reason, perhaps, radio will survive.

1 A approaches	B ways	C types	D roads
2 A suitable	B available	C disposable	D unavailable
3 A warning	B hazard	C threat	D injury
4 A listeners	B singers	C musicians	D DJs
5 A got	B sent	C started	D begun
6 A output	B log on	C upload	D download
7 A uploading	B downloading	C burning	D dealing
8 A gets	B puts	C has	D becomes
9 A do	B make	C have	D go
10 A makes	B takes	C costs	D has
11 A files	B CDs	C sites	D demos
12 A alone	B own	C even	D only

ho₂s

9 Do you like to keep track of your favourite bands? How do you get hold of new releases or find out about gigs? Do you download music off a particular website or do you go to stores to choose the music you want to buy like the girl in this photograph? Tell your partner.

CD 1 5

10 You will hear an interview with a musician about the effects the Internet has had on local bands. For questions 1-10, complete the sentences.

LOCAL BANDS AND THE INTERNET

The advent of the [_____ **1**] has greatly influenced local music.

Similar sites allowed bands to [_____ **2**] their music while others provided a place to make friends.

The key to MySpace's success is the combination of these [_____ **3**] factors.

The people who use this site are able to [_____ **4**] of their favourite bands however famous they might be.

The site does experience some difficulties with its [_____ **5**] because of the large number of users.

Unsigned bands needn't spend enormous amounts of money to enlarge their [_____ **6**] any longer.

There is huge potential for bands to establish a [_____ **7**] with their audience.

Knowing how many friends a band has, allows you to [_____ **8**] future sales figures when a new song is released.

A number of leading record labels intend to begin [_____ **9**] bands on the web.

Bands are now able to produce and issue their own music thanks to [_____ **10**] software.

11 Listen to the interview again, then decide if the following statements are true (T) or false (F).

	T	F
1 Bands have been promoting their music differently for over ten years now.	☐	☐
2 There had never been websites for bands to upload their music on before MySpace.com.	☐	☐
3 On MySpace.com people can either make friends or upload their music but not both.	☐	☐
4 The server sometimes crashes due to the number of people logging onto the site.	☐	☐
5 It's a more prolific way for bands to promote their music.	☐	☐
6 It's unlikely that major record labels will start scouting bands online.	☐	☐

12 In the recording you heard the expression *to sort the wheat from the chaff.* Read the expression in context and decide what the speaker meant.

The site often suffers from server problems due to its intense traffic. Plus it's not always easy to sort the wheat from the chaff when browsing, due to the proliferation of unsigned bands.

A to make sure people browse before they buy

B to prevent poor quality music from being uploaded onto the server

C to distinguish good quality music from worthless music

Speaking Part 2

> In Speaking Part 2 the examiner gives you a pair of photographs to talk about on your own for about one minute. You also have to answer a short question about your partner's photographs. Speaking Part 2 assess your ability to compare, describe and express opinions.

Practical Tips

- Compare the two photographs and say something which relates directly to them.
- Produce more extended, coherent language by using comparatives and linking words.
- Practice talking for one minute so that you are aware of the amount of language you are expected to produce in the time available.
- Be ready to answer the examiner's questions about your partner's photographs.

13 Read the text below which compares these two photographs and fill the gaps with the missing words.

Both photographs show people performing to music. In the first photo we can see two dancers dancing in a square in an **1** .... part of a town. It might be a tango, but I'm not sure. We can't see the musician but I would imagine there's a group of people playing **2** .... instruments or maybe just one person playing a violin somewhere in the background. The woman is dressed from head to foot in black with a **3** .... leotard, footless tights and high-heeled dancing shoes. Her jet black hair is tied in a bun at the back of her head and she's wearing a watch, or perhaps it's a bracelet, and several rings. She's very attractive. Her dancing partner is wearing a white shirt, black trousers with **4** .... and shoes. We can't see his face as he has his **5** .... to us, but he's dark haired like the woman. They probably come from a

Mediterranean country such as Spain or Italy or perhaps they're Cuban or then again, maybe they're from Argentina. In the background, watching them dance are several people. The man on the far right is probably a tourist as he's got a camera hanging round his neck. Next to him is an **6** .... man holding a couple of white plastic bags with what looks like fruit inside. Perhaps he's on his way home from the market and has stopped to watch the dancers. Someone is sitting on the floor, with their legs **7** .... , opposite the two dancers, but I can't see their head so it's difficult to **8** .... whether it's a man or a woman, but judging from the person's hands, I would say it's a woman. On this person's left are three other people. The one with the hat is just walking past and doesn't seem particularly interested in the two dancers, while a couple, holding hands, has stopped to watch.

The second photograph was probably **9** .... in an African country. We can see a group of four people standing behind unusual looking musical instruments. The people most likely all belong to the same tribe as they are wearing similar brightly coloured costumes and **10** .... with feathers in them. The first three men are all playing drums whereas the last man on the right is playing a funny looking instrument. I'm not sure what it is. On the floor, in front of them, are some weird looking objects which could be musical instruments, too. They might be for **11** .... Behind the men is a hut which looks like it's made out of a mixture of cement, bricks and wood. In the top right hand corner we can see a **12** .... which could be advertising a bar or restaurant of some sort.

14 Now take it in turns to describe the photographs in your own words.

Reading Part 3

1 You are going to read 4 excerpts from interviews with contemporary writers. Read them once quickly and choose the sentence that best summarises them.

1 Writing is a natural and individual gift. No person or background can encourage you to write. ☐
2 Writing is all about routine. ☐
3 All writers have different attitudes towards writing. ☐

The Charm of Writing

A - Louis de Bernières

Was there someone that got you interested in writing?
My father writes poetry and he wrote one poem for each of us children. My mother also has a wonderful style of writing, although mainly it is in letters. I did have a succession of amazing English teachers who were in love with language and literature and they passed that on to me.

Do you find writing easy?
I find it easy because I love doing it. When I first started, I had a great backlog waiting to be released. I wrote four books in four years and then I felt emptied out. So then I concentrated on short stories and music while I waited for the waters in the lake to fill up again. Now I feel full up again and ready to go.

What makes you write now?
I am not under any pressure from anybody. I write because the urge comes on me and that is all I can say.

How do you write?
I've no routine at all. I only write when I feel like it. I've got a summerhouse at the bottom of the garden which is solar powered and I can write down there. That's the best place to write if I'm doing something that doesn't need any research.

B - Anne Fine

Was there someone who got you interested in writing?
We did a lot of creative writing at school. We were made to sit down to write a story, in quiet, at least twice a week. They don't do creative writing in school now. It is an absolute tragedy.

Do you find writing easy?
No. I sit there, like everybody else, chewing over the pencil and getting stuck and thinking, 'How am I going to get out of this?' Sometimes it comes in floods and then I go back and tinker with it for six weeks. It is satisfying and absorbing, but not easy.

What makes you write now?
The germ of the book comes and then I don't have any choice – I am not satisfied until it is finished!

How do you write? Do you have a daily routine?
It's almost impossible to have a routine because children's authors are seen as an educational resource, so there is quite a lot we have to do. And there is my family, so I cannot be precious and say I must sit down at my desk at nine but I do work as often as I can, which is almost every day. I don't distinguish between the week and weekends and I work much better in the morning.

C – Philip Pullman

Was there someone who got you interested in reading and writing?
Not especially. They had the best attitude, which was to take no interest whatever: neither encourage nor forbid. Consequently I thought I'd discovered the world of books for myself, and it was my own big secret.

Do you find writing easy?
It gets harder and harder. Every day is a turning point. Every day I have to force myself to go and write, and every day (more or less) I still do.

What makes you write now?
Habit.

How do you write?
I go to my table and sit down and pick up my pen, and write three sides of A4 paper – and then I stop.

2 Read the texts again. For questions 1-15, choose from the writers (A-D). The writers may be chosen more than once.

Which writer

- finds their writing routine affected by their family? `1` `[ ]`

- writes best in a place that is separate from their house? `2` `[ ]`

- writes to support their family? `3` `[ ]`

- doesn't feel happy until their work is complete? `4` `[ ]`

- has times when they don't know what to write and other times when they have lots of inspiration? `5` `[ ]`

- works until they have written a certain number of pages each day? `6` `[ ]`

- doesn't feel fulfilled if they don't work enough each day? `7` `[ ]`

- was influenced by their parents' writing? `8` `[ ]`

- finds it less of a challenge to go back and make changes to their work than to begin a piece of work? `9` `[ ]`

- is finding their work increasingly difficult? `10` `[ ]`

- had a relative whose life was changed by books? `11` `[ ]`

- only works when they want to? `12` `[ ]`

- is disappointed that a subject they studied is no longer on the educational curriculum for children? `13` `[ ]`

- feels that no one influenced them in reading and writing? `14` `[ ]`

- needed time to think of ideas again after a long period of intensive writing? `15` `[ ]`

D – Adam Thorpe

Was there someone who got you interested in reading and writing?
My grandmother was an English teacher in secondary schools and would quote Shakespeare (mainly Hamlet) at least once a day in a dramatic tone at appropriate moments. She escaped poverty in Sheffield through literature and this inspired me more than anything else.

Do you find writing easy?
Easy is not a word in my lexicon. The initial creation is just as hard but my revision swing is more practised. That being said, I have worked on some poems for decades.

What makes you write now?
To keep my family in food and shelter (just), and some peculiar obsessional impulse that I first felt when writing out my alphabet letters over and over aged about four.

How do you write?
I try to start early in my study, and if I don't do several hours a day I feel incomplete.

3
Complete the sentences below with the correct word for different types of publication.

> album   atlas   biography   diary
> dictionary   encyclopaedia   guidebook
> logbook   manual   novel

1 If you don't know what that word means, look it up in the ....

2 That new .... about the last President of the U.S.A. was fascinating. I'd no idea that he'd had such a difficult childhood.

3 My son uses an on-line .... for any research he needs to do for school work – there's so much information on it about every single topic you could think of.

4 What did we do with that .... that came with the DVD player? I want to program it to record that new series tonight.

5 My grandmother has got hundreds of .... , with photos starting from when she was a baby through to ones of all her grandchildren.

6 I'm going on holiday to Egypt next month and I'd like a .... that, as well as giving all the usual tourist information, tells me something about the history of the place, too.

7 I think that writing a .... must be the most difficult kind of book to write. I mean, sitting there at a computer, day after day, creating a story and characters that other people will want to read about – that's hard!

8 I used to spend hours as a child looking at the maps in my .... I was fascinated by the idea of all those different places.

9 She kept a .... on her expedition to Everest, noting down all the details of the journey – the distance they covered each day, the food they ate, any difficulties they had.

10 I've never kept a .... I've always been too worried that someone else would read it and find out all my private thoughts and feelings!

4
Decide which of the conjunctions of time are possible in each sentence. In some sentences, more than one is possible, often with a change in meaning.

1 Tell me .... he arrives, please, as I'd like to speak to him.
A after   B before   C as soon as   D when   E until

2 I'm not doing any more work .... you pay me.
A after   B before   C as soon as   D when   E until

3 If you phone me about half an hour .... you think you're going to arrive, I can start cooking the dinner.
A after   B before   C as soon as   D when   E until

4 I'll come to the park with you .... I finish my homework – I really must get it done first.
A after   B before   C as soon as   D when   E until

5 I didn't go back to work full-time .... my children were old enough to be left on their own.
A after   B before   C as soon as   D when   E until

5
Match each rule for narrative tenses with its example sentence.

1 a continuous situation at a specific time in the past

2 actions/situations in progress at the same time in the past

3 an action in progress in the past, interrupted by another action or event

4 an event in the past happening at an earlier time, before another event in the past

5 background description in a story

6 emphasising the continuation of long activities which started and finished in the past

7 habitual actions in the past

8 narrating a series of events

a When I was at University, I played football every Saturday. ☐

b The alarm clock went off. She woke up and realized it was very late. ☐

c The protesters were demonstrating loudly in the street, the police were guarding the embassy, the Saturday afternoon shoppers were wandering in and out of the shops... ☐

d I was sitting in the sun when I heard somebody ring the door bell. ☐

e When I got off the bus, I realised that somebody had stolen my purse. ☐

f I'd been working very hard for weeks and not sleeping much when I went down with flu. ☐

g She was doing her homework at 7 p.m. yesterday. ☐

h While I was living in Canada, my brother was working in Sweden. ☐

6 Now underline the examples of the tenses in sentences a–h.

7 Complete the story with an appropriate narrative tense from Exercise 5, using the verb given in brackets.

1 .... (*already live*) in Vancouver for a few years when I **2** .... (*meet*) Jim. I **3** .... (*rush*) to work one day – I **4** .... (*oversleep*) again – standing at some traffic lights trying to get a cab. One finally **5** .... (*stop*) for me, but before **6** .... (*realise*) what **7** .... (*go on*), this man **8** .... (*run*) in front of me, **9** .... (*open*) the door of the taxi, **10** .... (*jump*) in and **11** .... (*slam*) the door shut. Well, I **12** .... (*be*) furious! **13** .... (*pull*) the door open and **14** .... (*ask*) the man what he **15** .... (*do*), stealing a cab from someone like that. He **16** .... (*not apologise*), but he **17** .... (*ask*) me where I **18** .... (*go*) and **19** .... (*invite*) me to share the cab with him. I **20** .... (*be*) still pretty angry, but **21** .... (*cannot*) be bothered to argue about it, so I **22** .... (*agree*) to share it with him. Anyway, on the journey, we **23** .... (*get*) talking and he **24** .... (*turn out*) to be a lot nicer than he **25** .... (*seem*) from his behaviour before. Well, one thing **26** .... (*lead*) to another – and we've now been married two years and are expecting a baby in the summer!

8 Read the text below and think of one word which best fits each gap.

Top Libraries

Libraries in the past were synonymous with conservation and archiving. You went to a library, chose a book, read it and then put it back on the shelf. **1** .... time has gone on, however, libraries have taken **2** .... additional functions – some recently built libraries around the world are testament to **3** .... changing role of libraries in our society.

The ultra-modern library in Seattle, U.S.A., is one such example. Its designer, Rem Koolhaas, wanted it to be a venue for meeting people as well **4** .... a place for immersing yourself completely in the world of books. Koolhaas recognised that, in today's Internet world, you hardly need to go to a library to get a book – you can download it with a click of your mouse. For this reason, he didn't fill his library with shelves, but, **5** .... , built a huge spiral which takes **6** .... four of the eleven floors in the library. Then, on the tenth floor, there is a wonderful reading room surrounded by windows **7** .... look out onto an amazing view of **8** .... city.

Another library with a non-traditional function is in the town of Malmö, in Sweden. Unlike in some libraries **9** .... silence is the rule, in this light and airy library (in 1999 voted one of the top twelve **10** .... beautiful libraries in the world), people are encouraged **11** .... talk. Malmö is running a project called the 'Living Library Project', **12** .... aims to break down prejudice against people from minority groups – such as the disabled, Romanies, and the homeless – by encouraging dialogue between people perceived as "outsiders" and visitors to the library.

no 6 on C.D .

Listening Part 3

9 How much time do you spend a day reading? What type of books do you enjoy reading? Do you belong to your local library?

10 You will hear five different people talking about books they recently bought. For questions 1–5, choose from the list (A–F), what each person said about their purchase. Use the letters only once. There is one extra letter which you do not need to use.

A   This book doesn't deserve such a high rating.

B   It captured my attention from the very beginning.

C   It should have won an award.

D   The story was easy to relate to.

E   It should definitely be recommended to other parents.

F   It's most likely to have a negative effect on teenagers.

Speaker 1		1
Speaker 2		2
Speaker 3		3
Speaker 4		4
Speaker 5		5

11 Listen to the five speakers again and answer the questions.

1 Who didn't have a good word for the book?   Speaker ....
2 Who thought the first half was much better than the second half?   Speaker ....
3 Whose son read the book she bought overnight?   Speaker ....
4 Who had already read the first two books in the sequel?   Speaker ....
5 Who would recommend this book to high school girls?   Speaker ....

12 The words in the box were mentioned in the recording. Can you match them to their meanings?

| sequel   snippet   disdain   tedious   drearily |

1 too long, slow, or dull; tiresome or monotonous   ....
2 a published work that develops the theme of an earlier one   ....
3 in a depressingly dull or repetitive way   ....
4 the feeling that someone is unworthy of one's consideration or respect   ....
5 a small piece or brief extract   ....

13 Now complete the sentences with one of the words from the previous exercise.

1 The storyline is .... predictable.
2 Bella treated her fellow classmates with ....
3 He read several .... of the book aloud to me.
4 The second half of the book is a .... uneventful read.
5 The .... of the book is bound to be just as good.

14 Now tell your partner about a book that you read recently.

Speaking Part 3

15 Here are some pictures showing different book covers. The sentences in the dialogue below are all in the wrong order. Number them from 1–13 and say which book(s) the speakers choose at the end of the dialogue.

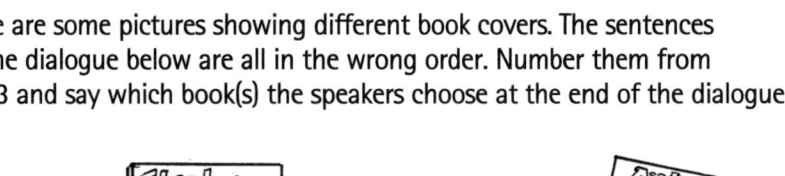

Sue:	Ah yes, that's not a bad idea. They would both make nice presents.	12
Sue:	Hmm. It sounds fascinating and really exciting, but what about this science fiction book called *Aliens!*? That'd look great in the shop window and would attract all sorts of customers from teenagers to adults.	4
Paul:	Do you want to start or shall I?	1
Sue:	Hmm. Maybe you're right, but there are so many travel books out there! How about a novel? There's this one *P.S. I love you*. It's the story of a young woman whose husband dies with a brain tumour. On her thirtieth birthday, she receives a tape recorded message and a birthday cake from her late husband followed by a succession of letters instructing her to perform unusual requests. These letters take her on a journey, her husband planned, to help her discover who she is without him.	10
Paul:	That's settled then.	13
Paul:	Right. Well, what about Coraline? It's a brilliant story about a girl who finds a passage to another life through a secret door in her house. This new world seems perfect at first but then she realizes she is in danger and has to find a way back to the secret door and her old life. Most kids and teenagers would love it.	3
Paul:	I don't think a comic would really do the trick. I know! What about a book on hobbies? That might be more suitable for the shop window. How about this one on cooking or this other one about Art and Photography?	9
Paul:	I don't know. It sounds a bit depressing if you ask me. Anyway, that would probably only attract female customers. Let's face it, you're not going to get many men going into the shop to enquire about *P.S. I love you!* unless they wanted to buy it for their wife or girlfriend!	11
Paul:	What about a good old mystery story instead? Everybody likes those. And you can't beat good old Sherlock Holmes. This collection of detective stories would be popular and it would certainly attract all sorts of people into the bookshop, children, teenagers and adults alike.	7
Sue:	No, you go ahead.	2
Sue:	Yeah. But don't you think it's a bit dated. We need a more modern hero like Spiderman. Comics will always be popular and they appeal to readers of all ages.	8
Paul:	I'm not sure that I agree with you there. I mean, not everyone's keen on science fiction, I think most people, nowadays, would rather read something factual. I, personally, would go more for a book which tells us all about the world we live in like this one by National Geographic. It gives lots of useful information about all sorts of interesting things and would attract anyone from teachers to travellers.	5
Sue:	Hmm. I see what you mean. The title might put them off. What do you suggest then?	6

16 Now talk to a partner. Take it in turns to talk about each book and say which you think should be placed on display in the local bookshop window and why.

17 Have you read any of the books featured in the picture above? Tell your partner about one of them or say which one you would like to read and explain why.

Tomorrow's World

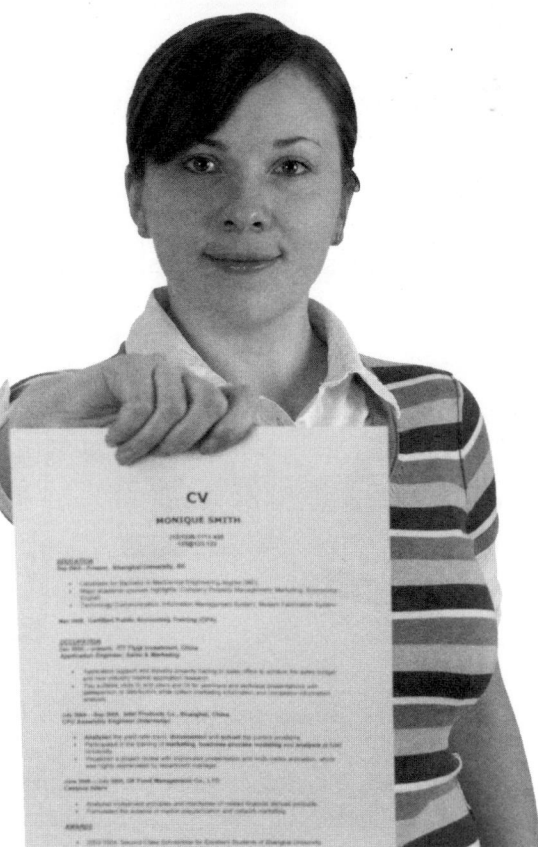

1 Read the text (paragraphs 1-6) about writing CVs and match the headings with the correct paragraphs.

1 Be honest — *D*
2 Check, double-check and triple-check for mistakes — ☐
3 How to write the Perfect CV — ☐
4 Keep it short — ☐
5 Made to measure — ☐
6 Stand out from the crowd — ☐

Building Your Future

A

You've identified your dream job, found a vacancy and are going to submit an application. The only problem is your CV: you haven't updated it since you applied for that summer job two years ago. There are a lot of other people out there who would like your dream job, so your CV needs to impress the recruiter to get you even to interview stage. Make sure that your application goes on the interview pile, and not in the rubbish bin. Here's how:

B

An obvious point, perhaps. But you would be amazed how many CVs employers receive with typos and spelling mistakes. According to a survey of recruitment professionals carried out in Britain by the Recruitment and Employment Confederation, 47% reported that 50% of the CVs they received contained grammar mistakes, with most errors found in CVs from 21- to 25-year-olds. For a busy recruiter with a pile of CVs to get through, finding even a minor error is a good excuse for discarding an application. Look out for these common mistakes:

spelling	*grammar*
recieve	could of, should of etc
correspondance	it's / its
definately	practice / to practise
Febuary	advice / to advise
	their / there / they're

C

You might feel that you can't possibly squeeze all your achievements into less than a short book. According to the experts, however, two pages is perfect, three acceptable if you have years of experience. Remember that you're selling yourself on paper to a recruiter with limited time. Showcase your strengths – and demonstrate your ability to edit at the same time.

2 Read the text again. For questions 1-8, choose the answer (A, B, C or D) which you think fits best according to the text.

1 In a survey about the quality of CVs, just under half of the respondents said that there were problems with use of grammar in

A all of the CVs they received. ☐

B 47% of the CVs they received. ☐

C half of the CVs they received from 21- to 25-year-olds. ☐

D half of all the CVs they received. ☐

2 For a recruiter, finding errors in CVs can be

A unexpected. ☐

B amazing. ☐

C useful. ☐

D annoying. ☐

D

It's fine to edit your experience so that you only include the most relevant information for the job. But don't be tempted to try and make yourself seem better qualified, or more experienced, to fit the role on offer. You will invariably be found out, either through employers checking information, or being caught out later on the job when your skills are put to the test.

E

With hundreds of black-and-white CVs to struggle through, an original approach can catch a recruiter's eye. You might not want to go as far as the aspiring – and successful – applicant who designed an 'employ me' invitation to send to the PR company she'd set her sights on. But do think about creative use of layout and colour to give your CV an edge over all the others.

F

Research your prospective employer. Find out what they like and what they don't like, what their company outlook is. This will help you gear your CV towards them. Some recruiters like to get a flavour of an applicant's personality through a personal summary in a CV, for example, where hobbies and interests are included but others don't. Remember that a CV needs to be tailored to fit every position you apply for – sending identical versions round to various employers by email will usually get you no further than their spam folder.

3 Which phrase best summarises the advice about the length of a CV?

A Three's a crowd. ☐

B Less is more. ☐

C Practice makes perfect. ☐

D More or less. ☐

4 Which sentence best summarises the advice about the content of a CV?

A Highlight what you're good at and don't include unnecessary detail. ☐

B Mention everything you're good at, giving lots of detail. ☐

C Don't leave out any details of your work experience. ☐

D Leave it to the recruiter to pick out the most important information. ☐

5 According to the text, being untruthful about your abilities in a CV

A could be helpful in the long-term. ☐

B is never helpful in the long-term. ☐

C could mean that your employer asks you to do an exam. ☐

D is the sensible option if you're not qualified for the job. ☐

6 The woman whose application was unconventional

A got as far as the interview stage but no further. ☐

B got the job she applied for. ☐

C invited lots of companies to meet her. ☐

D was looking for a job as a designer. ☐

7 Getting information about a prospective employer will help you with your CV by

A enabling you to find out if you like the company or not. ☐

B enabling you to find out where to send it to. ☐

C enabling you to style it so that it has more chance of success with a particular company. ☐

D providing you with information about the kind of personality they like. ☐

8 CVs sent round to prospective employers by email are unlikely to be well-received if they

A are not customised to the company. ☐

B include information about hobbies and interests. ☐

C aren't in summary form. ☐

D don't include information about hobbies and interests. ☐

Unit 6

Vocabulary

Jobs

3 Match the two halves of the sentences to make definitions for words / phrases to do with jobs and work.

1 The money you get each month from working is
2 When you are asked to leave your job because you're not doing it well,
3 When you are without a job and getting money to live on from the state,
4 When you are without a job,
5 When you change from one position to a higher level one,
6 When you choose to voluntarily leave your job,
7 When you complete a piece of paper with details of your qualifications, skills and experience,
8 When you have to leave your job because there isn't enough work for you,
9 When you receive money each month to live on after you have stopped working because you are older,
10 When you stop working because you are older, in lots of countries at the age of 65,
11 When you've applied for a job and you go to a meeting where you are asked questions about your skills and professional experience,

a you get the sack.
b you get made redundant.
c you resign.
d you are unemployed.
e you are on the dole.
f you retire.
g your salary.
h you get a pension.
i you fill in / out an application form.
j you have an interview.
k you get a promotion.

4 Complete the following sentences with words / phrases from Exercise 3, putting them in the correct form as necessary.

1 I was so fed up with the way they were treating me at work that I ....
2 I can't imagine .... at sixty-five – that seems so young nowadays to stop working!
3 My .... really isn't enough to live on – I may be seventy-one, but I'm going to have to try and get some part-time work, I think.
4 I've got an .... next week for a job. I hope they don't ask me too many difficult questions!
5 She's got a really good .... She's going from being a teacher to head teacher of the school.
6 My .... hasn't gone up since I started in the job – I still get the same amount each month as I was getting when I started there.
7 I can't believe that the .... for this job is so difficult – I've got to write down every job I've ever done, from the age of sixteen!
8 I still don't understand why I .... I thought I was doing a really good job.
9 They've made two hundred people .... They say it's due to the recession.
10 I've been .... ever since I lost my last job. At least I'm getting some money each month, but it's not very much.
11 The latest government figures have revealed that there are now more than two million people .... in this country – all those poor people without jobs.

Grammar

Future Tenses

5 Decide which sentences use a future form incorrectly and correct them.

1 She's having her birthday party on Saturday afternoon.
2 By 2010, we will live in Spain for ten years.
3 I'm going to stay in and watch TV tonight.
4 Come round at about 9 o'clock tonight – the children will have had dinner by then.
5 This time tomorrow, we are lying on a beach sunbathing.
6 I pick you up at 8 p.m., OK?
7 I'm sure he phones tomorrow, so don't worry.
8 Will you still love me when I'm old?
9 The Brighton train leaves at 10.30 a.m.
10 Feel how cold it is – it will snow, I'm sure!

6 Complete the following dialogues with the correct form of the verb, adding any pronouns as necessary.

1

Ben: So, you **1** .... (*get married*) on Saturday. How exciting! Where **2** .... (*go*) for the honeymoon?

Tom: I don't know yet – it's a surprise. But Anna did tell me that this time next week, we **3** .... (*relax*) on a beach somewhere, so I **4** .... (*look forward to*) that!

2

Jane: So, what time **5** .... (*be*) the flight again?

Isobel: Well, it was supposed to be 12.30, but I've just looked it up on the Internet, and now it looks like it **6** .... (*take off*) off late.

Jane: Oh no, how late **7** .... (*be*)?

3

Jill: So what are your plans? What **8** .... (*do*), now you've been made redundant?

John: I'm not really sure, to be honest. But I've got my redundancy money, which **9** .... (*last*) me a while, so I think I **10** .... (*take*) some time off to think about what to do next.

Jill: That sounds like a good idea.

4

Emma: Have you ever thought about what you **11** .... (*do*) when you retire? I mean, how **12** .... (*live*)?

Mick: Not really. I know I should. By the time we retire, there **13** .... (*not be*) any money for state pensions, I'm sure of that.

Emma: Do you really think it **14** .... (*be*) that bad? So, you reckon that we **15** .... (*live*) on the streets, then, because we **16** .... (*not have*) any money?

Mick: Well, I don't want to be pessimistic or anything, but I really can't see what solution the state **17** .... (*come up with*).

Emma: Well, they **18** .... (*just have to*) think of something, **19** .... they?

Mick: Don't worry. I **20** .... (*share*) my shop doorway with you!

Use of English Part 3

7 Read the text below. Use the word given in capitals at the end of some of the lines to form a word that fits in the gap in the same line.

What skills and qualities do you need in the workplace to **1** .... today? Is it enough simply to do your job well? Apparently not. Here's what the experts say you need for the jobs of the future, in no particular order of importance:	SUCCESS
Be a good member of a team.	
Have a good understanding of **2**	REAL
Be creative and **3**	IMAGINATION
Be **4** .... , both on a personal and professional level.	ETHICS
Have good taste.	
Be able to express your **5**	EMOTIONAL
Be **6** .... to change.	ADAPT
Be able to maintain a realistic view of yourself and your **7** .... even when working as a team.	CONTRIBUTE
Be willing to learn new things.	
Be open to new ideas.	
Be **8**	RESOURCE
Be a good **9**	COMUNICATE
Have good IT skills.	
Be **10**	RELY

8 Did you use to go to the circus as a small child? Which was your favourite act? Was there anything that you didn't like about the circus or that frightened you? Are you familiar with the names of the acts being performed in the photographs below? Describe the photographs and discuss the answers to the questions with a partner.

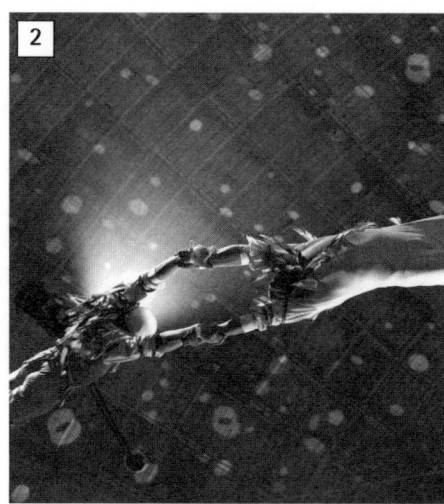

 9 You will hear a radio interview with a man who has an extremely unusual job. For questions 1-7, choose the best answer (A, B or C).

1 David Zebor
   A makes his living firing cannons.
   B makes cannonballs.
   C earns his wages being shot from a cannon.   `1`

2 While David flies through the air, his full concentration is focused on
   A the speed he is traveling at.
   B the safety net.
   C the audience down below.   `2`

3 If he gets the timings wrong,
   A he might lose his job.
   B he could get hurt.
   C he won't get it 100% right.   `3`

4 He started training
   A when he was just a small child.
   B with his parents in an acrobatic act in Eastern Europe.
   C when he was grown up.   `4`

5 Air is pumped at high pressure into the space
   A underneath where David is standing.
   B above the platform.
   C on top of the cannon.   `5`

6 He has to be careful he
   A doesn't land on his back.
   B doesn't get caught up in the wires.
   C isn't fired straight into the canopy.   `6`

7 People contemplating this line of work should bear in mind that
   A they won't earn a fortune.
   B they will have to spend a lot of time in Guyana.
   C they may not have enough strength in their knees and back.   `7`

10 Listen to the interview again and complete the gaps in the sentences.

1 David feels .... before each show.
2 David compares being fired from a cannon to ....
3 During his act he has to know exactly when to ....
4 Accidents are avoided by test firing a .... of David.
5 Preparation includes constantly reinforcing his back and ....
6 He also had to get his body used to being .... at such high speeds.

11 List the advantages and disadvantages of such an unusual job and discuss them in pairs or small groups.

What a Brainwave!

1 You are going to read an article about Tim Berners-Lee, the inventor of the Internet. Seven sentences have been removed from the article. Choose from the sentences A-H the one which fits each gap (1-7). There is one extra sentence which you do not need to use.

Movers and Shakers: Tim Berners-Lee

Sir Tim Berners-Lee was born in London in June 1955. [1] His parents were both mathematicians and they had been part of the team which built one of the earliest computers, the *Manchester Mark 1*. They had mathematics running through their blood and never wasted an opportunity to teach their son, even when he was eating his dinner.

[2] While he was at university, he was banned from using the university computer because he had been caught hacking. After graduation in 1977, he had a series of jobs in information technology. In 1980, he got a contract job at CERN, the world's largest particle physics laboratory based near Geneva, Switzerland. [3]

While working at CERN, Berners-Lee developed a project called ENQUIRE, to make it easier to share and update information between researchers and their computers. [4] The first web site ever built was put online at CERN in August 1991. Its aim was to provide information about the World Wide Web itself.

CERN agreed with Berners-Lee that the WWW idea had to be made available for free, which was probably one of the most important decisions made in recent history. [5] That has been one of the reasons behind the extraordinary growth of the Internet.

Tim Berners-Lee has strong ideas about the Web and how it should develop. He says it is just as important to be able to edit or add to the Web as it is simply to browse it. The structure of the Internet, he believes, has to resemble a spider's web and not a hierarchy and again this ensures that everyone can, in theory, access everything on the Internet, if they have access privileges. [6] He also believes that computer scientists have a moral responsibility to make sure their inventions and developments work for the best interests of all.

[7] These are the people and organisations that protect the democratic nature of the Internet, preventing any one person or company from having too much control over it.

A After school, Tim Berners-Lee studied physics at the University of Oxford.

B Berners-Lee has also founded the World Wide Web Consortium, also known as W3C, which creates standards and recommendations to improve the quality of the Web and uses partners throughout the world to do this.

C He is an idealist and believes that computers can help people work together better.

D It was here that the biggest and most important technological development the world has ever seen began.

E He was brought up in a house where everyone breathed mathematics with their oxygen.

F His invention has become so much a part of out lives that it is difficult to believe that life even existed before the Internet.

G It meant that everyone with a computer and access to the internet could use it for free.

H Not long after that, the World Wide Web (WWW) was born.

Vocabulary

Phrasal Verbs

2 Choose the correct particle to add to *come* to form a phrasal verb to match the definition.

across	up with	down with	into	out	over	round	round	up against

1 find by chance	come _across_ sth
2 become ill with	come .... sth
3 inherit	come .... sth
4 be faced with a problem / difficulty in doing sth	come .... sth
5 visit sb at their home (two phrasal verbs)	come .... / ....
6 regain consciousness	come ....
7 be published (book), first shown (film)	come ....
8 think of sth	come .... sth

3 Match the two halves of the sentences.

1 He doesn't look well. I think
2 It's the premiere in London on Friday,
3 It's difficult to know what to do,
4 I must tidy up the flat,
5 After her grandmother died,
6 It can be tough for women working in certain professions,
7 I was cleaning out a cupboard,
8 He collapsed after running the marathon

a and never came round, I'm sorry to say. ☐
b as my parents are coming round / over! ☐
c as they still come up against a lot of discrimination. ☐
d but I'd like everyone to try and come up with a possible solution. ☐
e he's coming down with something. ☐
f she came into a bit of money. ☐
g but it won't come out in my town until next week. ☐
h when I came across an old book that I'd thought I lost years before. ☐

Grammar

Passive Forms

4 Match what the speakers say with the inventions listed below (there is one extra invention), then complete each comment by putting the verb in brackets into the correct passive form.

1 television ☐
2 MP3 player ☐
3 mobile phone ☐
4 cashpoint machine ☐
5 video game console ☐
6 CD player ☐
7 microwave oven ☐
8 the Internet ☐

a My Mum remembers when it first started .... (*use*) by ordinary people – I mean, not just scientists – and that was only in the mid 90s. Can you imagine life today without email or YouTube?

b I'm sorry that these .... (*ever invent*). I never use them. I really worry about what they do to food.

c I wish these .... (*never invent*). I'm not into them at all, but my sister is completely addicted – she doesn't want to do anything else except play with these.

d I think these .... (*make*) obsolete, really, by newer ways of getting and listening to music. I mean, I play all my music through the computer now. Don't you?

e I reckon that by the end of the decade, everyone .... (*persuade*) that it's not worth bothering with one of these – we can just watch everything through the computer instead.

f I can't stand it when they .... (*turn off*) in class. I think it's so rude for students to take calls when the teacher's in the middle of a lesson!

g This must be one of the most useful things ever to .... (*invent*). I mean, to be able to get hold of your money wherever and whenever you want. That's amazing, really.

Use of English Part 4

5 Complete the second sentence so that it has a similar meaning to the first, using the keyword given.

1 It took him a long time to become accustomed to working such long hours.
USED
It took him a long time to ....
.... long hours.

2 The government is facing a lot of opposition to its plans to build a new runway.
AGAINST
The government is .... a lot of opposition to its plans to build a new runway.

3 I'll come with you if you take me out for dinner afterwards.
WON'T
I .... you take me out for dinner afterwards.

4 She refused him permission to come home late on Saturday night.
LET
She .... home late on Saturday night.

5 Please phone me immediately after you arrive.
AS
Please phone me .... you arrive.

6 Now Lucy's older, it's not necessary for her to wear a uniform to school.
DOES
Now Lucy's older, she .... wear a unifrom to school.

7 She doesn't like using microwave ovens.
ON
She's .... using microwave ovens.

8 They finally thought of a solution to the problem.
UP
They finally .... a solution to the problem.

Listening Part 4

6   Can you name these inventions? Which do you think is the most ingenious and why?

7   You will hear an interview about the man who invented the cash machine, John Shepherd-Barron. For questions 1-10, complete the sentences.

The Cash Machine

It was the [____1____] that first gave John Shepherd-Barron this idea.

The chief executive of the bank was totally [____2____] by his idea.

The machine worked on [____3____] rather than plastic cards then.

Although the substance the cheques were soaked in was radioactive, it wasn't [____4____] for the users.

The machine worked by linking a [____5____] to the cheque.

You couldn't [____6____] more than £10 a time.

The machines being [____7____] was the first difficulty installers had to face.

Mr Shepherd-Barron's wife was responsible for the invention of the four [____8____] Pin number.

Even though there's a [____9____] commemorating its 25th anniversary, most people are unaware of the cash dispenser's historical significance.

The security expert believes people will soon start using their mobile phones instead of [____10____] for their purchases.

8   Listen to the interview again and answer the following questions.

1 When does this invention date back to? ....
2 Where was it first installed? ....
3 Who was the first withdrawal made by? ....
4 Where did the inventor happen to be when he came up with the idea? ....
5 Who showed no hesitation whatsoever regarding this invention? ....
6 What did the machine take instead of the cards we use today? ....
7 How did the carbon 14 work? ....
8 Who came up with the idea of the four figure pin number? ....
9 How many cash machines are there in the world today? ....
10 What does the speaker feel cash will be replaced by in the future? ....

9   Which invention do you think man could never do without today? Discuss your ideas with a partner.

48

In Speaking Part 4 thé examiner asks you questions about the topic dealt with in Part 3. This part of the Speaking Paper tests your ability to engage in a more in-depth discussion.

Practical Tips

- Try to give full answers to the questions you are asked.
- Make sure you don't dominate the conversation or interrupt when your partner is speaking.
- Remember to initiate, listen and respond as you did in Part 3.
- Tell the examiner if you are not familiar with the topic he is asking you about!

10 Read the following questions carefully and write down the answers. Then discuss them with a partner and give a reason for each answer.

1 Which invention do you think has had the greatest influence on the way we live our lives today?
....

2 Who, in your opinion, is the greatest inventor of all times? Why?
....

3 Can you name any inventions which have saved people's lives?
....

4 Do you believe we would have been better off without some inventions?
....

5 Do you know how people can protect their inventions from being copied by someone else?
....

6 Have you ever watched a programme featuring modern inventors and their inventions? What was it like?
....

7 Who do you think is more gifted? Inventors of the past or the inventors of today?
....

8 What qualities should an inventor have in order to make his or her invention a success?
....

9 What sort of difficulties do you think inventors face when trying to persuade people to sponsor their inventions?
....

10 Have you or any of your friends ever entered a competition where you had to invent something?
....

11 If you were to invent something, what do you think people would benefit from most today?
....

12 Do you know of any Nobel Prize Winners who have been awarded prizes for their inventions?
....

Happy Holidays!

Reading Part 1

1 Read the article and choose the best travel information below to describe the writer's rail and sea journey.

1 Leave Paris at 4.15 p.m., arrive in London at 12.15 a.m. ☐
2 Leave Paris just before 7 a.m., arrive in London around 3 p.m. ☐
3 Leave Paris at 6 a.m., arrive in London just before 1 p.m. ☐

The Good Old Times

The champagne was coming around for the second time on the 16.13 Eurostar from Paris Gare du Nord to London St Pancras when we came to a halt. The guard announced that there had been an incident in the tunnel, necessitating a return to Paris. 'Terrorist attack,' the executive next to me asserted. Seemingly untroubled, he took out his Blackberry and arranged for his 'people' to book him a London-bound flight from Paris Charles de Gaulle.

As news filtered through that it wasn't a terrorist attack, but a fire in the tunnel, I saw the possibility of revisiting a journey I thought I'd enjoyed for the last time some years before: the old rail-sea-rail route. This was the last survivor of the boat train era, in that you caught a train from Paris to Calais, took the cross-Channel ferry, then another train from Dover to London or vice versa. And you used to be able to do it on a single ticket. I liked to buy this from Charing Cross Station, partly just for the fun of registering the shock of the people queuing behind me for tickets to the London suburbs as I confidently asked for one to Paris; surprise that soon turned to irritation, because the rail-sea-rail ticket had to be written out by hand, which took about 10 minutes.

The journey in either direction took roughly eight hours, but for a while the price (about £60 for a return)

compared favourably with Eurostar fares. When Eurostar began to make their cheapest fares more widely available, however, the rail-sea-rail ticket began to die a painful death.

The rail-sea-rail was heir of the Golden Arrow (1929-1972), which was called *Flèche d'Or* on the French side and ran directly to the docks at Dover Marine and Calais Maritime, both now closed. To me, the route still carried an echo of that glamour, although it was a very faint echo as I entered a gloomy Gare du Nord at 6 a.m. the morning after the fire. The Eurostar section was closed off, and a crowd of passengers contemplated a notice informing them that no service would operate that day. I wondered how many of them had learnt that their Eurostar tickets would be valid on the ordinary train to the coast.

The SNCF train service between Paris and Calais has gradually been downgraded, so that a change en route is inevitable. The 6.58 involved a change at Lille. It was packed with displaced Eurostar passengers debating whether they needed to head for Calais Frethun or Calais Ville station in order to catch a ferry. I knew it was Calais Ville, and I was torn between showing off my knowledge and keeping it to myself, because I knew there'd be quite a bottleneck of people there.

At Lille Flandres, I boarded the 9.14 for Calais Frethun, and it seemed that many other Eurostar passengers had also made it. I predicted we would have to take a further train connection from Frethun to Calais Ville, and when this proved correct, I began to be regarded as something of a travel expert by the Eurostar passengers.

It was strange to see this crowd, with their stylish clothes and suitcases, streaming through the concourse of Calais Ville station, which is normally inhabited by a couple of sleeping tramps, a ticket clerk and the bloke who keeps the station bar. Emerging from the station, I pointed out to my companions the bus stop to the left from where buses left for the ferry terminal. But knowing what I do about those buses, I climbed into a taxi.

I arrived at the ferry terminal at 10.45 and bought a ticket for the next departure, at 11.05. During the crossing, the sun glimmered on the Channel, and I recalled the words of a Eurostar refusnik I'd met on a rail-sea-rail trip in about 2002: 'I'd rather be on the sea than under it.'

At Dover Priory station, I caught the 12.50, which arrived in London, at Charing Cross station, two hours later. That night, I went to bed at 9 p.m. and slept until lunchtime, which is part of the appeal of the rail-sea-rail route: you really know you've made a journey.

2 Read the article again. For questions 1–8, choose the answer (A, B, C or D) which you think fits best according to the text.

1 What happened to stop the 16.13 Eurostar train getting to London St. Pancras?

A There was a terrorist attack. ☐
B There was a problem with the guard. ☐
C There was a fire. ☐
D The train broke down. ☐

2 What alternative travel plans did the writer's fellow passenger on the Eurostar make?

A to go to London on another train ☐
B to go to London by plane ☐
C to stay in Paris ☐
D to go to Paris by plane ☐

3 For the writer, the idea of travelling by train and ferry to London is

A depressing. ☐
B funny. ☐
C shocking. ☐
D appealing. ☐

4 What happened to the single ticket train and ferry route between Paris and London?

A In the end, it couldn't compete with Eurostar ticket prices. ☐
B It stopped in 1972. ☐
C It stopped as soon as the Eurostar train service began. ☐
D It stopped because passengers preferred the speed of the Eurostar train. ☐

5 Nowadays, non-Eurostar train services between Paris and London

A continue to stations at the ports in Dover and Calais. ☐
B continue to a station at the port only on the French side. ☐
C continue to a station at the port only on the British side. ☐
D don't continue to stations at the ports either in Dover or Calais. ☐

6 In relation to his fellow passengers the morning after the incident on the Eurostar, the writer

A was rather reluctant to share his knowledge of the rail-sea-rail route to London with them. ☐
B was happy to share his superior knowledge of the route with them. ☐
C felt as displaced as they did, after changing trains at Lille. ☐
D wanted to discuss with them the best route to take from Lille to Calais. ☐

7 Calais Ville train station is usually

A full of people. ☐
B quite empty. ☐
C used mainly by homeless people. ☐
D a popular place for fashionable people. ☐

8 The writer remembers a fellow passenger from a previous train and ferry journey between London and Paris who

A usually refused to travel anywhere. ☐
B didn't like travelling on trains. ☐
C didn't like the idea of travelling in the Eurostar tunnel. ☐
D didn't like travelling on boats. ☐

Unit 8

Vocabulary

Holidays

3 Find 8 words connected with holidays and travel in the wordsearch to match the definitions below.

```
N T P K B K Y R M O M G
G N I E E S T H G I S N
H I O K P S E Y C Q J I
J N M I A I E H R C T K
V L N F T N R R U O T K
K O A J R I M T I D Q E
R R Y U W J D X S W I R
I E O A J F K E E X P T
M J C P G C A M P I N G
L P V B B E U N T X D M
X I K A J V L H Q D E R
Q A H P Z U N I O W H L
```

1 When you stay in a tent on holiday.
2 A holiday where you stay and travel on a ship.
3 A holiday where you walk a long distance, usually through mountains or forests.
4 A holiday where you look at wild animals in their natural habitat.
5 Visiting places of interest, e.g. the main monuments in a place.
6 A visit to a place or an area, often with a guide.
7 When you go somewhere, usually for a short time, then come back again.
8 A long journey by ship or in space.

4 Choose the correct word to complete the sentences about travel.

1 Last summer, we went on a .... round the Caribbean on a friend's yacht – it was wonderful.
  A trek   **B** cruise   **C** drive
2 Since they started the roadworks on the motorway, the .... to work takes me so long every morning.
  A excursion   **B** voyage   **C** journey
3 I love .... holidays – I really like just being able to pack up the accommodation when you feel like it, and move on to the next place.
  A sightseeing   **B** camping   **C** fly and drive
4 The .... of the castle was very interesting – the guide really knew what she was talking about.
  A tour   **B** trip   **C** sightseeing

5 My parents are going to Africa on a .... this summer – my mother's always wanted to see lions in a natural setting, I mean, away from the zoo!
  A trek   **B** trip   **C** safari
6 I'm going on a shopping .... to New York at Christmas. Three days of nothing but shopping – I can't wait!
  A trek   **B** trip   **C** excursion
7 My children don't much like .... holidays in cities in summer – all that walking around hot streets looking at things makes them very bad-tempered!
  A sightseeing   **B** trekking   **C** fly and drive
8 It's good to .... – to get away from everyday life and see something different.
  A journey   **B** travel   **C** tour

Grammar

Wh- questions

5 Complete the questions with a word from the box, and use the correct form of the verb provided.

| where   what (x 2)   when   whose |
| which   who (x 2)   How many   How much |

1 .... (drive) to the party last night? You or her?
2 .... (happen) to you? You look terrible.
3 .... (you get back) from the U.S.A.? On Monday?
4 .... (you go) on the cruise with? Your husband?
5 .... house .... (you stay) at in France? Jane's again?
6 .... (be) the weather like on your holiday?
7 .... (you go) on holiday last summer? Turkey again?
8 .... country .... (you like) best – Spain, Italy or France?
9 .... people .... (go) on the trip last week? Lots?
10 .... the holiday .... (cost) altogether?

6 Match the following answers to a question in Exercise 5.

1 No, we went to Slovenia, actually. ☐
2 Terrible. Rained every day! ☐
3 No, early this morning. I'm exhausted! ☐
4 Yeah, that's right. She's so kind lending us her place whenever we want it. ☐
5 I really couldn't pick one in particular. I love them all! ☐
6 I've got terrible jet-lag. I've just arrived back from Australia. I just need to sleep. ☐
7 Yeah, that's right. It was like a second honeymoon! ☐
8 I did. She was too tired. ☐
9 No, not that many, really. A lot cancelled at the last moment. ☐
10 I'd say about a thousand pounds in total. ☐

Grammar

Question Tags

7 Complete the following sentences with the correct question tag.

1 You don't like sightseeing very much, ... ?
2 Camping in the UK in the summer can be very wet, ... ?
3 We're not going to miss the flight, ... ?
4 I'm not too late, ... ?
5 You wouldn't be able to give me a lift to the station, ... ?
6 You weren't in Mumbai during the terrorist attacks, ... ?
7 He didn't cancel the holiday, ... ?
8 You won't forget to phone me when you arrive, ... ?

8 Read the recommendations below for a safe holiday. Use the words given in capitals at the end of some of the lines to form a word that fits in the gap in the same line.

Before you go...

Read lots of different **1** .... guides about the place or country you are going to, and take what you	TRAVELLING
think is the **2** .... one with you.	GOOD
Buy some good, **3** .... maps of the area you are going to.	DETAIL
Take as few clothes with you as possible. If you need any more when you are away you can buy things at local markets. They will be cheap and	
4 .... of the place you are staying.	CHARACTER
Take all your personal **5**	HYGIENIC
and washing products with you, as well as any **6** .... you might need.	MEDICINE
Take at least two pairs of good quality walking shoes – they should be lightweight and **7**	COMFORT
Take a book to read while waiting for the next **8** .... or train, and	FLY
your own travel journal to write in. Never put your money, passport or travel tickets together – put them	
9 .... in different parts of	SECURE
your luggage. Even **10** .... ,	GOOD
a money pouch or belt will keep important things safe.	

9 Read the clues and complete the crossword.

Across

3 make a choice from a range of possibilities
6 a person who steals from a house or building
7 the outer edge of a circular object
8 the first appearance of light in the sky before sunrise
10 a sudden large increase, typically a temporary one

Down

1 a unit used to measure the intensity of a sound
2 a stand used for the sale of goods in a market or large covered area
4 preconceived opinion that is not based on reason or actual experience
5 a minor illness
9 when it grows dark

10 You will hear people talking in eight different situations. For questions 1–8, choose the best answer (A, B or C).

1 You hear a young man talking.
Why did he decide to take part in the campaign?
A He wanted to make some money working on the stalls.
B He wanted an opportunity to fight discrimination.
C He lives in an intolerant community.

2 You hear part of a lecture about the chilli pepper.
What is the lecturer describing?
A How the chilli pepper reduces inflammation in arthritis.
B The benefits you can get from eating chilli peppers.
C How to prepare tasty dishes with chilli peppers.

3 You hear a woman talking about training for the Olympics.
How does she feel?
A She regrets taking part.
B She thinks all the hard work was worthwhile.
C She wishes she'd done better.

4 You hear a doctor being interviewed on the radio.
What is he concerned about?
A the decibels some mp3 players are unable to reach.
B the noise safety levels imposed upon users.
C the increasing number of people listening to dangerously loud music.

5 You hear a woman talking about the famous writer, Beatrix Potter.
What difficulties does she say Beatrix Potter came across?
A Publishers were unwilling to accept her work.
B She was unable to replace the black and white sketches.
C She couldn't publish the letter without Noel Moore's consent.

6 You hear a man talking on the radio.
What is he?
A a restaurant manager
B a chef
C a waiter

7 You hear a man talking about an exhibition he recently went to.
Which invention appealed to him the most?
A the glasses
B the bell
C the burglar alarm

8 You hear a woman talking about a holiday experience.
Why did she miss her flight?
A She forgot to pick up her tickets.
B Her alarm didn't go off.
C She didn't get a good night's sleep.

11 Listen again and decide if the following statements are T (True) or F (False).

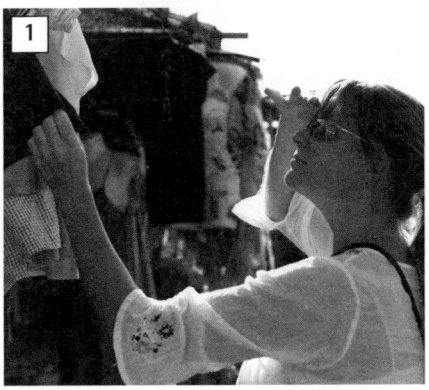  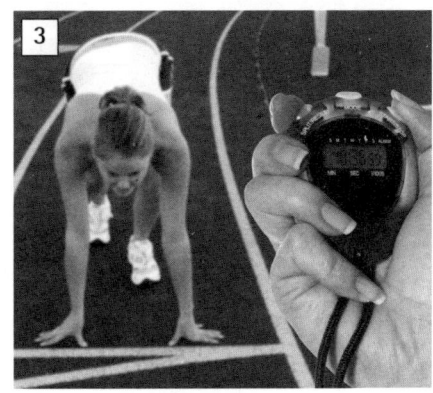

	T	F
1 Speaker 1 works on a market stall selling clothes.	☐	☐
2 Speaker 2 advises people to wear goggles when cutting up chilli peppers.	☐	☐
3 Speaker 3 would rather have seen more of her trainer before the Olympics.	☐	☐
4 According to the doctor it's impossible to hack through the sound limiters on ipods.	☐	☐
5 Speaker 5 claims Beatrix Potter did the sketches in the story of Peter Rabbit herself.	☐	☐
6 Speaker 6 was fired by the manager for spilling food on one of the customers.	☐	☐
7 Speaker 7 was put off the night time reading glasses by the battery.	☐	☐
8 Speaker 8 said she was given a fine for speeding on the motorway.	☐	☐

12 You heard the idioms *throw in the towel* and *spic and span* in the recording. Discuss their meanings with a partner and then match the idioms (1–10) to their meanings (a–j).

1 a blessing in disguise
2 a chip on your shoulder
3 at the drop of a hat
4 back to the drawing board
5 drive someone up the wall
6 hit the nail on the head
7 know the ropes
8 let bygones be bygones
9 pass the buck
10 under the weather

a forget about a disagreement that happened in the past ☐
b when an attempt fails and you have to start again ☐
c feel ill or sick ☐
d irritate or annoy someone very much ☐
e avoid responsibility by giving it to someone else ☐
f understand how to do something ☐
g when bad luck or misfortune results in something positive ☐
h being upset or angry due to something that happened in the past ☐
i do or say exactly the right thing ☐
j do something immediately ☐

Man's Best Friend

1 Match the words and phrases below with the picture that illustrates them.

1 a perch ☐
2 a food trough ☐
3 a paw ☐
4 bars ☐
5 a barn ☐
6 a roe-deer ☐

2 You are going to read an extract from a novel. Seven sentences have been removed from the extract. Choose from the sentences A-H the one which fits each gap (1-7). There is one extra sentence which you do not need to use.

Life at the Zoo

There will always be animals that seek to escape from zoos. ☐1☐ Every animal has particular habitat needs that must be met. If its enclosure is too sunny or too wet or too empty, if its perch is too high or too exposed, if the ground is too sandy, if there are too few branches to make a nest, if the food trough is too low, if there is not enough mud to wallow in - and so many other ifs - then the animal will not be at peace. It is not so much a question of constructing an imitation of conditions in the wild as of getting to the essence of these conditions. ☐2☐ A plague upon bad zoos with bad enclosures! They bring all zoos into disrepute.

Wild animals that are captured when they are fully mature are another example of escape-prone animals; often they are too set in their ways to reconstruct their subjective worlds and adapt to a new environment.

But even animals that were bred in zoos and have never known the wild, that are perfectly adapted to their enclosures and feel no tension in the presence of humans, will have moments of excitement that push them to escape. All living things contain a measure of madness that moves them in strange, sometimes inexplicable ways. ☐3☐ Without it, no species would survive.

Whatever the reason for wanting to escape, sane or insane, zoo detractors should realize that animals don't escape to somewhere but from something. Something within their territory has frightened them - the intrusion of an enemy, the assault of a dominant animal, a startling noise - and set off a flight reaction. ☐4☐ I was surprised to read at the Toronto Zoo - a very fine zoo, I might add - that leopards can jump eighteen feet straight up. ☐5☐ I surmise that Rosie

and Copycat never jumped out not because of constitutional weakness but simply because they had no reason to. Animals that escape go from the known into the unknown - and if there is one thing an animal hates above all else, it is the unknown. Escaping animals usually hide in the very first place they find that gives them a sense of security, and they are dangerous only to those who happen to get between them and their reckoned safe spot. ☐6☐ She was new to the zoo and seemed to get along with the male leopard. But various paw injuries hinted at matrimonial strife. Before any decision could be taken about what to do, she squeezed through a break in the roof bars of her cage and vanished in the

night. ☐7☐ Traps were set and hunting dogs were let loose. Not a trace of the leopard was found for ten weeks. Finally, a casual labourer came upon it under a barn twenty-five miles away and shot it. Remains of roe-deer were found nearby. That a big, black tropical cat managed to survive for more than two months in a Swiss winter without being seen by anyone, let alone attacking anyone, speaks plainly to the fact that escaped zoo animals are not dangerous absconding criminals but simply wild creatures seeking to fit in.

A Animals that are kept in unsuitable enclosures are the most obvious example.

B Consider the case of the female black leopard that escaped from the Zurich Zoo in the winter of 1933.

C Everything in an enclosure must be just right; in other words, within the limits of the animal's capacity to adapt.

D If you city of Tokyo and turned it upside down and shook it, you would be amazed at the animals that would fall out.

E Our leopard enclosure in Pondicherry had a wall sixteen feet high at the back.

F The animal flees, or tries to.

G The discovery that a wild carnivore was free in their midst created an uproar among the citizens of Zurich.

H This madness can be saving; it is part and parcel of the ability to adapt.

Vocabulary

Animal Idioms

3 Match the following animal idioms and sayings with their definition

1 A wolf in sheep's clothing.
2 Catch / kill two birds with one stone.
3 Like a bear with a sore head.
4 Like a lamb to the slaughter.
5 Curiosity killed the cat.
6 You can lead a horse to water, but you can't make it drink.
7 You can't teach an old dog new tricks.
8 Running round like a headless chicken.

a When you warn someone not to ask too many questions about something. ☐

b It's difficult to change someone's habits or character. ☐

c You can make it easy for someone to do something, but you can't make them do it. ☐

d When you're in a bad mood and being unpleasant to other people because of it. ☐

e When you manage to do two things with a single action. ☐

f When someone conceals the fact that they're not a nice person by being charming and friendly. ☐

g When you're very busy doing lots of things, but in an ineffective way. ☐

h When someone does something or goes somewhere calmly and without protesting, because they don't know that something bad is going to happen. ☐

4 Complete the following sentences with an idiom or saying from exercise 3, making any necessary changes in form.

1 He seemed so nice when I first met him, but then turned out to be so horrible. He was a real

....

2 If we go and visit my parents on Saturday, my brother and his family will be there too, so we'll

....

3 Look, you can't possibly clean the house, get that report finished and look after the kids all at the same time. You're .... and nothing's getting done properly.

4 Are you sure you want to know the answers to all those questions? Remember that

.... !

5 He had no idea what she was like when he first got involved with her, how awful she could be to boyfriends. He was ....
.... , poor man.

6 I've shown him how to use it, and given him lots of advice, but he doesn't seem to have taken any notice of what I've said. Still, I suppose you

....

7 I gave her my home phone number, my mobile number, my email, but she still hasn't called – well, you .... !

8 What on earth's the matter with you today? You're in a lousy mood and you're being foul to everybody. You're ....

Grammar

Determiners

5 Complete the dialogues below with the following determiners.

both	each	each of	either
enough	every	most	several
most of	neither	none	none of

1 A Which one would you like?
   B .... I really don't mind.

2 A Shall we go shopping or shall we study for the exam?
   B I think we've got time to do .... But we'd better get some studying done first, before we go shopping, otherwise my mum will get cross with me!

3 A Which skirt do you think would be better for the party – this black one or that red one?
   B .... of them, to be honest! I think you need something completely different.

4 A Have you got .... money to pay the train fare?
   B No, actually I haven't. Could you lend me ten pounds?

5 A So, did you know all the people at the dinner?
   B .... them. There were only a couple that I didn't know.

6 A Do your three sisters all look like you?
   B No, ... us is completely different! Looking at us, you'd never guess we were related.

7 A How much is the bill?
   B It's just over fifty-five pounds – split amongst the six of us, with a tip, that's ten pounds ....

8 A Could you just check to see if we've got any milk left? I'm going shopping later and can get some if we haven't.

B No, there's .... in the fridge at all.

9 A What do you spend .... money on each month, would you say?

B Well, apart from the mortgage, probably heating bills – in winter, at least.

10 A Where do you usually go for your summer holidays?

B Oh, we go to the same place .... single year – to my mother-in-law's in the north of England. I wish we could go somewhere different for once!

11 A Did you have many students in your class tonight?

B No, ... them turned up – not even one! I think it was something to do with the football match.

12 A So, how's the diet going? Have you lost much weight, yet?

B Yes, actually, I've already lost .... kilos. Can't you tell?

6 Rewrite the sentences using a word from the box.

| whatever | whichever | whenever |
| however | whoever | wherever |

1 Come and see me at any time. I'm free the whole week.
Come and see me whenever you like .
I'm free the whole week.

2 I don't mind who you bring to the party – as many people as you want.
.... –
as many people as you like.

3 It doesn't matter which dress you choose – with your figure, they'll all look good on you.
.... – with your
figure, ...

4 I don't care how you do the work, just get it done, even if you have to stay up all night!
.... even if you have
to stay up all night!

5 It doesn't matter where we go skiing, it's going to be expensive. It's not a cheap sport!
....
It's not a cheap sport!

6 It doesn't matter what we say, he won't change his mind. He's so obstinate.
....
He's so obstinate.

7 For questions 1–12, read the text below and decide which answer (A, B, C or D) best fits each gap.

Our Furry Friends

A pet is an animal kept for companionship and 1 .... The most popular pets are noted for their loyal or playful characteristics, for their attractive appearance, or for their 2 .... While in theory any animal might be a pet, in 3 .... only a small number of species of mammals and other small animals, such as birds, fish, or lizards, are practical. One reason for this is that large animals are not able to 4 .... inside small dwellings.

A number of health benefits have been linked with pet ownership. 5 .... an animal around can stimulate the caregiver, in 6 .... the elderly, giving people someone to take care 7 .... , someone to exercise with, and someone to help them heal from a physically or psychologically troubled past. Walking a dog, for example, can provide the owner with exercise, fresh air, and social interaction. 8 .... a pet may help people 9 .... health goals, such as lowered blood pressure, or mental goals, such as decreased 10 .... There appears to be strong evidence that having a pet can help a person lead a longer, healthier life. A recent study 11 .... that owning a pet can reduce the risk of a heart attack by 2% and that pets are better than medication in reducing blood 12 .... There is now a medically-approved class of 'therapy animals', mostly dogs, who are brought to visit confined humans.

	A	B	C	D
1	A enjoy	B enjoying	C enjoyable	D enjoyment
2	A song	B tune	C music	D noise
3	A practical	B practice	C practise	D practising
4	A size	B fit	C reach	D have
5	A Showing	B Coming	C Having	D Being
6	A particular	B special	C private	D fact
7	A in	B at	C with	D of
8	A Caring	B Taking	C Dealing	D Owning
9	A achieve	B live	C make	D challenge
10	A stressful	B stress	C distressing	D stressed
11	A finalised	B ended	C concluded	D terminated
12	A pressure	B tension	C strain	D force

8 Read the definitions and circle the corresponding word in the wordsearch below. Then write the word on the line.

1 a piece of mechanical or electronic equipment

....

2 a set of straps fastened to a dog's body to restrain it

....

3 a sheepdog originating near the border between England and Scotland

....

4 disorderly and disruptive and not amenable to discipline or control

....

5 a line separating two countries, administrative divisions or other areas

....

6 a series of questions about a completed mission or undertaking

....

7 very worried and upset

....

8 give professional help and advice to someone

....

```
Z T K U T W D D G J D B Y F O
L S H R M E U O I C H O E J T
L D U T V H G P Z X C R R O J
T O E I E Z O H H O K D E X B
G R C B F D A I U N P E D R W
S E X H R R U N X Q K R R Q C
A P L V N I S X F A C C O J D
M C G E X E E B U B B O B C U
E P S E L S C F Y W N L G A I
H S T L M K C P I I U L H D U
S X I U N R U L Y N M I J M K
Q N C T O P F O S P G E A Z G
G T H G U A R T S I D X U W E
P H U H V G L E B E Z T W N A
Y S W J R E S O C E D F X W W
```

9 Now complete the sentences with one of the words in Exercise 8.

1 He decided to seek .... as he had been suffering from depression.
2 I do wish you would learn to control your .... behaviour.
3 Guide dogs are trained to wear a ....
4 The kennel we'll be visiting next week breeds ....
5 Sharon was so .... she did nothing but sob all night long.
6 That's a funny looking .... ! Whatever is it for?
7 They won't be safe until they've crossed the .... into Mexico.
8 How long is the .... for the new employees expected to take?

10 Imagine you're the proud owner of a dog! How often would you take it out for walks? Who would be in control? You or the dog? Would the scene be like the one shown in the first or second photograph?

11 You will hear Dr Robert Townsend, an animal psychologist talking about working with animals and their owners. For questions 1-7, choose the best answer (A, B or C).

1 When Dr. Townsend encounters a snarling dog

A he knows he might get bitten.

B he has to overcome his fear.

C he considers it a test of his abilities.

2 The animal centre

A treats all kinds of animals from birds to bears.

B is for owners of disobedient dogs seeking advice.

C sells equipment for pet owners.

3 Dr Townsend was required to give a woman some advice on

A an invention she was designing.

B travel arrangements to and from Northern Ireland.

C how to create a less hectic schedule.

4 Max's owners were worried that

A they knew too little about their dog's background.

B their dog might turn on them or someone else.

C they wouldn't be able to put a stop to all the barking.

5 Dr Townsend's last client that day

A was a distraught neighbour.

B couldn't stop her dog from running round in circles.

C used to live in Germany.

6 Dr Townsend advises would-be animal psychologists

A to charge between £80 and £200.

B never to appear in court on their clients' behalf.

C to get qualified veterinary training.

7 He sums up saying that

A some people have a natural gift when it comes to animals.

B counselling takes a lot of energy.

C not all dog owners can consider themselves so privileged.

12 Can you recall what Dr Townsend did yesterday? Read the text and fill the gaps with the missing words. Then listen and check.

I lead a very busy life with an extremely tight schedule. Let's take yesterday, for example. The first task of the day involved giving an inventor some feedback and advice on a prototype **1** .... she has just developed and wanted me to try out. She travelled all the way from **2** .... , in Northern Ireland for the consultation and when she was leaving she thanked me and said it had been very useful and that I had inspired her to make some crucial **2** .... I was pleased to be of help.

Then I saw Max, a one year-old border collie who had been brought in by his worried owners concerned that his **4** .... behaviour was starting to border on dangerous. Amid constant barking, I questioned Max's owners to find out about his **5** .... and then came to the conclusion that Max was simply **6** .... and in need of firm guidance.

To confirm my assessment I then put a special **7** .... on the dog and I took him outside for a walk. I introduced him to various stimuli along the way - from cows and chicken on the farm to other dogs - in an attempt to get a profile of the dog's **8** ....

After the walk I returned to my office where I observed the dog's reactions to **9** .... and then I gave Max's owners a **10** .... session with suggestions on how to control their dog's unruly behaviour.

After seeing Max, I saw two more dogs and then I had to rush over to Wentworth, a town nearby, to visit a **11** .... client whose German shepherd wouldn't stop **12** .... its own tail!

13 Have you ever considered working with dogs either professionally or voluntarily? Discuss your ideas with a partner.

Are you a Fashion Fanatic?

Reading Part 3

1 Read the four texts (A-D) below from a magazine article where people talk about the most expensive item of clothing or accessory that they have ever bought. Match the texts to the items they describe. There is one extra item.

1 a coat ☐
2 a hat ☐
3 a suit ☐
4 a skirt ☐
5 a wedding dress ☐

Money Well Spent

A - Emma

I bought it to wear to a wedding. A friend of mine was marrying some kind of minor celebrity, so it was a fairly smart affair - in fact, I even made it into a couple of those celebrity gossip magazines, as I happened to be standing next to someone half-famous when the paparazzi took a photo! But, anyway, it was a very striking emerald green, made of a kind of felt material, and it was what I think is called a 'pillbox' style, with a matching green net that sort of draped over the top of your face, like a little veil - very 1940's, really. I wore it with a matching green dress - by some miracle, I'd managed to find one in exactly the same shade - and a black coat. I paid £350 for it, which would be a lot to pay nowadays, even, but fifteen years ago, that was a fortune to spend on an accessory, especially as I wasn't earning very much at the time. But I don't regret it. I wore it lots of times after that, to other weddings or events where I had to look dressed up, and it always used to make me feel really stylish. And still, today, it gets some use, as it's in my daughter's dressing-up box!

B - Lucy

It took me months to find the right one, but, when I finally did, it was perfect. It was sleeveless, quite high-necked and full-length, right down to the floor, with a train so long that it had to be carried by four bridesmaids. It was made of thick silk, with lace edging around the neck and lace panels in the train.
I knew as soon as I tried it on that that was the one - it made me look just how I'd always imagined I'd look on that day.
I don't even want to say how much I paid for it, but let's just say it wasn't exactly cut-price. And then it took me another few weeks to find shoes that matched. I actually ended up going on a trip to Paris to get them, as I couldn't find what I wanted in London. Was it worth all the expense? Well, we'd split up before our third anniversary, so I suppose it wasn't. But, I did look gorgeous wearing it that day, even though I say so myself! And, after I got divorced, I managed to sell it for quite a good price - about half what I paid for it, which wasn't bad.

C - Geoffrey

It was a dark beige colour and made out of linen, which, of course, used to crease terribly after one had had it on for a while. However, with linen, one expected that - and, with the heat in summer, a few wrinkles in one's clothes were a small price to pay for the coolness that the fabric afforded. It was cut beautifully, with both the trousers and jacket hanging perfectly. I'd never had anything custom-made before and one could certainly tell the difference in quality between something made-to-measure compared to off-the-peg I can't remember exactly how much it cost - it was too long ago, now. It was quite costly, though, I do remember that; it was my first posting abroad, and I really

wasn't very well off, so it was a struggle to afford it - something like a week's salary, perhaps. But I wore it for years and years, so I would certainly say that it was worth every penny I paid for it. It's still hanging in my wardrobe today; if I were the slim young man that I was back then, I would happily wear it again!

D - Elizabeth

I bought this in Italy nearly twenty years ago, now, when I was living in Milan. Winters are really cold there, much colder than I had expected, with an added dampness to the air that makes it feel as if the cold is creeping into your bones. I remember going out shopping with the intention of getting something cheap and functional, like an anorak - something sensible, anyway, to beat the cold. But then I saw it in a shop window - dark grey, almost like a cape, with wide sleeves and a hood and a big shawl collar - thousands and thousands of Lira's worth (this was pre-Euro days) of beautiful, warm wool falling to just below the knee. Not exactly a cheap anorak - but

I loved the 1950's look that it had about it and thought that I would just try it on. It was even more beautiful close up, with a black silk lining, and a parka-style draw-string at the back for nipping in the waist if you wanted to. It was far more than I could afford at the time, but it was gorgeous. I just had to buy it, even if it did mean having to borrow money to pay my rent that month. And I've never regretted it. It's nearly two decades old now, and the lining could do with some repair work, but the rest of it looks as good as ever. And I've still never got round to buying that sensible anorak!

2 For questions 1-15, choose from the people (A-D). The people may be chosen more than once.

Which person

• bought the item to wear as a guest at a formal celebration?	1
• doubts whether it was worth spending so much on an item?	2
• had planned to buy something in a very different style?	3
• had to travel to another country to complete her/his outfit?	4
• has gained financially from passing the item on to another person?	5
• mentions the item as being good for protection from the extreme weather?	6
• would wear the item now if it still fitted?	7
• was surprised to have managed to find something that matched the item?	8
• still uses the item for its original purpose?	9
• mentions how wear changed the look of the item?	10
• found themselves inadvertently in the public eye whilst wearing the item?	11
• doesn't mention any difficulty in being able to afford the item?	12
• mentions a feature that allows the item to be modified in shape?	13
• fulfilled a dream with the way they looked when wearing the item?	14
• didn't buy the item already made?	15

Unit 10

Vocabulary

Fashion and Clothes

3 Choose the correct word/expression about fashion to complete the sentences below, changing the form where necessary.

> above the knee   accessory
> break all the rules   loose-fitting   match
> outrageous   smart-casual   timeless

1 Giorgio Armani invented the fashion concept of ' .... ' – easy-to-wear but elegant working clothes.
2 These jeans are too tight. I want something more ....
3 I wore skirts well .... when I was younger, but now I think I'm too old for minis.
4 A classic style will never look dated. It's ....
5 Jean Paul Gaultier .... in the fashion book – he even got men wearing skirts!
6 Punk style, combining razor blades and safety pins with fabrics like tartan, was considered to be .... when it first came out in the 1970's.
7 Christian Dior was the first designer to combine the sale of clothes with .... , such as shoes, handbags and scarves.
8 She gives a lot of attention to small details, like her handbag and shoes always .... perfectly in colour.

Vocabulary

Phrasal Verbs

4 Match the following phrasal verbs with their definition.

1 look back
2 set up sth
3 turn your back on sth
4 pay off
5 turn sth into
6 start off
7 come up with sth

a become sth else
b begin to do
c establish sth
d get good results
e ignore or reject sth
f produce sth especially when challenged
g think about the past

5 Complete the following sentences with a phrasal verb from Exercise 2, putting it in the correct form.

1 He .... his talents .... a multi-million pound fashion empire.
2 She .... as a fashion model, before becoming an actress later on.
3 Mary Quant .... her first shop in the King's Road selling stylish, but inexpensive designs.
4 All that hard work .... in the end – I passed my exams with top grades!
5 After years as a glamorous top model, she .... her .... that whole life and went to live very simply on a farm in the middle of nowhere.
6 If you want to be a success in the fashion world, it's all about .... an idea that no one else has thought of.
7 They launched their first collection in the 1990's and have never .... – every collection since has been a great success.

Grammar

Past Habits

6 Complete the conversation below by using the following verbs with an expression for talking about past habits.

> dress   get   have   help   let
> like   send   take   wear (x 3)

Anna: So, has your style changed at all over the years, Aunty?
Beatrice: Oh yes, definitely! I don't dress nowadays anything like I **1**  *used to dress* when I was younger.
Anna: Really? What kind of things **2** .... you .... back then?
Beatrice: Well, in the 1970's, I was a punk, so I **3** .... all sorts of outrageous stuff!
Anna: You, a punk! Cool!
Beatrice: Yeah, it was great fun. I **4** .... lots of black stuff and tartan, I remember. Mini skirts, bondage trousers – the legs were joined together at the knees with a bicycle chain! And my hair – I **5** .... a green mohican, you know, where all the hair is standing up in the middle of your head and then shaved at the sides.

Anna: Really? That's hard to believe looking at you now, Aunty!

Beatrice: Well, you know, people change. It **6** .... me ages to get ready to go out, to get the hair just right – all that work with extra strong hair gel. My brother **7** .... me do it.

Anna: And what about at school? **8** .... they .... you in school with a hairstyle like that?

Beatrice: Oh, I **9** .... always .... into trouble at school for how I looked and dressed. They **10** .... me to the toilets to wash the gel out and flatten my hair down. And they **11** .... the mini skirts, either!

Anna: So why did you stop being a punk, Aunty?

Beatrice: Well, it wasn't really a conscious decision. It just sort of happened. You know, fashion changes.

Grammar

Emphatic structures with *what*

7 Put the words into the correct order to make sentences with what for emphasis.

1 about / face / hated / I / pins / punks / safety / the / the / through / was / what
   What I hated about punks was the safety pins through the face!

2 about / constantly / fashion / how / I / is / it's / love / what
   ....
   .... changing.

3 do / is / newspaper / should / to / what / write / you / your
   ....
   ....

4 a / he / told / lie / us / was / what
   ....
   ....

5 about / annoys / arrogance / him / his / is / me / most / what
   ....
   ....

6 what / do / our / punks / spray / to / used / was / we / we / were / when
   ....
   .... hair green!

Use of English Part 2

8 Read the text below and think of one word which best fits each gap.

Jeans

Is it the constantly evolving style of jeans that ensures they never go out of fashion? During the 70s they **1** .... tight at the top and wide at the bottom – the infamous flares. In the 80s they were tight and went straight down the leg – a style called 'drainpipes' in the UK. **2** .... of the biggest innovations in jeans style came **3** .... France in the 90s – faded jeans, **4** .... had been washed before you bought them to give a worn, used look. Since the beginning of the 21st **5** .... , jeans **6** .... tended to be worn low on the hips – these are called low-rise jeans or hipsters. Now, towards the end of the first decade of the new millennium, a higher wasted shape is starting **7** ....be increasingly popular. **8** .... latest in the jeans revolution is Eco jeans. These are made from organically cultivated cotton, have buttons made from coconut fibres and the fabric **9** .... dyed using a combination of mimosa flowers and potatoes. These new jeans **10** .... becoming a world-wide phenomenon, **11** .... there is still some way to go to make them the perfect eco product. Unfortunately, the chemical used to fix the colour on to the fabric is highly damaging to **12** .... environment.

9 Describe the photographs and tell your partner which outfit you would rather wear and for what occasion. Then say which you wouldn't even contemplate dressing up in and why.

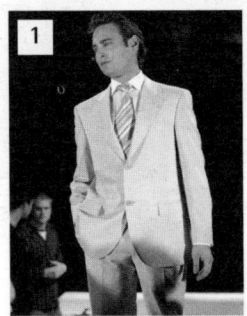 

10 Read the definitions and guess each item of clothing.

1 a close-fitting garment made of nylon or wool covering the legs, hips, and bottom

....

2 an undergarment worn on the upper part of the body, typically having no sleeves

....

3 a coloured summer jacket worn by schoolchildren or sports players as part of a uniform

....

4 trousers made out of ribbed fabric

....

5 a loose set of clothes worn when exercising or as casual wear

....

6 a strip of leather or other material worn, round the waist, to support or hold in clothes

....

7 a sturdy item of footwear covering the foot and ankle, and sometimes also the lower leg

....

8 a knitted jumper fastening down the front

....

9 a strip of material worn round the collar and tied in a knot at the front

....

10 a set of outer clothes made of the same fabric and designed to be worn together

....

11 You will hear five different people talking about fashion. For questions 1–5, choose from the list (A–F), what each person thinks about the clothes they wear. Use the letters only once. There is one extra letter which you do not need to use.

A This person does not want to be stereotyped.

Speaker ☐ 1

B This person isn't bothered about being untidy.

Speaker ☐ 2

C This person pays a lot of attention to detail.

Speaker ☐ 3

D This person would rather follow fashion locally.

Speaker ☐ 4

E This person isn't always able to dress as he / she wishes.

Speaker ☐ 5

F This person will only wear one brand name when it comes to footwear.

12 Listen again and decide if the sentences are true or false.

	T	F
1 Speaker 1 wears a cardigan as part of her school uniform.	☐	☐
2 Speaker 2 doesn't think he looks scruffy.	☐	☐
3 The way Speaker 3 dresses makes him look dull.	☐	☐
4 Speaker 4 feels that following fashion helps you stay young.	☐	☐
5 Speaker 5 believes dark colours are better suited to her complexion.	☐	☐

13 Which Speaker shares your own dress sense? Exchange your opinion with a partner.

Speaking Part 4

14 Look at the photographs, then say how fashionable you think the clothes in the shop window are and what it would be like to be a window dresser.

15 Read the following questions carefully and write down the answers. Then discuss them with a partner and give a reason for each answer.

1 Do you think that fashion can have a negative effect on people? How?

2 Have you got or would you ever have a tattoo or piercing done because it's fashionable?

3 Are teenagers easily influenced by the way their favourite pop stars dress?

4 What does it take to be fashionable in your opinion?

5 Do you feel teenagers spend far too much money on clothes and fashion accessories?

6 If a friend of yours was wearing an item of clothing that didn't suit them, would you tell them?

7 Do you think some fashions are ridiculous? Which ones? Why?

8 Have you ever felt uncomfortable or uneasy in the clothes you were wearing? In what way?

9 Who's the smartest and most stylish person you know?

10 Do you like shopping for clothes? Do you always try them on before you buy them?

11 Do you agree that the models you see on the catwalks today look unhealthy and too skinny?

12 What would you wear if you had to go for a job interview?

13 What do you think of television programmes that advise people how to dress?

14 Would you seek the advice of an expert if you felt your dress sense needed improving?

15 Have you ever bought anything and deeply regretted it afterwards?

16 What do you think of people who spend ridiculous amounts of money on clothes and shoes?

17 Do you check that the clothes you buy haven't been produced in sweatshops?

18 Do you own any items of clothing, shoes or bags that have been made out of recycled material? If so, what?

19 Have you ever bought any second hand clothes at a jumble sale, car boot sale or a charity shop?

20 Have you ever queued outside a store, waiting for it to open when there is a sale? Did you get a good discount?

Keep up Appearances

1 Read the interview with a life coach. For questions 1-8, choose the answer (A, B, C or D) which you think fits best according to the text.

Change Your Life
with a Life Coach

Do you want a successful, happy life? Do you want to improve your self-confidence, get more focus into your life, control your own destiny, realise your ambitions? If the answer to any of these questions is yes, then a life coach could be just what you are looking for. To find out more, we spoke to Carole Williams, a leading UK coach who specialises in working with teenagers and young people.

'A coach is like a mentor who you work with to achieve particular goals in your life, to overcome difficulties and generally make yourself a happier, more successful person.

To try and achieve this, we first look at the young person's life to see if there are any areas where they feel dissatisfied or unhappy. From this we can see if there are any imbalances in their life as well as what they really want from life. Our main aim is to get people to 'think outside the box', rather than in old, safe, familiar ways.

My advice to young people is - be inspired, be ambitious for yourself. One of the problems facing young people are the expectations of family, teachers and the outside world. Another big problem is peer group pressure. It takes a certain amount of self-confidence not to do what everyone else is planning to do. Coaching is about breaking through those expectations and fears.

Most teenagers are incredibly motivated and enthusiastic, but very often this is not recognised. We need to harness that potential. I know that young people have much more to offer society than we normally believe. Some teenagers are very focused, but we are all unique individuals! Celebrate who you are and don't compare yourself to anyone else. Teenagers often compare themselves with pop or fashion icons, people we see on the TV and so on. But they are not comparing like with like. We should really be looking at ourselves, exploring how best we can fulfill our own potential. My advice is to model yourself on yourself!

Many teenagers may not know what they want to do. If that is you, don't panic, simply take the time to explore what you do like doing. What do you get totally absorbed in? What makes you really happy? The answers to these questions will give you some clues about what direction to start looking in. You need to get these decisions right when you are young because when you are older it is much more difficult to change direction. Take time to sit and explore what you want to do. Try and ignore pressure from parents, teachers and your peer group. You have to try to lift yourself out of that. If you are going to follow a dream, surround yourself with people who will support and encourage you.

Life coaching can help and encourage you. I try to get the young people I work with to set goals that they really want, and I hope to give them the structure, tools and support to be truly successful people - in every aspect of their lives.

It's not as difficult as it sounds. Believe in yourself and you will find that everything you need to achieve your goals is within you.

So, what three pieces of advice would Carole give to someone for a successful life?
Well, that's difficult as there's so much I could say! If I had to choose, though, I'd say live without regrets, live in the present and be forgiving.'

1 The phrase 'to think outside the box' means
A to think about all the things that make you feel unhappy with your life.
B to think in new and unexpected ways.
C to brainstorm ideas.
D when your thoughts are chaotic rather than orderly and tidy.

2 Life coaching can help young people
A feel confident enough to decide things for themselves, rather than be influenced by the people around them.
B influence their friends, instead of their friends influencing them.
C follow the advice of their friends and family more confidentally.
D meet the expectations of friends and family.

3 Carole Williams believes that
A people expect too much of youngsters.
B young people suffer from lack of motivation.
C people aren't doing enough to help youngsters.
D people tend to underestimate youngsters.

4 Carole thinks that comparing themselves with famous people is
A motivating for youngsters.
B unhelpful for youngsters.
C good for providing a role model for youngsters.
D good if you want to become a celebrity.

5 When deciding what to do with their lives, young people should
A talk to a careers advisor.
B make a list of questions to ask people about jobs.
C look for clues in their lives to point them in the right direction.
D start off by really thinking about what activities engage and satisfy them.

6 Carole says that
A life is easier for young people than it is for older people.
B it is never too late to make changes in your career.
C it is not easy to make changes in your career when you are older.
D making changes in their lives is good for people.

7 Carole advises young people that if they want to achieve their goals,
A the best people to help them are not necessarily those closest to them.
B they should follow the advice of family and friends.
C they should be guided by their teachers.
D they should leave their familiar environment.

8 Carole finds it hard to
A live without wishing she had done something different in the past.
B think of three pieces of advice for a successful life.
C limit herself to only three pieces of advice for a successful life.
D make choices in her life.

Unit 11

Vocabulary

Personality Adjectives

2 Complete the crossword with adjectives of personality using the clues below.

Across

2 Someone who is generally happy and positive.

4 Someone who is determined to do what they want, who refuses to change their mind about something.

5 Someone who is kind and helpful.

6 someone who thinks that they are more important or better at something than they really are.

7 Someone who likes being around and spending time with other people.

10 Someone who behaves in an angry or violent way to another person.

12 Someone who can be depended on, or trusted, because they behave in a way that you expect.

13 Someone who makes people laugh.

Down

1 Someone who is uncomfortably aware of themselves and their actions.

3 Someone who always assumes that good things will happen.

4 Someone who has good judgment, based on practical ideas.

8 Someone who really wants to be successful, powerful or wealthy.

9 Someone who doesn't like working or making an effort.

11 Someone who is willing to give money or time to other people, often more than is usual or expected.

3 Complete what Phillippa says about some of her friends and family with words from Exercise 2.

1 He drives me mad most of the time. He never agrees with what I say and always refuses to change his mind, even when it's so obvious that he's wrong. He's just so 1 .... , honestly! And he can be very 2 .... – .... He thinks he's great at everything, but he's not, I can tell you. I really wish I had a sister instead!

2 He's so cool! Everyone thinks he's great. He's always telling jokes, making people laugh – even the teachers think he's 3 .... ! He's very 4 .... He loves being with other people, you never see him on his own. And he's incredibly 5 .... He'll always help you out, if you need it, like with homework or something. He's just the perfect guy, really, but he's not interested in me, I know.

3 She's great. I think we get on really well – much better than some of my friends get on with theirs. One of the things I love about her most is that she's always so 6 .... Whenever I'm feeling down, she always manages to think of something nice for me to look forward to. She's always very busy. Even when she's not working, she's always doing something around the house, cleaning or fixing something. You couldn't call her 7 .... ! Even though home and family is important to her, I think that she's quite 8 .... in her career. I know she wants to become managing director before she's 50!

4 I would say that she's the most **9** .... person I know. If I suggest doing something a bit wild, she usually always manages to talk me out of it, convincing me that it's really not a good idea, it's dangerous, whatever. She's one hundred percent **10** .... , too – you can trust her completely to do what she says, she'll never let you down. She's also just about the most **11** .... person I know – she'll give up her time to help anyone with anything, and she'll always pay, like at a café or something, if I've run out of money. She's a really good person.

4 Who do you think Phillippa is talking about in Exercise 3? Write your answers here.

1 ....
2 ....
3 ....
4 ....

5 Describe two of your friends and family in the same way as Phillippa.

Grammar

Suffixes

6 Add the correct suffix/es to the words below to form adjectives. Change the base form of the noun where necessary.

-ful	-able	-ate	-less

1 affection	5 grate	9 rely
2 care (x 2)	6 hope (x 2)	10 skill
3 cheer	7 misery	11 thought (x 2)
4 enjoy	8 passion	12 use (x 2)

7 Complete the following sentences with a word from exercise 6.

1 He's not a very .... child. He doesn't like being kissed or cuddled at all.
2 I've had flu for a week and it's rained every day. If anyone should feel .... , it's me!
3 It would be .... to have chains for the car, in case it snows.
4 She's .... at languages. She's lived in France for ten years, but she still doesn't speak French properly.

5 I'm very .... for all the help you've given me. Thank you so much.
6 Fiona's .... about sailing. She's got a boat and she spends all her spare time and money out on the water.
7 For me, there's nothing more .... than lying on a hot beach with a good book – pure pleasure!
8 I've never known anyone so .... Doesn't he bother checking any of his work?

Use of English Part 1

8 For questions 1–12, read the text below about gossip and decide which answer (A, B, C or D) best fits each gap.

Where would we be without a bit of gossip? It's fun, interesting and it sells newspapers and magazines. In **1** .... , at times, it seems that half of the British media would disappear overnight without celebrity gossip. It all **2** .... harmless enough, but scientists have discovered some interesting things about just how powerful gossip can be.

Researchers in Germany carried out a test on students using a computer game. They found that gossip was very important when people were making decisions about things. The researchers gave students some money which they then gave to other **3** .... in turn, writing comments **4** .... each other as they played. The study **5** .... that students gave less money to people described in these notes as mean and more to those described as generous. This even **6** .... when they were shown false gossip invented by the researchers and against the evidence they saw with their own eyes. 'People only saw the gossip and not the past decisions', the researchers **7** ....

Another group of researchers in America have uncovered some good in bad gossip, however. They say that **8** .... gossip between friends makes their friendship stronger and brings people closer together. The gossipers **9** .... their friendships by telling secret information to each other, whether real or **10** .... , with the person being gossiped about kept on the **11** .... of the group. This of course does not take into account the effect of all this on the person being talked **12** ....

1	A fact	B point	C all	D deed
2	A sees	B feels	C looks	D like
3	A jokers	B gamers	C players	D fans
4	A relation	B around	C of	D about
5	A appeared	B showed	C seemed	D looked
6	A caused	B existed	C passed	D happened
7	A concluded	B summarised	C denied	D drew
8	A dividing	B changing	C allocating	D sharing
9	A carry	B strengthen	C inform	D encourage
10	A nought	B none	C not	D no
11	A outside	B outskirts	C underneath	D outer
12	A around	B in	C about	D behind

9 What type of personality do you think the people portrayed in the photographs below might have? Discuss your ideas with a partner.

    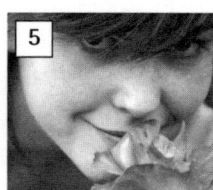

10 Fill the gaps in the sentences below with one of the words in the box.

gaudy	dress sense	traits	at ease	fuss	laid back

1 I've never met anyone with such awful taste. She has no .... whatsoever!
2 I do wish you wouldn't wear such .... outfits.
3 Generosity is one of her more likeable ....
4 I really can't make out what all the .... is about!
5 Robert never gets upset about anything. He's always so ....
6 We have never felt completely .... with each other.

11 You will hear a woman talking about personality types. For questions 1-10, complete the sentences.

Psychology and Personality Types

How we [1] is influenced by our personality.

People with almost identical distinguishing qualities are unlikely to have the same [2].

We are given our personality traits and characteristics at [3].

As we grow, our personality evolves [4] to our circumstances.

A bashful person may need to learn to have more [5].

The way some people behave in later years can undergo quite a radical [6].

People might be able to [7] their personality by developing certain traits.

Worriers could learn to become a little less [8].

Selfish people would benefit from acquiring some of the [9] of the over-anxious.

You have to be [10] if you really want to change your personality.

12 Listen again and answer the following questions.

1 What does our personality affect?
2 Do people who display similar personality traits behave in the same way?
3 How can you discover your personality type?
4 Why do our surroundings affect the way our personality develops?
5 In what way do people change as they get older?

13 Describe your personality to your partner and say whether you think it could be modified by developing different traits and how you would change it, if you could.

Speaking Part 2

14 What are the most significant and influential moments in a person's life? Number the events below from 1 (most important) to 10 (least important).

Learning to walk and talk. ☐

Going to school for the first time. ☐

Making new friends. ☐

Being awarded a diploma or degree. ☐

Going for an interview. ☐

Starting a new job. ☐

Leaving home. ☐

Getting engaged. ☐

Getting married. ☐

Having a child. ☐

15 These two photographs show people at very important and extremely happy moments in their lives. Read the descriptions of the photographs and answer the questions.

In the first photograph, we see a young man clutching the degree he has obviously just been awarded. The way he is standing, holding the degree aloft, fists clenched and head raised, wearing a broad grin, show us just how much this moment means to him. All that hard work has finally paid off and this is his moment of triumph! I wonder if the boy is English, but, then again, he looks quite dark so he might be from Italy or Spain. He's wearing a black gown and mortar board. If I'm not mistaken the colour of the gown and mortar board depends on the university the student attends because they vary from brown and black to navy and even purple and red. He can now hopefully go on a happy and successful career thanks to all the hard work and dedication he put in to getting his degree.

The second photograph was taken on a beach and I don't think it was a particularly warm day. The sea looks very grey and the bride looks as though she might be feeling quite cold. I suppose the photographer thought photographs on the beach would be a nice way to remember their wedding day. The girl is slim and attractive in her strapless wedding gown. She is carrying the train of her dress draped over her arm to protect it from the sand and water. Her veil is being lifted by the breeze and her hair looks quite windswept. She might even be wondering how she is going to look when she gets to her reception and has to greet all her guests! I am sure, like most girls, she wants to look her best on the most important day of her life. The bridegroom is wearing what is probably a very nice outfit except that he has discarded his jacket, shoes, and socks and has his trouser legs rolled up. Still... his bow tie looks very smart! They are laughing and both look very happy as they run up the beach holding hands, with the groom leading the bride.

1 What is the boy clenching in his fist?

2 What is he wearing on his face?

3 Was he paid any money for all his hard work?

4 Are there any clues as to which university he has been attending?

5 What is a mortar board and gown?

6 Whose idea was it to go on the beach?

7 Why is the girl draping the train of her wedding gown over her arm?

8 What is lifting the bride's veil?

16 Now compare the photos in your own words and say in what way the events depicted will influence each person's life.

It all Ads up!

1 You are going to read an article about *Shopaholics and Buy Nothing Day*. Seven sentences have been removed from the article. Choose from the sentences A-H the one which fits each gap (9-15). There is one extra sentence which you do not need to use.

Shopaholics and Buy Nothing Day!

What precisely is a *shopaholic*? We can define the term as someone who loves shopping. [1] It doesn't matter what they buy as long as they are shopping.

Research carried out by the National Consumer Council (NCC) in Britain showed that almost 80% of 10 to 12 year olds are fond of shopping whilst 95% of girls aged 10 to 19 actually say they have developed a passion for it. [2]

According to the survey, many teenagers seemed to believe that if they owned more things, they would be happier. They associated material things with power, status and identity. [3] Kids as young as 10 are attracted by fashionable labels and must-have gadgets thanks to advertising. The study revealed that, on average, a child will cost his or her parents £38,488 between the ages of six and 11.

The results of the survey also predict that teenagers who are addicted to shopping at this stage of their life, may have problems with debt and spending later on in life. [4]

How would the average shopaholic survive on *Buy Nothing Day*, the world day dedicated to not buying anything when people are invited to reflect upon the role of consumerism in their lives? [5] Thus, this day that was totally dedicated to shopping in the past has now been transformed into a day when people are encouraged not to buy anything.

Canadian artist, Ted Dave, first came up with the idea in the 1990s. [6] The first *Buy Nothing Day* was held in September 1992 and the rules were simple: 24 hours without buying anything - absolutely nothing! The theory was

that the time saved could be used in other ways, such as dedicating ourselves to our hobbies or simply detoxifying ourselves from shopping. Even if it seems easy, *Buy Nothing Day* is a real challenge for most of us, and even more so for those *shopaholics* out there!

7 ☐ Other similar initiatives are *credit card cut up*, where volunteers stand in a shopping mall with a pair of scissors and a sign offering a simple service: to put an end to extortionate interest rates and mounting debt by cutting your credit card in half. Another initiative is *Zombie Walk*, where men and women dress as zombies and walk next to the people who are doing their shopping to try and put them off. Last but not least, is *Whirl-mart*, where long queues of people with empty trolleys wander around the supermarkets without buying anything.

A This is also a consequence of advertising strategies that lead people to believe that by owning a particular product, their lives will be enriched.

B He wanted to turn a long-standing tradition upside down, in order to provoke and make people reflect.

C In fact, they love it so much that they are addicted to it.

D *Buy Nothing Day* is celebrated at the end of November, the Friday after Thanksgiving Day, which is traditionally known as *Black Friday* since it marks the beginning of Christmas shopping and is one of the 10 busiest shopping days in the United States.

E And even though most of the time they buy things they don't need, they just can't put a stop to their frenzied spending.

F Some people were reluctant to take part in the protest march for fear of being arrested.

G It's important that they learn to manage their money at a young age and spend wisely, resisting the temptation to buy things they don't really need.

H *Buy Nothing Day* can be a personal experiment as well as a collective form of protest.

Unit 12

Vocabulary

Advertising and the Media

2 Complete the sentences below with the correct word or phrase for TV and Media, changing the form as necessary.

bombard with news	press coverage
breaking news	quiz programme
freedom of the press	soap opera
keep up-to-date with the news	switch channel
on the air	the headlines
presenter	weather forecast

1 Did you know that over a third of the world's population live in countries where there's no .... The right to inform and be informed just doesn't exist!

2 Even in today's world of technology, newspapers are still the main way of .... for most people. There are thousands of newspapers printed throughout the world every day.

3 I never watch those 24-hours-a-day channels that claim to be showing the latest ' .... '. It seems to me that they frequently just show the same news story, over and over again.

4 He's a .... of one of those reality TV shows. I wouldn't want his job, having to deal with all those difficult celebrities!

5 I think that a lot of people feel that they're .... nowadays with the radio, TV, newspapers and the Internet. There's just no escape from being told about all the awful things going on in the world.

6 My kids love that .... where people try and win a million pounds by answering questions about general knowledge.

7 The first TV advert went .... in the 1950s. It was for toothpaste.

8 Bias can be created in a newspaper article by the facts that are included or left out, and even by how .... – the title at the top of the article that gets people's attention, or not – are phrased.

9 .... of celebrities and their lives is just so over-the-top. I mean, the most tedious details about these people's lives are all over the newspapers and magazines. Who wants to know this stuff?

10 He always .... when the adverts come on, then flicks from one channel to another until the programme starts again. It drives me mad!

11 I think my grandmother is addicted to .... She watches at least five a day, and knows all about the characters' lives and problems. I'm getting a bit worried that she thinks they're real people!

12 Shall we bother watching the .... ? I mean, last week they said that temperatures were going to be around 35 degrees, and then it snowed!

3 Write in the full forms of these acronyms.

1 BBC ....
2 CIA ....
3 CNN ....
4 FAO ....
5 MA ....
6 MTV ....
7 NATO ....
8 UNICEF ....
9 WHO ....
10 WWW ....

Grammar

Relative Pronouns and Clauses

4 Choose the correct relative pronoun/s to complete the sentences. In some sentences more than one answer is possible.

1 Advertisers want to reach into the hearts and minds of the people .... watch the ads.
A who   B that   C which

2 The experts .... analyse the world of advertising say that the latest ads don't just sell products, they sell lifestyles.
A who   B that   C which

3 If a journalist doesn't follow certain guidelines, they may be brought to court by the person or people .... they're writing about.
A who   B that   C what

4 Freelance International Press is an organisation .... defends human rights and freedom of information.
A which   B that   C what.

5 Advertising really started to develop .... handbills were used in the fifteenth and sixteenth century, after the invention of the printing press.

A which   B that   C when

6 That's the producer .... soap operas have won drama awards.

A which   B whose   C who

7 This is the moment we've all been waiting for, ... Anne has to answer the million-dollar question!

A what   B when   C where

8 That's the village .... I was born.

A that   B when   C where

5 Answer the following questions about the sentences in Exercise 4.

1 Which word or words do the relative clauses in the sentences in Exercise 4 above refer to? Underline them.

2 In which sentences do the relative clauses give essential information to understand the main clause, i.e. which are defining relative clauses?

Sentence/s number ....

3 In which of the sentences you identified in b is the relative pronoun the object of the clause?

Sentence/s number ....

4 In which of the sentences in Exercise 4 can the relative pronoun be left out?

Sentence/s number ....

6 Complete the following sentences with a suitable relative clause. If it's possible to leave the relative pronoun out, write it down and then circle it.

1 Look! There's the man .... I met at the party last week. Shall I say hello?

2 He's the presenter .... quiz programmes get millions of viewers each week. You know the one I mean, don't you?

3 CNN, ... is an American news channel, broadcasts breaking news 24 hours a day.

4 My boss, ... used to work in Mexico, speaks excellent Spanish.

5 The new flat-screen TV .... they bought is fantastic. The picture is so much better than on their old telly.

6 MTV is a TV music channel .... can be watched all over the world.

7 Looking back, the happiest time of my life was .... I lived in Rome.

8 My children watch a lot of television, ... really worries me.

Use of English Part 4

7 Complete the second sentence so that it has a similar meaning to the first sentence, using the word that is given without changing it at all. Use between two and five words.

1 It's not a good idea for young children to watch TV by themselves, as something unsuitable could come on.
OWN
It's not a good idea for young children to watch TV .... , as something unsuitable could come on.

2 Although people complained about the adverts, the campaign wasn't stopped.
EVEN
They didn't stop the campaign, ... people complained about the adverts.

3 The advertising agency produced a series of adverts aimed specifically at families with children.
CAME
The advertising agency .... a series of adverts aimed specifically at families with children.

4 'Why don't we go to the cinema instead of watching another soap opera on the TV?', asked Lucy.
SUGGESTED
Lucy .... to the cinema instead of watching another soap opera on the TV.

5 They put a device on the TV so that the children couldn't watch it too much.
PREVENT
They put a device on the TV to .... it too much.

6 Considering that it's the first time she's presented this quiz show, I think she's doing quite well.
ACCOUNT
If you .... that it's the first time she's presented this quiz show, I think she's doing quite well.

7 We should switch over now if we're going to catch that programme on the other channel.
BETTER
.... now if we're going to catch that programme on the other channel.

8 You didn't do enough research before buying that TV. I don't think it was very good value for money.
OUGHT
You .... more research before buying that TV. I don't think it was very good value for money.

8 Do you know what the machine in this photograph was used for, who it was invented by and when it dates back to? Discuss your ideas with a partner.

9 Read the definitions and find the corresponding word in the wordsquare.

1 material used in sheets throughout the ancient Mediterranean world for writing or painting on
2 a large board in a public place, used to display advertisements
3 small printed advertisement or other notice distributed by hand
4 a machine for printing text or pictures from type or plates
5 portable object other than furniture or costumes used on the set of a play or film
6 an organization or company managed by members of a board
7 a person, object, or place selected as the aim of an attack
8 synonym for **2**
9 a printed publication consisting of folded unstapled sheets and containing news, articles, advertisements, and correspondence
10 an abbreviation for *advertisement*

```
W R H A N D B I L L
P R O P A D V E R T
O P A P Y R U S I P
L P R I N T I N G A
B R D M B A S E A P
I E I D K R C W U E
L S N T H G L S G R
L S G J D E S W D B
B O A R D T R U S T
```

10 You will hear an interview with Michael Harris, a representative of the Advertising Society. For questions 1–10, complete the sentences.

CD 1 13

Advertising

Advertising came into being in Ancient Egypt when [1] were written on Papyrus.

Television advertisements first [2] in the fifties with an ad for toothpaste.

Newspapers took to advertising in the [3] hundreds.

Advertising developed when advertisers started selling advertisement time to [4]

A more creative and scientific style in the sixties saw advertising [5]

The key to a [6] advert is that it has to be entertaining, self-explanatory and of an appropriate length.

Past advertisements and props are filed away in a huge [7] in the History of Advertising Trust.

There is a [8] on advertising of unhealthy food and drinks when children's programmes are on.

The interviewer asks if ready-made meals, which are made to look just as fresh as homemade meals, is [9]

Michael Harris believes that thanks to the high standards of advertising today, adverts are able to give people [10]

11 Listen again and decide if the following statements are T (true) or F (false).

	T	F
a Handbills were brought into practice in Egyptian times.	☐	☐
b The printing press was devised before the fifteenth century.	☐	☐
c Adverts were first published in newspapers in the sixteenth century.	☐	☐
d Sponsors could purchase advertisement time in the fifties.	☐	☐
e Advertising prospered in the sixties thanks to a more creative approach.	☐	☐
f The key to success in advertising is making the most of the time available.	☐	☐

12 Is there an advertisement that particularly stands out in your memory? Describe it to your partner and say what it is that struck you about this advert and why.

Speaking Part 2

13 Look at the photos below and discuss the following questions with a partner.

1 Where do you think the two photographs were taken?
2 Do you recognise any of the items being advertised?
3 Do you think the amount of advertising could be harmful?
4 What time of day do you think it is?
5 Where would you rather be?

14 Now read what this person said about the two photographs and compare it to your answers.

I think the first photograph was taken in Times Square, in New York City. I know so because I've been there and I recognised it as well as the yellow cabs New York is notorious for. I've no idea where the second photograph was taken, it could be anywhere in the mountains and there are no clues in the background that could help me guess.

The first photograph is jam packed with brightly coloured advertisements. In the foreground on the left hand side of the photograph I recognize the camera company Kodak. It looks like they're advertising a film for digital cameras, then further back, on a tall building is the face of a dark haired woman who looks a bit like that actress... erm... Angelina Jolie and the word ARGENT. There's a funny looking blue sort of torch with a flame coming out of the top. Perhaps it's advertising a new perfume. The building in the foreground on the right must be a cinema as there seem to be several billboards showing scenes from some of the latest films. The word Virgin is written in large letters above the entrance to what must be a music store. In the middle of the photograph, towards the back, the façade of a narrow skyscraper is covered in billboards advertising different products but I can't quite make them out. There's only one advertisement in the second photograph and it is a definite product that a company is trying to sell. The little boy is holding a globe up in his right hand. It might be an ad promoting global issues such as global warming especially as it seems to have been put up in the middle of nowhere.

I don't think the advertising in either of the photographs could be harmful as it's proportional to its surroundings. In a large lively place like Times Square you can hardly expect to find a few advertisements dotted here and there and the mountains would be totally spoilt if there were placards nailed to every tree!

As regards the time of day, I would say that the first photograph was taken early on a summer morning. The pavements on both sides of the street are packed with people and there are people standing in the middle of the street waiting for a bus. Most of them are lightly dressed in short sleeved tops and one or two appear to be carrying what looks like a rolled up newspaper, but I could be mistaken. Most of the cars on the street are taxis, apart from one which is some sort of jeep with its headlights on so perhaps it's early evening. It's difficult to tell. As for the second photograph, it could have been taken anytime during the day before sunset.

If I could choose where to be right now, I think I would go for Times Square. I've never been there before and I would love to see it. I wouldn't want to be in the place in the second photograph because I have absolutely no idea where it is or what it is like, it could be anywhere and I wouldn't want to find myself stuck on the side of a mountain with no one around for miles on end.

15 Can you think of any other places which are bombarded with advertisements? Have you been to any of them? What are they like? Tell your partner.

Unit 13
Break a Leg!

1 Read the article about reality TV. For questions 1-8, choose the answer (A, B, C or D) which you think fits best according to the text.

Unreal... The Reality TV Phenomenon

Big Brother started the whole thing off with ordinary people, but we stopped watching. It would appear that we prefer to watch famous people - ordinary people are boring! Now in the UK any reality TV show that wants to be a success has to have its 'celebrities'. It has become something of a national joke that if your TV, music or media career is beginning to fade, then make sure you get on to a reality TV show. You will, if you are lucky, find yourself moving quickly from the celebrity 'C-list' to the top A-list.

Take the incredibly successful *Strictly Come Dancing*. Twelve million British people watched the final at the end of 2007. This show has seen celebrities from sports stars to pop stars learning how to dance, from the samba to the foxtrot, the waltz to the jive. The show's judges, along with viewers voting by phone, decide who wins the series. The current champion is Alesha Dixon, ex-member of R&B band *Mis-Teeq*, now a solo singer and film actress. On winning, Alesha said 'I am over the moon. It was worth all the bruises, all the lack of sleep, all the painful cuts and sore joints, all the tears and all the 380 hours of training.'

Audiences are fascinated to watch stars from sport, TV and music learning to dance to a high standard. This is perfect family viewing. In *Strictly Come Dancing*, there is no violence, embarrassing moments or swearing. We can escape into a sparkling, glamorous world, which is a satisfying mixture of make-believe and reality.

Another popular celebrity show is *I'm a Celebrity Get Me Out of Here* - what Malcolm Maclaren, former manager of the punk group the Sex Pistols, has recently called a 'pantomime torture camp'. The celebrities are flown into the jungle and have to go through a series of trials, including eating unusual parts of a kangaroo and sitting in a plastic box full of poisonous snakes. It can be a rather uncomfortable programme to watch. The whole thing looks so horrible that you wonder why these people would choose to be there. The latest series of *I'm a Celebrity* has been immersed in scandal after Malcolm McLaren left the show. He said, 'this is not a reality show. It's fake... They know who's going to win and lose. There are about 550 people in this 'jungle'. It might have been a jungle once upon a time, but now it's a film set... the trials are tricks to fool the public about a danger that isn't there. It proves this show is nothing more than a circus.'

The makers of the show have strongly denied McLaren's claims that the show is fake and that the contestants are never in any real danger. However, his claims come as little surprise to most people. Few believe it is simply a reality TV show about people surviving in the outback; they know it is scripted and organised. Is that a problem? Well, most people don't seem to mind – they're still happy to sit back and watch this piece of unreal reality TV. And, of course, the whole controversy is proving very good for publicity. In the battle for viewing figures and advertising revenue, any publicity is good publicity.

1 Appearing on a reality TV show
A makes celebrities laugh. ☐
B can improve the luck of a celebrity. ☐
C can help a celebrity whose career is not going well. ☐
D can help people become famous. ☐

2 The winner of the programme *Strictly Come Dancing* is decided
A only by specialist judges. ☐
B by judges and ordinary people watching at home. ☐
C by other celebrities. ☐
D by former champions of the programme. ☐

3 The most recent winner of *Strictly Come Dancing* feels
A very happy about winning, despite all the effort it took. ☐
B very happy about winning, but upset about all the injuries she sustained during the contest. ☐
C very happy and ready for a new career as a dancer. ☐
D disorientated after all the effort she put into the contest. ☐

4 The appeal of *Strictly Come Dancing* is that it gives people watching
A a break from the usual violence on television. ☐
B the chance of escapism into an exotic world, which is at the same time real. ☐
C the chance to learn to dance to a high standard. ☐
D the satisfaction of seeing celebrities learning to do something new. ☐

5 The show *I'm a Celebrity Get Me Out of Here* is
A designed for easy viewing. ☐
B hard to watch on occasion, given the extreme nature of the tasks expected of the contestants. ☐
C a comedy show, designed to make viewers laugh. ☐
D often the subject of scandal. ☐

6 A recent contestant on the programme *I'm a Celebrity Get Me Out of Here*
A has said that he would have preferred to have performed in a circus. ☐
B has accused the programme's producers of torturing him. ☐
C is angry because he didn't win. ☐
D has cast doubts on the authenticity of the programme. ☐

7 Viewers of *I'm a Celebrity Get Me Out of Here*
A won't be shocked by Malcolm Mclaren's revelations about the show. ☐
B will be shocked by Malcolm Mclaren's revelations about the show. ☐
C will refuse to believe Malcolm Mclaren's revelations about the show. ☐
D will be disappointed if they find out for sure that the contestants are never in danger. ☐

8 For a TV show, publicity
A can be controversial. ☐
B can be good, but can be bad too. ☐
C is always advantageous, whether it's good or bad. ☐
D is a battle that has to be fought. ☐

Unit 13

Vocabulary

Entertainment

2 Underline the odd one out in each list.

1 choreographer / audience / composer / vocalist / producer
2 standing ovation / applause / booing / cast
3 opera house / box / theatre / concert hall / cinema
4 review / stalls / stage / orchestra pit / wings / box / gallery
5 cast / director / playwright / play / choreographer
6 concert / play / composer / conductor / opera
7 ballet / concert / dress rehearsal / play / opera
8 audience / backing group / curtain / cast

3 Complete the following texts about artistic events using a word or phrase from Exercise 2.

I've got a friend who works at the 1 .... in town, and he got me into the 2 ....
yesterday of that new 3 .... It was an interesting production – a drama about a family, set in the 1950s – but it didn't seem to me like it was ready for the opening night tonight. Some of the 4 .... couldn't even remember their lines!

I wasn't sure that I was going to like 5 ....
– all that dramatic singing, with the elaborate costumes – it all seemed so formal and old-fashioned, and not something for young people. But then I was invited to see a production at the 6 .... in Milan – La Scala. I absolutely loved it, from the moment the 7 .... went up! I had a cheap seat in the 8 .... , so didn't have a brilliant view, but that didn't matter. I could still hear the beautiful singing perfectly. Something that surprised me, though, was when some people in the 9 .... started 10 .... when the main male 11 .... didn't quite reach one of the high notes in a song. I'd expected people at such a cultured event to be more polite! Still, his performance improved a lot, and at the end, he even got a 12 .... , he'd done so well.

I'm going to see a modern 13 .... on Saturday evening – so not a traditional one, like *Swan Lake*, but one that involves contemporary dance. It had a very good 14 .... in the paper. The critic said that the 15 .... , who's very young, has come up with some really original work. I've got a seat in the 16 .... It was quite expensive, but I think it'll be worth it, as I'll be close to the stage and able to see everything.

Grammar

Gerunds and Infinitives

4 Match the prepositions to the verbs and adjectives below.

on (x 2)	of (x 4)	for
in (x 2)	at (x 2)	about

1 insist ....
2 approve ....
3 apologise ....
4 believe ....
5 fantastic ....
6 terrified ....
7 awful ....
8 interested ....
9 capable ....
10 proud ....
11 keen ....
12 worried ....

5 Complete these sentences using a verb or adjective followed by a preposition from Exercise 4, and one of the verbs from the box in the correct form.

save up	keep	travel	try	get	live
draw	not pass	have	play	go	leave

1 He's .... on the underground – he feels claustrophobic down there, shut inside a train, inside a tunnel.
2 Can you believe it? He refused to .... me waiting for two hours.
I certainly won't be seeing him again!
3 I'm quite .... the idea of .... cross-country skiing. it looks like fun.
4 My grandmother doesn't .... people .... together instead of getting married – she's so old-fashioned!
5 They .... to buy something you want, rather than getting credit for it.
6 I'm quite .... this new job, I have to admit – lots of people applied, so I did pretty well!
7 I'm .... , I really am. I'm 35, but my artwork looks like something a 4-year-old child would do!
8 He .... for the airport at 5 o'clock in the morning, but when we got there we were so early that the check-in desk wasn't even open!
9 She's .... the exam. She doesn't think she did enough work for it.
10 Penelope is .... the guitar. She should think about doing it as a career.

11 I'm not sure that he's .... a normal relationship with anyone – he's very damaged emotionally.

12 I'm .... to Morocco on holiday at Easter – I've read lots about it and it sounds fascinating.

6 Put the verbs in the following sentences into the correct form.

1 I'm learning .... (play) the flute – I have a class every week.

2 Do you mind .... (work) at the weekend? I would hate it myself.

3 We asked .... (see) the manager, but they said he wasn't there.

4 I can't stand .... (listen) to my sister practising the violin – it sounds so awful!

5 She pretended .... (not see) me when we passed each other on the street.

6 They hadn't expected me .... (come) in to work today – they thought I was still ill.

7 I'd rather not .... (go out) tonight – I'm too tired.

8 I've chosen .... (work) part-time until my children are older.

9 I can't see. Move out the way and let me .... (have) a look.

10 My parents used to make me .... (eat) so many vegetables when I was a child – especially broccoli, which I hated!

11 I can't afford .... (buy) any new clothes this month – I'm broke!

12 It's not worth .... (go) out now. it's too late.

7 Correct any mistakes in the following sentences. Some sentences are correct.

1 Don't you remember meeting her at that party last year?

2 He's tried so many times taking his driving test, but he still can't manage to pass.

3 He stopped work for ten minutes having a coffee break.

4 She went on giving her speech, despite the interruptions from the audience.

5 Stop to make so much noise, everyone! I can't hear myself think!

6 You will remember turning off the heating when you leave, won't you?

7 What I regret is not studying Psychology at university. I'd have loved to have been a psychologist, rather than a lawyer.

Use of English Part 3

8 Use the word given in capital letters at the end of some of the lines to form an appropriate word to fit the gap.

The Oscars

Everyone who has ever been to the cinema or seen a film on TV knows that the Academy awards, 1 .... known as the Oscars, are the oldest, best known, most influential, most 2 .... and famous of all film awards. At the yearly Hollywood bash, which for the last two decades has been televised worldwide by satellite, the stars' outfits, the 3 .... , and the 4 .... speeches are hotly debated. No other award, for any 5 .... whatsoever, is followed by more people worldwide than the Academy Awards – and that includes soccer world championships.

AFFECTION

PRESTIGE

PRESENT
ACCEPT

ACHIEVE

The Academy has a major effect and influence upon the film industry. A 6 .... or award raises prestige and profits for a studio or 7 .... , so studios can be tempted to try and influence the voting with marketing and advertising campaigns. The Academy has tried to limit this kind of pressure on votes, as well as any influence from promotion, box office receipts and studio public relations and 8 .... departments. They also discourage voting for reasons of sentimentality, atonement for past mistakes, and personal 9 .... or prestige of actors. They haven't always been 10 .... , however. This is show business, after all!

NOMINATE

PERFORM

MARKET

POPULAR

SUCCESS

9 Look at the photographs and describe the different ways the people are being entertained.

10 You will hear five different people talking about what, in their opinion, constitutes good entertainment. For questions 1–5, choose from the list (A–F) what they say about different sorts of entertainment. Use the letters only once. There is one extra letter which you do not need to use.

A I don't have much in common with my partner.

B What I'd really love to do in my free time, I just can't afford.

C I do the sport I watch on TV.

D I can't say I think much of modern TV shows.

E There is a wider range of programmes for people who are either older or younger than me.

F I'm really quite the theatregoer.

Speaker 1 ☐ 1

Speaker 2 ☐ 2

Speaker 3 ☐ 3

Speaker 4 ☐ 4

Speaker 5 ☐ 5

11 Listen again and choose A, B or C.

1 Speaker 1 spends her Monday afternoons watching her favourite
  A soap opera. ☐
  B quiz programme. ☐
  C court room drama. ☐

2 Next weekend Speaker 2 will be taking his wife to
  A the theatre. ☐
  B a concert. ☐
  C a match. ☐

3 Speaker 3 thinks there aren't enough programmes available to
  A teenagers and children. ☐
  B elderly people. ☐
  C people her own age. ☐

4 Speaker 4 can't afford to
  A go to a concert. ☐
  B appear on the X factor. ☐
  C go out with her friends. ☐

5 Speaker 5 will soon be
  A taking part in a competition. ☐
  B taking part in Big Brother. ☐
  C a member of the audience on a celebrity show. ☐

12 How would you rather be entertained? Discuss your preferences with a partner.

Speaking Part 1

13 In pairs work with a partner and ask each other the questions from each topic.

Likes and Dislikes

Candidate A

1 What makes you laugh? Does anything shock or offend you?
2 Do you like it when it rains? What do you like or dislike about it?
3 Would you rather have dinner at home or in a restaurant? What sort of things do you like to eat?
4 Tell us about something you did recently that you particularly enjoyed.

Candidate B

1 Do you like foreign food? Tell us about a dish you are particularly fond of.
2 Do you prefer the winter or the summer? What do you like/dislike about these seasons?
3 What sort of clothes do you feel more at ease in? Is there anything you hate wearing, but have to?
4 Tell us about your most treasured possession.

Free Time

Candidate A

1 What is your idea of good entertainment? Why?
2 How do you spend a typical Saturday night?
3 Do you like spending time alone or with friends? Why?
4 Tell us about a place you visited recently. Who did you go there with?

Candidate B

1 Are you doing anything interesting this weekend? Tell us about your plans.
2 Do you have any hobbies? Are you a member of a club?
3 Do you have enough free time? What would you do, if you had more time to yourself?
4 Do you always stick to the same routine or do you prefer to change and do different things?

Holidays and Travel

Candidate A

1 Do you like travelling? Which means of transport do you prefer? Why?
2 Where did you go on your last holiday? Did you enjoy it? Who did you go with?
3 Would you rather book your holiday online or go through a travel agency? Why?
4 When you go on holiday do you take traveller's cheques? How do you usually pay for things?

Candidate B

1 Have you ever been abroad? Where did you go? What was it like?
2 Are you afraid of flying? Do you have to take travel sickness pills before your departure?
3 How often do you go on holiday? Do you prefer to stay in your own country or travel abroad?
4 Have you ever had to make a complaint about a hotel?

The Media

Candidate A

1 Do you read a daily newspaper? Which one?
2 Do you believe everything you read in the paper? Why? Why not?
3 How much television do you watch? Could too much be harmful?
4 Tell us about a piece of news you heard recently.

Candidate B

1 Do you watch the news on TV or listen to it on the radio? Which is your favourite news programme?
2 Would you say journalists and photographers invade people's privacy? What can be done about it?
3 Do you think the media has too much power? Why? Why not?
4 Have you ever thought of working for the media? What field would you be cut out for?

Education and Work

Candidate A

1 Would you rather work in a quiet place or have lots of things going on around you? Why?
2 Have you ever had a part-time job? What did you do? Did you enjoy it?
3 Do you like team work or do you prefer to work on your own? Why? Why not?
4 Can you remember your first day at school? Tell us about it?

Candidate B

1 What sort of school do/did you go to? Tell us about it?
2 Have you ever had evening classes or gone on a distance training course? What was it like?
3 Will English be necessary in your future job? Why? Why not?
4 Have you ever considered doing voluntary work? What sort of work would you volunteer for?

Get yourself an Education!

1 Which sentence best summarises what the article below is about?

1 I just want the best for my kids. ☐
2 Why I would never send my child to a private school. ☐
3 Private schools should be abolished. ☐

Private or State?

Sending your child off to school for the first time in their life is terrifying. You simply cannot imagine how this tiny little precious creature, for whom you have cared since birth, will manage in an unfamiliar environment surrounded by lots of other kids, some of whom might not be as gifted, genius and sweet as yours.

Assuming you have any choice at all, picking their first school is also a revealing moment for anyone who considers themselves to be a good, responsible citizen. ☐1☐ Suddenly you forget about everyone else; it is all about your baby and only your baby.

When it was our turn to decide, my husband and I were in the happy financial position of being able to consider private schools. ☐2☐ Neither of us was educated privately; plus which, we had some concerns about the possible long-term effects of a private education on a person's social and emotional development. For us, then, it was a choice between the two local state primaries equidistant from our house. ☐3☐ The other is much more representative of the area demographically. We chose the latter because we liked the school and because it felt like the right thing to do.

The catchment area includes three large council estates sitting between numerous streets filled with privately owned houses, the smallest of which would cost you several hundred thousand pounds. ☐4☐

Our daughter and son, aged 10 and 9, have now been there for six and five years respectively, and are doing very well, both socially and intellectually. It is through our contact and involvement with the school community, however, and, sadly, other locals finding reasons not to pick our school, that I have witnessed class division, unrealistic aspirations and covert racism the like of which I have never come across before in my life

☐5☐ At a state school your kids will learn to live alongside and appreciate other kids from many diverse and different cultures. They will learn that privilege is not a birthright, that it has to be earned, along with understanding that they need to earn their place in society and earn the right to succeed. ☐6☐ They will learn to make room for people of different abilities.

I do not pretend to know everybody's reasons for not sending their children to state schools but I would bet it has something to do with wanting the 'best' for their kids. There is a widely held belief that when it comes to our children, anything goes. ☐7☐

2 Read the article again. Seven sentences have been removed from the article. Choose from the sentences A-H the one which fits each gap (1-7). There is one extra sentence which you do not need to use.

A But we all want the best for our kids and only a tiny percentage can afford to opt for the 'best', so surely it is up to all of us to participate in driving up standards and expectations at our local schools?

B Friends of mine who educate their children privately have said they want their kids to be taught alongside children just like them - but why?

C It is a time when you find yourself assaulted by all sorts of terrors, nerves and unanswerable questions, most of which are so unpleasant you cannot believe you are thinking them.

D One is regarded as the perfect primary, principally because it has an extraordinarily low number of disadvantaged kids despite being opposite a massive council estate.

E The school's intake is, therefore, wide and socially mixed - 37% of its kids have English as a second language and 33% are eligible for free school meals, ie poor.

F There is so much that is positive, wonderful even, about state schools.

G They will learn street sense, who to be wary of, who to avoid, how to keep their heads down and how and when to stand up for themselves.

H We did not contemplate that option for long.

Vocabulary

Education

3 Complete these stories about experiences in education with the following words and phrases, changing the form as necessary.

---

academic (x 2)   boarding school
degree   drop out   expel   fail   fees
grade   lecture   lecturer
playing field   scholarship   state school

I got into university after getting good enough
1 .... in my A-level exams, but I pretty
soon realised I'd chosen the wrong **2** ....
subject - Astrophysics really wasn't my thing. I think
I was probably too young to take it all seriously. Even
when I managed to get up in time to go to a
3 .... , rather than sit there and take
notes like I should, listening to the **4** ....
going on and on, I'd often fall asleep! Anyway,
I **5** .... at the end of the first year, after
6 .... the end-of-year exams. I decided
that an **7** .... life wasn't for me and
I trained to become a chef instead.

I've got a friend who was taken out of his local
8 .... and sent away to **9** ....
at the age of nine - just imagine it, leaving your
family so young. His parents had put him forward for
a **10** .... , which he'd managed to get,
and it covered everything, so they didn't have to pay
any **11** .... at all. They thought he would
get a better education, what with the brilliant
12 .... reputation of the school and its
wonderful facilities - the **13** .... where
they did sport was enormous, apparently. But,
despite all that, he was so unhappy there that he
started behaving badly, being rude to the teachers,
that kind of thing. It got so bad that, by the time he
was twelve, he'd been **14** .... - the school
refused to have him there anymore!

Grammar

Modal Verbs

4 Choose the correct modal verb to complete the following sentences. For some, more than one answer is possible.

1 I .... phone my mother - we always
speak on a Sunday.
A must   B mustn't   C have to
D don't have to   E needn't

2 I .... do my homework tonight – it's
got to be in tomorrow.
A must   B mustn't   C have to
D don't have to   E needn't

3 She phoned to say that you .... pick
her up from the station – she's happy to walk.
A must   B mustn't   C have to
D don't have to   E needn't

4 I'll .... leave half an hour earlier in the
mornings when I start my new job.
A must   B mustn't   C have to
D don't have to   E needn't

5 You .... be late for school again! Your
teacher will be so cross if you are.
A must   B mustn't   C have to
D don't have to   E needn't

6 Of course you .... come to the family
dinner on Saturday, but it would be very nice for
everyone if you did.
A must   B mustn't   C have to
D don't have to   E needn't

7 We .... go to school yesterday,
because the teachers were on strike!
A must   B mustn't   C had to
D didn't have to   E needn't have

8 When I was a child, we .... help our
parents much more than children do today.
A must   B mustn't   C had to
D didn't have to   E needn't have

5 Complete the sentences with the correct form of the following modal verbs. Two or more modals are possible in some of the sentences.

could	may	might	ought to	should

1 You're putting on weight. You .... do more exercise.
2 That .... to be enough money for the shopping, I'm sure.
3 That .... not be enough money for the shopping. There's a lot of stuff on the list, you know.
4 I .... go to the party. I'll see how I'm feeling later on.
5 You .... be right - I'm not sure.
6 .... I look for another job? What would your advice be?
7 It's not suprising he failed his exams. He .... done more work.
8 Look, there's a light on in one of the rooms upstairs, so they .... be at home. Let's try ringing the bell again.
9 He .... get a scholarship. We won't know the verdict until August.
10 He .... got a scholarship, if he'd worked harder.

6 Correct the following sentences as necessary. Some sentences are correct.

1 Jim told me you can play the guitar. How long have you been learning?

2 I haven't able to go on holiday this year, as I've had too much work.

3 My mother could sing beautifully when she was younger.

4 My younger son used to be able to suck his toes when he was a baby!

5 After months of unsuccessful attempts to contact him, I could finally get in touch by email.

6 Will you can come to dinner on Friday, or are you working?

7 Richard just couldn't manage to pass his driving test when he was younger – he's 38 now and still having lessons!

8 Be able to speak another language really well is a wonderful skill to have.

Use of English Part 4

7 For questions 1-8, complete the second sentence so that it has a similar meaning to the first sentence, using the word given. Use between two and five words.

1 On the days you work, who looks after your children after school?
   CARE
   On the days you work, ...
   your children after school?

2 He managed to pass all his exams this year.
   SUCCEEDED
   He .... all his exams this year.

3 John didn't go to the lecture this morning because he didn't wake up in time.
   OVERSLEPT
   If John .... have gone to the lecture this morning.

4 Although he went to university, Julian works as a bus driver now.
   SPITE
   .... to university, Julian works as a bus driver now.

5 The last time I studied anything was when I did my degree course.
   HAVE
   I .... I did my degree course.

6 They're eager to finish school for the summer.
   LOOKING
   They're .... school for the summer.

7 There are lots of people who think that it's pointless paying all that money in fees for a private school, when you can go to a state school for free.
   WORTH
   There are lots of people who don't
   .... all that money in fees for a private school, when you can go to state school for free.

8 Janice is the only person at my university to have managed to get an Erasmus scholarship.
   NOBODY
   Apart .... ever got an Erasmus scholarship at my university.

8 The photographs below show St. John's College at Cambridge University. What do you think it would be like to study for a degree at a university like this? What would student life be like? Would you find it overpowering? Is there an equivalent institution in your country? Discuss your ideas with a partner.

9 Match the words on the left with the definitions on the right.

1 entrant   **a** an organization's involvement in social welfare
2 fit in   **b** abandon a course of study
3 deter   **c** the teaching of individual pupils or small groups
4 outreach   **d** an underlying basis or principle
5 foundation   **e** a person or group that takes part in something
6 drop out   **f** be socially compatible with other members of a group
7 tuition   **g** discourage someone from doing something by instilling fear of the consequences

10 Now complete the sentences with the correct form of a word from Exercise 9.

1 She .... of college when she had only two more exams to sit.
2 Give it some time and you'll soon .... at your new school.
3 Nothing would .... him from taking part in the competition.
4 How many .... schools have you traveled to so far?
5 I'm afraid we can't vouch for the standards of .... at that institution.
6 Susan has just started a .... course at the local college.
7 A large number of .... were turned away last year due to lack of places.

11 The words *drop out* and *fit in* are phrasal verbs. Read the phrasal verbs below and match them to their meanings.

1 drop off   **a** behind, fall back or get left behind
2 fit in/into   **b** call informally and briefly as a visitor
3 fit out/up   **c** pass quickly and easily into a habitual state or manner
4 drop back   **d** fall asleep easily, especially without intending to
5 drop by/in on   **e** find room or have sufficient space for someone or something
6 drop into   **f** provide the necessary items for a particular situation

12 Now fill the blanks with the correct form of a suitable phrasal verb from Exercise 11.

1 I could .... you .... at 3. 45 this afternoon.
2 The colt was struggling to stay with the pace and started to ....
3 Can you .... any more clothes .... that suitcase?
4 She couldn't help .... a Scottish accent.
5 Struggle as she might to stay awake, she kept ....
6 The cabin had been .... with all the latest mod cons.
7 I used to hate it when they would unexpectedly .... us.

CD 1 15

13 You will hear a radio interview with Director of Admissions, John Hampdon, about university applications. For questions 1-7, choose the best answer (A, B or C).

1 All young people should
  A   not throw their talent away on higher education.
  B   be given the chance to enter the most demanding universities.   `1`
  C   aim to get into higher education before they're too old.

2 The Government
  A   advises students not to be intimidated by their upbringing or social class.
  B   would rather universities didn't rely so strongly on its assistance.   `2`
  C   does not approve of schools interfering with university applications.

3 The number of places available to applicants from low-income backgrounds
  A   is a canon decided upon by the Government.
  B   depends on the number of grants available.   `3`
  C   is in line with the students the school is able to recruit.

4 Promising, talented students whose grades are not good enough for university entrance
  A   can go back to school to improve their education.
  B   should have chosen different subjects.   `4`
  C   might be able to go on a special course organized by the university.

5 Changes to the application process and entrance requirements
  A   have brought about a 15% rise in applicants over the last four years.
  B   have facilitated access to applicants lacking in language qualifications.   `5`
  C   have led to a fall in the university's application average.

6 A recent report stated that fifty percent of the
  A   population comes from poorer backgrounds.
  B   people attend full time higher education.   `6`
  C   admissions were from state schools and colleges.

7 The number of admissions from lower-income backgrounds proves that students with a poor upbringing
  A   are easily put off applying for a place at university.
  B   can make the most of their abilities.   `7`
  C   may never feel completely at ease.

14 Now listen again and answer the following questions.

1 Why is the Government encouraging universities to work with schools?
....

2 Does the Government have a say in the running of the universities?
....

3 Do universities have to provide places for a certain number of students from low-income backgrounds?
....

4 What is the extra money universities receive spent on?
....

5 What are foundation courses?
....

6 How much has the average number of applicants to Cambridge University gone up by in the last four years?
....

7 What made this increase possible?
....

8 Was an increase in applications from low-income backgrounds also reported?
....

1 You are going to read a newspaper article about sleep. Seven sentences have been removed from the article. Choose from the sentences A-H the one which fits each gap (1-7). There is one extra sentence which you do not need to use.

How Did You Sleep Last Night?

From the moment a baby arrives, sleep becomes an obsession. But, as John Crace discovers, the broken nights that so many parents experience may have little to do with the kids. Sleeplessness – like wrinkles and grey hair – is simply part of the process of ageing If you're getting enough, you barely give it a moment's thought. But once you're not, it dominates your waking life. **1** ☐
A third of all adults have sleeping problems and, more

often than not, we blame having children. Not that people necessarily sleep that brilliantly before they have children. It's just that sleep rarely becomes a big issue. You have a good night, you have a bad night. No problem. All that changes when a baby comes along.

Leah Jewett, mother of Copey, five, and one-year-old Dare, knows just how this feels. 'I've always had unusual sleeping patterns, but it was easier to cope before the children were born. If I woke up in the night, it was just my problem and I could catch up with my sleep later.' 2 ☐

So what is a normal night's sleep? 3 ☐ 'People tend to have a fixed idea of how much sleep they need that stays with them throughout their lives,' says Kevin Morgan, professor of gerontology at the Sleep Research Centre at Loughborough University. 'But sleep changes over time. The ageing process is just as evident in the unconscious as it is in the physical manifestations of wrinkles and grey hair.'

As virtually no one thinks they need less sleep than they are actually getting, and most adults claim to experience life past the age of 30 as one long battle against fatigue, you might also assume sleep deprivation was part of the human condition. 4 ☐ 'We can all sleep more than we need,' says Jim Horne, director of the Sleep Research Centre. 'Ask someone about their holiday and they will often talk in terms of 'catching up' with their sleep. This doesn't square with the facts. 5 ☐ Sleep is just a way of passing the time. Only a quarter of those with sleeping difficulties can be described as sleep-deprived.'

Not that this is of much comfort to anyone who is having trouble sleeping. 'You can try telling a young mother that she's actually getting enough sleep each night,' says Morgan. 'It's just that she's getting it in interrupted packets rather than in a single stretch, but she'll still feel exhausted and may worry that she's not coping.'

In this respect, sleep is like pain. It exists on its own continuum; if anyone thinks they have a problem, then they have a problem and what's tolerable for one person may be intolerable to another. Even so, as the graph of average sleeping patterns shows, there is typically a steady decline in the number of hours we sleep each night the older we get.

Sleep begins in the womb and changes both in character and length throughout our lives. 6 ☐ The four stages of non-REM sleep follow a similar pattern with the transition to stages three and four, the deeper stages of sleep, becoming less common the older we get.

This does not, however, answer the basic question: why do some people seem to need more sleep than others? In any random sample of 24 babies there will be one that sleeps for 18 or more hours each day and another that sleeps for just nine or 10. And the patterns of sleep we adopt in childhood will most likely carry on into adulthood.

Teenagers are a special case, however. Many spend hour upon hour in bed - but for a good reason. The neural networks of the cortex are going through a process of intense reconfiguration and the brain needs some time out. 7 ☐ Periods of extended sleep can be associated with depression. On the other hand it might just be down to normal adolescent boredom.

A Almost to the point of obsession.

B As their teens slumber, parents in turn lose further sleep worrying that their children are sleeping so much because there is something wrong with them.

C Babies can spend up to 80% of their sleep in rapid eye movement (REM) mode - the state most associated with dreaming - while REM will only account for about 10% of a 70-year-old's sleep.

D But you'd be wrong.

E Sadly, our sleep is unlikely to improve once the kids finally leave home.

F Now there is the added anxiety both of being woken up by the children and having to be on hand for them in the daytime. I worry about my sleep constantly'.

G Seven hours is often quoted as a good night's sleep for an adult, but in reality there is no such thing as a standard night's sleep.

H We sleep more on holiday simply because the brain's got less to do.

Unit 15

Vocabulary

Dreams and Sleep

2 Choose the correct word or phrase to complete the sentences.

1 Never in my .... did I imagine that I would win the lottery! It's incredible. I can't believe it!
   A nightmares   B wildest dreams
   C vivid dreams

2 My job is just a .... at the moment. I've got so much work, I don't even get time to eat!
   A nightmare   B daydream   C vivid dream

3 The baby gets very .... in the afternoons, so I put her down for a nap.
   A sleepy   B sleepiness
   C asleep

4 You really think that one day you'll be able to afford a big house like that? .... ! You'll never have enough money.
   A Sweet dreams!   B Dream on!
   C Get some sleep!

5 To help me .... , I try and relax before I got to bed by having a hot bath then drinking a cup of camomile tea.
   A daydream   B sleepy
   C get to sleep

6 You can't speak to her now, I'm afraid. She's in bed .... and I don't want to wake her up.
   A daydreaming   B asleep   C sleepy

7 I have this really strange .... at least one night a week. I'm on a ship in the middle of the ocean, and then this boy I used to know from school appears, and he always says to me...
   A sleepiness   B daydream
   C recurring dream

8 It was such a .... It felt like I could actually smell and taste the food.
   A vivid dream   B daydream   C sleepiness

3 Complete the following sentences with one of the words or phrases from the answer options in Exercise 2 in the correct form, plus any other words that are needed.

1 A 12-hour flight, in charge of three children under the age of five? What .... !

2 Don't phone after ten tonight, will you? I'm having an early night and I'll ....

3 Hey, what are you .... about? By the look on your face, it's something nice!

4 I can't believe I got the job! Earning all that money! I never imagined I'd get it, not .... !

5 I'm going to have a siesta. I feel so ....

6 Stay out at a party till 3 a.m.? At the age of 14? .... , sweetheart! Perhaps when you're 18.

7 You look exhausted! What time .... last night? It must have been very late by the way you're yawning!

8 It felt like I was really there, it was incredible! It was such .... !

Grammar

Obligation, Necessity and Permission

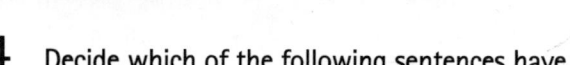

4 Decide which of the following sentences have mistakes and correct them.

1 Were you allowed to wear trousers when you were at school?

2 Do your parents make you stay out late at weekends, or do you have to come home early?

3 I got my children to be good in the supermarket by bribing them with sweets!

4 Please don't let me tidy up my bedroom. You know how much I hate doing it!

5 We needn't rush to the station. The train's leaving in about a minute!

6 I'm allowed to take as long as I want for lunch. It can't be more than an hour.

7 Will you let me help you with that?

8 I didn't make her clean the car. She did it because she wanted to!

5 Complete the sentences below so that they mean the same as the first, using the key word for each one.

1 This is a library. There's a no talking rule!
   ALLOWED
   This is a library. You .... talk!

2 My son doesn't do his homework willingly.
   MAKE
   I have to .... his homework.

3 I'm sure I can persuade her to come to the party.
   GET
   I'm sure I can .... to the party.

4 Can we take photos of the paintings?
   ALLOWED
   .... photos of the paintings?

5 Melanie's parents don't mind if she stays out till late.
   LET
   Melanie's parents .... till late.

6 To stay healthy, it is essential for us to eat plenty of fruit and vegetables.
   NEED
   To stay healthy, we .... plenty of fruit and vegetables.

7 I said that he couldn't borrow my car.
   LET
   I .... my car.

8 My boss said that I didn't have to work late yesterday after all.
   MAKE
   My boss .... work late yesterday after all.

9 It's not necessary for you to have so much sleep.
   NEED
   You .... so much sleep.

10 Ask her to come round at 8 o'clock.
   GET
   .... at 8 o'clock.

6 Complete the sentences below using one of the following verbs in the correct form with the causative structure *get/have* + object + past participle. In two sentences, the causative structure isn't possible with *get*.

brake into	clean	cut	make	paint
repair	send	service	smash	steal

1 We need to .... the house .... We're both hopeless at decorating, so we can't do it ourselves, can we?
2 I knew we should have .... the boiler .... before the cold weather started – now it's broken and we haven't got any central heating!
3 I need to buy a new car – it keeps breaking down and I keep having to .... it .... I'm just wasting money on it.
4 I've .... my car windows .... three times in the past month, when it's been parked outside my house. This area is getting really bad for vandalism.
5 She always .... paperwork .... by courier. She doesn't trust the postal service!
6 Miguel .... his house .... when he was on holiday last summer. They stole everything, even some food he had in his freezer.
7 I can't find anything I like in the shops, so I'm going to .... my wedding dress .... for me.

8 Your hair's a bit of a mess! You really ought to .... it .... I know a good hairdresser.
9 Excuse me. I've just .... my handbag .... It had everything in it, including my phone. Could I borrow your mobile to call the police?
10 The car's so dirty. We really must take it to the garage to .... it .... Or I suppose we could do it ourselves!

7 Can you work out why isn't it possible to use get in three of these sentences?

Use of English Part 2

8 Read the text below and think of one word which best fits each gap.

Sleepless Nights

Daniel Newnham is an insomniac. When his insomnia is at **1** .... worst he gets just four hours' sleep a week. 'It started about three years ago **2** .... I went to California. I did a lot of travelling and my body clock just **3** .... returned to normal. I would lie in bed, feeling more and more exhausted, but my brain would be racing. I became very depressed. I try to avoid becoming fixated on going to sleep, but it's still a struggle.' While no one rules **4** .... the use of medication as a quick fix, few argue for it as a long-term solution. 'We can exercise some control **5** .... establishing good routines,' says Jim Horne, Director of the Sleep Research Centre. **6** .... than lying in bed thinking, you should get up and do something quiet, **7** .... as reading, and go back to bed once you're tired. If the same thing happens again, get up again. And don't try to **8** .... up with your sleep; start your day at a set time each day. You may feel tired for a bit, but eventually your sleeping patterns should return to normal. 'Older people should try to keep mentally and physically active. It's the people who do less that tend to doze **9** .... in the day – which makes sleeping at night that much more difficult.' Most sleep problems, says Morgan, can be sorted **10** .... with cognitive behavioural therapy – the only drawback being **11** .... , assuming you can find a doctor who takes your problem seriously, there can be a two-year waiting list to get referred to a therapist on the NHS. And time can be critical. 'The only guarantee with sleep,' says Morgan, 'is that problems will only get **12** .... if left untreated.'

Listening Part 4

9 What would you do if you couldn't get to sleep at night. Look at the photographs and discuss your ideas with a partner.

 1  2  3 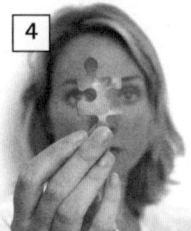 4  5 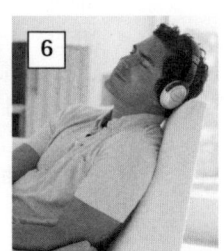 6

10 Circle the words in the *word snake* and match them to the definitions below.

cognitivedisorderissuetummyrumblingtriggeratstake

1 cause an event or situation to happen or exist ....
2 an important topic or problem for debate or discussion ....
3 a person's stomach or abdomen ....
4 at risk ....
5 make a continuous deep, resonant sound ....
6 the mental process of acquiring knowledge and understanding ....
7 an illness that disrupts normal physical or mental functions ....

CD 1 16

11 You will hear a doctor speaking about the importance of getting a good night's sleep. For questions 1-10, complete the sentences.

GOOD NIGHT – SLEEP TIGHT!

The [____ **1**] develops during sleep and some people can survive on as little as four hours a night.

Difficulty sleeping might be due to unsuitable [____ **2**] in which people sleep.

Lack of [____ **3**] can be a threat to both physical and mental health.

Appetite and weight increase are regulated by the [____ **4**] set off during sleep.

Shortage of sleep is more than just a [____ **5**], in some cases the repercussions have been dire.

The organ of the brain that regulates [____ **6**] planning, as well as sense of time, can be badly damaged by denial of sleep.

You become grumpy and absent-minded, your attention span shortens and you find it hard to concentrate after a [____ **7**] night.

Exercise generates [____ **8**] which prevent the brain from unwinding therefore it should not be done too near bedtime.

People who feel hungry shortly before going to bed should eat food which [____ **9**] serotonin.

It is wise to [____ **10**] the help of a doctor if lack of sleep does not allow you to live a normal life.

12 Listen again and decide if the following statements are true (T) or false (F).

		T	F
1	Four hours' sleep is all the brain needs to maintain its cognitive skills.	☐	☐
2	Having a TV in the bedroom may help you become more restful or relaxed.	☐	☐
3	Sleep deprivation doesn't affect us physically or emotionally.	☐	☐
4	People who don't get enough sleep are more likely to put on weight.	☐	☐
5	The consequences of lack of sleep are much more dangerous than one may believe.	☐	☐
6	The Challenger Shuttle explosion was thought to have been caused by sleep deprivation.	☐	☐
7	It takes more than one sleepless night to make a person irritable and forgetful.	☐	☐
8	Exercise should be avoided too near bedtime.	☐	☐
9	Snoring reduces the amount of oxygen in the blood by restricting the airflow into the lungs.	☐	☐

13 Have you ever gone a whole night without sleep? How did you feel the next day? Did you experience any of the consequences of sleep deprivation mentioned by the speaker? Tell your partner.

Speaking Part 2

14 Does this man look comfortable? Do you think he'll feel rested when he wakes up? What's the most uncomfortable place you've fallen asleep in? Tell your partner.

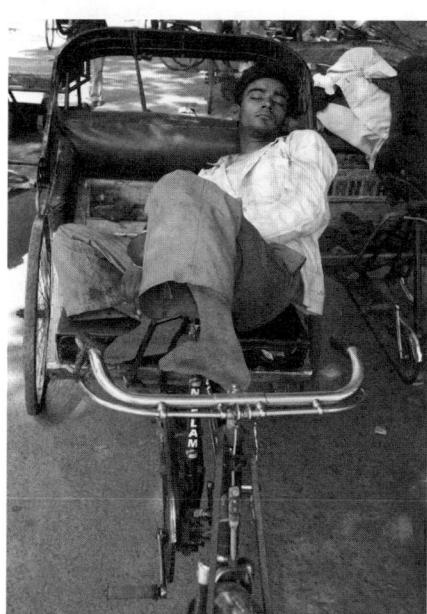

15 Both photographs show people sleeping in unusual places. Read the description below and find ten differences between the information in the text and the situation portrayed in the photographs.

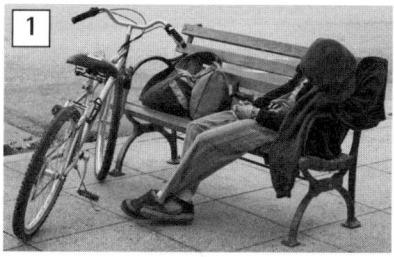

The first photograph shows a man asleep or resting on a public bench. He is wearing trousers, trainers and what appears to be a hooded jacket. He is slumped on the edge of the bench and he is leaning against either a blanket or a towel. On the bench underneath him are two bags. One is a holdall and the other is a smaller bag. Well, I think it's a bag, but it is so plump, it could almost be a cushion. Propped against the wall, is a bicycle which seems quite new. The ground looks quite dry, as though it has been raining and it's rather dull. It doesn't look like a particularly nice day, weather wise, at all. I don't know why this person has chosen to rest here. There could be any number of reasons, I suppose. I don't think he is just out for a cycle ride because he has too much stuff with him, although, he could be on a cycling holiday. On the other hand, it could be that he has nowhere else to go; nowhere else even to sleep. I wonder if the bulky bag is, in fact, a sleeping bag and he does seem to have a tent with him, the one he is leaning on. This bench, would, I think, be extremely uncomfortable, if you were trying to rest or sleep for any length of time.

The second photograph is rather strange. I am not really at all sure what is going on. It could be some sort of indoor gym. There seem to be what look like large storage chests down one side of the area. On the other side there appear to be lights which would suggest the place is used at night time as well as during the day. There are about eighty people standing on the type of mats you would use in a gym. Some people are walking over the rows of people on the ground. Perhaps they are instructors of some sort but, then again, quite a lot of people lying down seem to be dressed in similar clothes. I get the impression that it is far from the sea. It looks like there are some cliffs and possibly a bay with some trees. I can see some sort of brick and wood structure at the end of the area where the people are lying. I can't actually make out what it is they are doing. Yoga, perhaps. They certainly appear to be lying very still. Perhaps they are just learning to relax. I wonder if it could be a 'sit in' in protest against an issue of some sort. I really don't know, but it certainly doesn't look like a very comfortable way to rest or sleep.

16 Now compare the photographs and say how comfortable these places might be for sleeping or resting.

1 You are going to read an article about silence. For questions 1-15, choose from the four sections (A-D) of the text. The sections may be chosen more than once.

Silence, Please!

What does silence mean to you? Do you enjoy silence or do you prefer to be surrounded by noise? Does silence still exist in our noisy world?

A - Naturally quiet?

The natural world is never silent. Even miles from civilisation, in the middle of the desert you will hear the rustling of an insect or the sound of the wind. The official definition of silence is a place where the background noise measures 20 decibels or less. It might seem quiet to you in the natural world but there are many sounds that are outside the hearing range of humans, such as infrasound communication between elephants in the savannah, or the ultrasound used by dolphins. The quietest sound is made by leaves rustling in the wind. This often measures only 10 decibels. The loudest natural sound is a man's voice, which can reach up to 60 decibels. One of the loudest artificial sounds is the noise of a jet aircraft as it takes off and lands: 130 decibels. Sirens and pneumatic drills are also extremely noisy, producing 120 decibels. Have you ever thought that most of the noise we make might be completely unnecessary?

B - Going deep within

In Western culture, silence usually means simply an absence of sound, and it is often associated with being alone and being afraid. For many people in the East, however, silence is a necessary part of their spiritual life, for example, in daily meditation. Whatever your feelings about silence, it is true that if you want to listen to someone you have to stop talking. Silence is an important part of understanding the people around you. You also need silence if you want to listen to yourself, to hear your inner voice and your own thoughts. Making a friend of silence will help you find inner peace and calm. Not only that, but silence could make you more intelligent: the brain cannot function properly if it is continously processing noise - it needs quiet.

C - The search for silence

More and more people are feeling the need for silence. A new trend from the US is the silence party. There is no music or small talk at these parties. They are totally silent. Two New York artists came up with this idea in 2002, and their quiet parties were a big success. Dotted in quiet places around the world, you will find 'hotels du silence'. These hotels are set on the peaceful shores of a lake or in the middle of a forest and there are no mobile phones, no TVs and traffic. If you still can't find any peace then try using the 'map of silence' - something created by a group of researchers in the UK, mapping the quietest places in Britain using research information from 1300 people living in the countryside.

D - The sound of silence

Silence can be found in the most unexpected places. Avant-guarde musician, John Cage, has explored the meaning of silence in one of his most famous pieces - music without music. In this work, all you hear are people coughing and the other noises that an audience makes as they sit, settling themselves into their seats, waiting for a concert to begin.

Which section

- mentions noise that, for people, is inaudible?　　　1 ☐
- defines what silence is officially?　　　2 ☐
- explains how a lack of silence can stop a part of the body working properly?　　　3 ☐
- reports on an unusually silent social occasion?　　　4 ☐
- mentions a very noisy machine?　　　5 ☐
- mentions a discipline of which silence is an intrinsic part?　　　6 ☐
- reports on an event where the silence itself is what you listen to?　　　7 ☐
- mentions the different ways that silence is viewed in different parts of the world?　　　8 ☐
- mentions the least noisy natural sound?　　　9 ☐
- mentions something that can tell you the geographical location of particularly quiet places?　　　10 ☐
- reveals the noisiest sound produced by humans?　　　11 ☐
- mentions an artistic work that examines the nature of silence?　　　12 ☐
- mentions special quiet places to stay?　　　13 ☐
- mentions the noisiness of nature?　　　14 ☐
- points out how you have to be silent to hear other people?　　　15 ☐

Vocabulary

Musical Instruments

2 Put the following instruments into the correct group according to the type of instrument they are.

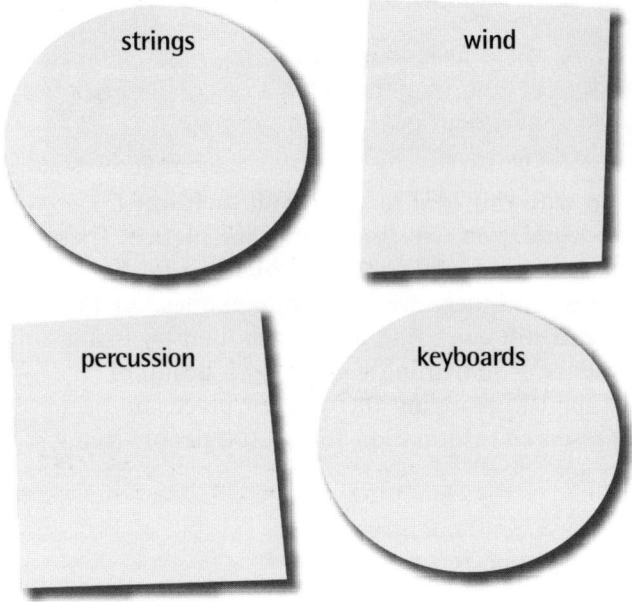

cello	guitar	recorder
clarinet	harmonica	saxophone
cymbals	harp	synthesizer
didgeridoo	harpsichord	trumpet
double-bass	maracas	viola
drums	organ	violin
flute	piano	xylophone

Vocabulary and Grammar

Phrasal verbs

3 Match the phrasal verbs with their definitions.

1 break down	8 look after sth / sb
2 come back	9 look into sth
3 eat out	10 put off sth
4 get over sth	11 run into sb
5 get up	12 take after sb
6 go on	13 turn down sth
7 go through sth	14 turn up

a when you leave your bed ☐
b when your car stops working ☐
c to postpone something ☐
d to reject something ☐
e when something happens or somebody arrives somewhere unexpectedly, or in a way that was not planned ☐

f return ☐
g recover from an illness or difficult emotional situation ☐
h investigate or examine a situation in more detail. ☐
i be similar to an older relative in character or appearance ☐
j experience a difficult situation ☐
k take responsibility for somebody or something ☐
l have a meal at a restaurant ☐
m to meet someone you know unexpectedly ☐
n continue ☐

4 Decide which answer options are possible to complete the following sentences. For some sentences, more than one answer is possible.

1 The music teacher was ill, so they .... until next week.
   A put the concert off   B put off the concert
   C put it off   D put off it

2 They had to .... yesterday morning, to get to the airport by 7a.m.
   A get very early up   B get up very early
   C get it up very early   D get up very early it

3 He's very upset about her leaving him – I think it's going to be a long time before he ....
   A gets over it.   B get it over.
   C gets over.   D gets over the relationship.

4 She really .... She's got the same red hair and green eyes.
   A takes after her father B takes her father after
   C takes after him   D takes him after

5 The Browns .... on their way up to Scotland – their car overheated, apparently.
   A broke the car down   B broke down the car
   C broke down   D broke it down

6 We .... Our favourite restaurant is that Italian place in the High Street.
   A eat out a lot   B eat a lot out
   C eat the restaurant out D eat out the restaurant

7 Why don't you two go out for the evening and leave the children with me? I'll ....
   A look them after.   B look after them.
   C look after the children. D look the children after.

8 Gilly's .... at the moment. She's having trouble at work and her father's very ill. I feel really sorry for her.
   A going through a difficult time
   B going a difficult time through
   C going through it   D going it through

9 I was amazed! I hadn't seen him since we left school, and then he just .... last weekend!
   A turned it up   B turned up it
   C turned my house up   D turned up at my house

10 Honestly, he just .... about himself and didn't ask me a thing about myself. I'm not going out with him again!
   A went talking on   B went on talking
   C went on (and on)   D went on it

5 Add a preposition from the box below to form a 3-word phrasal verb (1-12). Then match it with its definition (a-l).

up	with	on	of	to

1 catch up .... sth / sb
2 cut down / back .... sth
3 get along .... sb
4 get away .... sth
5 get rid .... sth / sb
6 get through .... sb
7 look down .... sb
8 look forward .... sth
9 look up .... sb
10 put up .... sth / sb
11 run out .... sth
12 take care .... sth / sb

a when you do something wrong and manage to escape without punishment
b reduce consumption or use of something
c tolerate something or someone
d take responsibility for something or someone
e discard, throw away something you don't need anymore
f get to the same place or the same standard as other people
g think with pleasure about something that's going to happen
h when the supply of something finishes
i feel superior to someone
j respect and admire someone
k have a good relationship with someone
l manage to make someone understand something

6 Complete the following sentences using a 3-word phrasal verb from Exercise 5 in the correct form.

1 Why don't we .... all those CDs? All our music's on the computer now, so we don't need them, really, do we?
2 I' .... the dinner tonight. You go and sit down and watch the telly.

3 I don't know how much longer I can .... my boss. She's just so unreasonable and so demanding! I should start looking for another job.
4 I hadn't done my homework for school today, but the teacher was off sick, so I .... it!
5 Jo missed two weeks of classes at university when she had the flu, but she's worked really hard since she came back and .... all the work she missed.
6 We're going to have to .... our heating, after that last bill we got. We'll just have to wear extra jumpers instead!
7 I'm really .... going on holiday. I haven't been away anywhere for five years!
8 You .... toothpaste two days ago? So you haven't cleaned your teeth since then. Oh, yuk!

Use of English Part 4

7 For questions 1-8, complete the second sentence so that it has a similar meaning to the first sentence, using the word given.

1 I'd prefer us to go to see the Arctic Monkeys than Shakira.
RATHER
.... to see the Arctic Monkeys than Shakira.

2 Who's responsible for the accounts in the company?
CHARGE
Who .... the accounts in the company?

3 I threw out loads of old clothes and bought lots of new stuff.
RID
I .... loads of old clothes and bought lots of new stuff.

4 I'm not sure if he's working today.
MIGHT
He .... today.

5 There was enough food and drink at the party for everybody.
RUN
We .... food and drink at the party.

6 Michael has given Nicola a beautiful silver bracelet.
HAS
Nicola .... a beautiful silver bracelet by Michael.

7 Ruth had a really good idea for solving the problem.
UP
Ruth .... such a good solution to the problem.

8 What a pity you didn't carry on with your guitar lessons.
SHOULD
You .... your guitar lessons.

8 Read the definitions and find the words in the wordsquare.

```
A C O W C G L W F M T C S V U
M M E R J W N E L I Z J C S V
B A A Q Y H Q I U S C V R E U
T A C T L E S S R S H N U Q V
Z C X E E V L Q W E H N F I O
Y L T X J U O U S L T K F G L
C P G Q Z G R B U T S T Y X J
I Z D A D M E F M N W I A Z A
R J Q S E W E E W I M N E L T
P T Q H A C T R A O R Y D R F
X Z R R R A E F B P J S C H J
C B E O E T A B E D A K I J K
U B F A S A C O H C M X D N R
F A P J M E N A G E Q F I Q C
L H E S H Z R U D I X Z S G J
```

1 costing a lot of money
2 enhance the features, figure, or character of someone (verb)
3 shabby and untidy or dirty
4 adopt an extreme or undesirable course of action so as to resolve a difficult situation
5 having little or no sense, use, or purpose
6 strong and assertive; vigorous and powerful
7 an argument about a particular subject in which many people are involved
8 enhancing someone's appearance (adjective)
9 a person who engages in an occupation or sport on an unpaid basis
10 harass someone constantly to do something that they don't want to do
11 showing a lack of sensitivity in dealing with others or with difficult issues
12 be cautious and alert to risks or dangers

9 Complete the gaps in the sentences with the correct form of one of the words found in the wordsquare in Exercise 8.

1 Aunt Charlotte always was a .... personality.
2 There was no need to make such a .... remark.
3 The dress didn't .... her and I told her so!
4 Do you always have to look so .... !
5 I don't think sleeveless tops are very .... at my age.
6 Mum was always .... me to give her a hand with the housework
7 It's .... trying to plan so far ahead.
8 I wouldn't trust that bunch of stumbling .... if I were you!
9 I'm afraid I can't afford the .... clothes in that new boutique.
10 Shoppers were told to .... of cut-price fakes.
11 There has been much .... over the rate of inflation.
12 The workers had every intention of .... to force if negotiation failed.

10 You will hear people talking in eight different situations. For questions 1–8, choose the best answer (A, B or C).

1 You overhear a woman talking to a friend. What does she say about the clothes she wears?
A She doesn't care what she looks like as long as she's fashionable. ☐
B She dresses for the occasion. ☐
C She doesn't think she looks scruffy when she's casually dressed. ☐

2 You hear a man talking about domestic animals. What does he say about dogs?
A They provide an opportunity for the elderly to exercise. ☐
B They are good company for only children. ☐
C They can be trained to be useful to society. ☐

3 You overhear a woman talking on a radio program. What form of entertainment can most people afford?

A amateur plays ☐
B pop concerts ☐
C debates on the radio ☐

4 You hear a man talking about advertising. What is he doing?

A complaining about something ☐
B making a suggestion ☐
C giving advice ☐

5 You hear part of a talk on the radio about schooling.
What is the man's conclusion?

A Skilled pupils should be given the opportunity to attend special schools. ☐
B Grammar and comprehensive schools should be regarded more highly. ☐
C Schools should be chosen according to individual needs. ☐

6 You hear an elderly woman talking on the phone. What is she trying to do?

A convince her son about something ☐
B persuade her son to do something ☐
C warn her son about something ☐

7 You hear part of a radio program about feelings. Why are shy people so reluctant to take up something new?

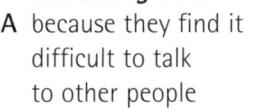

A because they find it difficult to talk to other people ☐
B because they are afraid of making a fool of themselves ☐
C because they might hurt themselves ☐

8 You hear a woman talking about having difficulty sleeping at night.
What was she once obliged to do as a last resort?

A sit up all night doing a puzzle ☐
B drink a couple of glasses of wine ☐
C wander around the house ☐

11 You heard the proverb *Clothes maketh the man* in the recording. Discuss its meaning with a partner and whether or not you agree with it. Then match the other proverbs (1-10) to their meanings (a-j).

1 Empty vessels make the most noise.
2 A rolling stone gathers no moss.
3 A bird in hand is worth two in the bush.
4 Every cloud has a silver lining.
5 All that glitters is not gold.
6 Don't count your chickens before they're hatched.
7 Fools rush in where angels fear to tread.
8 However long the night, the dawn will break.
9 Kill the goose that lays the golden egg.
10 Look before you leap.

a Inexperienced people act in situations that more intelligent people would avoid. ☐
b Consider possible consequences before taking action. ☐
c There is a positive or hopeful side to every unpleasant situation. ☐
d Destroy something that would be a source of wealth or success. ☐
e You must not be too confident that something will be successful. ☐
f If a person keeps moving from place to place, they gain neither friends nor possessions. ☐
g Bad things don't last forever. ☐
h The least intelligent people are often the most talkative or noisy. ☐
i Appearances can be deceptive. ☐
j It's better to keep what you have than to risk losing it by searching for something better. ☐

Big Spender!

1 Read the following extract from a short story by D.H. Lawrence. For questions 1-8, choose the answer (A, B, C or D) which you think fits best according to the text.

The Rocking Horse Winner

There was a woman who was beautiful, who started with all the advantages, yet she had no luck. She married for love, and the love turned to dust. She had bonny children, yet she felt they had been thrust upon her, and she could not love them. They looked at her coldly, as if they were finding fault with her. And hurriedly she felt she must cover up some fault in herself. Yet what it was that she must cover up she never knew. Nevertheless, when her children were present, she always felt the centre of her heart go hard. This troubled her, and in her manner she was all the more gentle and anxious for her children, as if she loved them very much. Only she herself knew that at the centre of her heart was a hard little place that could not feel love, no, not for anybody. Everybody else said of her: 'She is such a good mother. She adores her children.' Only she herself, and her children themselves, knew it was not so. They read it in each other's eyes.

There were a boy and two little girls. They lived in a pleasant house, with a garden, and they had discreet servants, and felt themselves superior to anyone in the neighbourhood.

Although they lived in style, they felt always an anxiety in the house. There was never enough money. The mother had a small income, and the father had a small income, but not nearly enough for the social position which they had

to keep up. The father went into town to some office. But though he had good prospects, these prospects never materialised. There was always the grinding sense of the shortage of money, though the style was always kept up.

At last the mother said: 'I will see if I can't make something.' But she did not know where to begin. She racked her brains, and tried this thing and the other, but could not find anything successful. The failure made deep lines come into her face. Her children were growing up, they would have to go to school. There must be more money, there must be more money. The father, who was always very handsome and expensive in his tastes, seemed as if he never would be able to do anything worth doing. And the mother, who had a great belief in herself, did not succeed any better, and her tastes were just as expensive.

And so the house came to be haunted by the unspoken phrase: There must be more money! There must be more money! The children could hear it all the time though nobody said it aloud. They heard it at Christmas, when the expensive and splendid toys filled the nursery. Behind the shining modern rocking-horse, behind the smart doll's house, a voice would start whispering: 'There must be more money! There must be more money!' And the children would stop playing, to listen for a moment. They would look into each other's eyes, to see if they had all heard. And each one saw in the eyes of the other two that they too had heard. 'There must be more money! There must be more money!'

It came whispering from the springs of the still-swaying rocking-horse, and even the horse, bending his wooden, champing head, heard it. The big doll, sitting so pink and smirking in her new pram, could hear it quite plainly, and seemed to be smirking all the more self-consciously because of it. The foolish puppy, too, that took the place of the teddy-bear, he was looking so extraordinarily foolish for no other reason but that he heard the secret whisper all over the house: 'There must be more money!'

Yet nobody ever said it aloud. The whisper was everywhere, and therefore no one spoke it. Just as no one ever says: 'We are breathing!' in spite of the fact that breath is coming and going all the time.

1 The feelings between the woman and her husband
   A were as strong as they were when they first got married. ☐
   B hadn't lasted. ☐
   C had changed because of the children. ☐
   D had changed due to bad luck. ☐

2 The children could sense
   A how much their mother loved them. ☐
   B their mother's feeling towards their father. ☐
   C their mother's true feelings towards them. ☐
   D what a good mother they had. ☐

3 Financially, the family lived
   A according to their means. ☐
   B an uncomfortable life of poverty. ☐
   C beyond their means. ☐
   D comfortably on the parents' incomes. ☐

4 In his career, the father
   A had lived up to people's expectations of him. ☐
   B hadn't done as well as expected. ☐
   C hadn't ever had any hope of achieving much. ☐
   D would have done better if he hadn't been so concerned with keeping up appearances. ☐

5 In an attempt to generate more income, the mother
   A tried hard to think of what she could do, but failed to come up with anything that worked. ☐
   B was very resourceful. ☐
   C tried unsuccessfully to get a job. ☐
   D made things to sell. ☐

6 Compared to the father, the mother
   A wasn't at all extravagant. ☐
   B had less expensive tastes. ☐
   C found it equally as difficult to live frugally. ☐
   D was much better at budgeting. ☐

7 For the children, the shortage of money in the household
   A was not something that they were aware of at all. ☐
   B caused them anxiety, too. ☐
   C made them upset because they didn't get the presents they wanted. ☐
   D meant that they didn't feel like playing very much. ☐

8 The shortage of money was something that
   A the family discussed openly. ☐
   B made some members of the family have difficulty breathing. ☐
   C the family felt they had to whisper about. ☐
   D the family didn't speak to each other about. ☐

Vocabulary

Money and Shopping

2 Where would you go to buy the following items? Write in the name of the shop or store.

1 a bunch of lilies

....

2 some wholemeal bread rolls

....

3 some paperclips and glue

....

4 a kilo of organic chicken breast

....

5 a tube of antiseptic cream

....

6 a kilo of Granny Smith apples

....

7 a tin of cat food

....

8 an armchair from the 1930s

....

9 a comic

....

10 a pair of earrings

....

11 a packet of fruit pastilles

....

12 a screwdriver

....

13 some fresh trout

....

14 a tin of tomatoes

....

15 a lighter

....

3 Complete the conversation with an item from the box, putting it into the correct form as necessary.

| bargain (x2) | cheap | expensive | knock off |
| quid | reduce | sales | sell off | value |

A I love your coat. Is it new?

B Thanks, yeah, it is actually. I got it last month in the January **1** .... The shop was **2** .... all the winter stuff really **3** .... , ready for the new spring stock, and this was **4** .... from just over £200 to £50!

A Wow, what a **5** .... ! £150 off the price!

B I know, I was amazed. And my sister, who came shopping with me, found a beautiful pair of boots in that shop *Cobblers* – you know, that shoe shop that's usually really **6** .... , with nothing under about a hundred **7** .... ? Well, her boots had about 90% **8** .... the price - instead of £200, they were £25!

A Really! And their stuff is such good quality, too, so that's fantastic **9** .... for money. Next time you and your sister go shopping, can I come too? I can see that you've both got a real eye for a **10** .... !

4 Match the sentences.

1 Come on! If we don't hurry,
2 I'd go and see the doctor
3 If I didn't have to work this Saturday,
4 If I don't get to bed by 11p.m.,
5 If I had loads of money,
6 If we save up some money each month,
7 If you could live anywhere in the world,
8 If you mix blue and yellow,
9 If you turn on this switch here,
10 Unless you start working harder,
11 What job would you do
12 You might get the job
13 You'll have the whole weekend free
14 If they sell their house now

a I'm exhausted the next day.
b you get green.
c the light over there comes on.
d we'll miss the train!
e you won't pass your exams.
f if you do your homework tonight.
g we may be able to afford a holiday next summer.
h I'd buy a new car.
i if I were you – you might need antibiotics.
j how much will they get for it?
k where would you choose?
l if you had the choice?
m I could go away for the weekend.
n if you apply for it - give it a go!

Grammar

Zero, First and Second Conditionals

5 Complete the following conditional sentences with the most appropriate form of the verb in brackets.

1 If I .... (not / get) enough sleep, I .... (be / always) really grumpy the next day.
2 What .... (you / buy) if you .... (win) the lottery?
3 If it .... (snow) tonight, we .... (not / be able to) drive to school tomorrow.
  We .... (have to) get the bus instead.
4 If I .... (be) you, I' .... (try) and save £100 a month - saving is a good idea!
5 What .... (you / do) if you .... (never / have to) work again in your life?
6 I .... (usually / get) spots if I .... (eat) too much chocolate.
7 You .... (go) out tonight unless you .... (promise) to be home by midnight!
8 If you .... (not / start) saving money when you're young, you .... (not / have) enough for
  your retirement.
9 I' .... (let) you stay up and watch that programme tonight if you .... (help) me with the
  washing up first.
10 Jenny .... (come) to the party, if you .... (invite) her. Phone her and ask!
11 Would you .... (go) and see your grandparents more, if they .... (not / live) so far away?
12 Things at work aren't looking good. How .... (we / manage) for money, if I .... (lose) my job?

Use of English Part 1

6 Read the text below about saving money and decide
which answer (A, B, C or D) best fits each gap.

Saving Your Money

Whether you're a high school student on an allowance from your parents, or already working part-time, or a college
1 .... venturing out into the world, learning to plan your **2** .... is an important skill. And saving **3**
.... be an integral part of your financial planning. Starting saving while you're young **4** .... a lot of
sense. If you start saving now, it will build to a larger amount by the time you reach **5** .... age than if you
wait to start saving later on. Another good reason to get into the habit of saving early on is that people who save a
lot get used to a lower rate of consumption while working, so they need less money when they retire.

Here's some simple advice to help you get on the right track:

- Put 10% of your monthly **6** .... into savings before anything else.
- If you are already working, ignore any **7** .... in salary that you get and put them into savings.
- Never borrow money to pay for a depreciating **8** .... , like a car.
- Find a partner and stay together. Studies show that two can live more cheaply together than
  each alone – and that divorce is the greatest destroyer of **9** ....

Remember, however, that saving is a lot easier if there are small rewards along the way.
Don't **10** .... yourself of daily treats like going for a coffee or a drink with a friend,
otherwise life seems dull and boring, which makes saving that much more difficult.

1	A degree	B graduate	C career	D graduation
2	A money	B income	C budget	D cash
3	A will	B has	C should	D need
4	A is	B has	C seems	D makes
5	A retire	B retirement	C retiring	D retired
6	A receipts	B income	C bill	D account
7	A raises	B rises	C uprisings	D rising
8	A earnings	B share	C ownership	D asset
9	A rich	B wealth	C comfort	D materialism
10	A limit	B stop	C cut	D deprive

7 What sort of relationship do you have with money? Do you save every penny or do you spend money like there's no tomorrow? Tell your partner.

8 The sentences below all contain words and expressions which refer to money. Read the first half of each one (1-10) and find its corresponding second half (a-j).

1 Andrew lost his job and...
2 I wouldn't work there if I were you...
3 When we were young we didn't have...
4 The company was in so much debt...
5 David got ripped off...
6 I went to the sales and...
7 It turns out that the painting...
8 He's so tight fisted...
9 Kevin's new house must have...
10 You haven't got any...

a lose change on you, have you?
b blew a month's wages in one day.
c cost him an arm and a leg.
d two pennies to rub together.
e had to sign on the dole.
f it had to declare bankruptcy.
g they pay peanuts.
h Jan picked up at the sale is worth a fortune.
i at the restaurant last night.
j he wouldn't even buy me a drink.

9 Read the definitions and match them to the words in the box.

loan	☐	repossess	☐
owing	☐	recession	☐
debt	☐	mortgage	☐
reckless	☐	weakness	☐
outcome	☐	default	☐

1 a disadvantage or fault
2 a period of temporary economic decline
3 money lent by a bank in order to buy property
4 a sum of money that is borrowed and has to be paid back with interest
5 failure to repay a loan
6 the way something turns out
7 to be obliged to pay money in return for something received
8 a sum of money that is due
9 retake possession of something when the owner is unable to settle his debts
10 heedless of the consequences of one's actions

10 Read the sentences and fill the gaps with a suitable word from Exercise 9.

1 The firm intends to restructure its debts in order to avoid ....
2 I put down fifty thousand in cash and took out a .... for the rest.
3 Borrowers are able to take out a .... for £99,000.
4 The company I work for is heavily in ....
5 741 homes were .... for non-payment of mortgages last year.
6 They denied .... any money to the company.
7 All this .... spending will get you into trouble.
8 What really counts is the .... of the vote.
9 It's about time you recognized your product's strengths and ....
10 This country is in the depths of a ....

11 You will hear a radio interview with a financial expert about the economic crisis in Britain and the USA. For questions 1-7, choose the best answer (A, B or C).

1 The 'lending and spending boom' refers to a period when
 A banks supplied extremely competitive credit.
 B people never had to worry about the consequences of their spending.
 C people blamed the banks for their debts rather than themselves.

`1`

2 To stop the economy from going into recession
 A outstanding payments on homes have to be brought down.
 B business investment has to be intensified.
 C the public has to be given the incentive to spend more.

`2`

3 People who take cheap credit for granted
 A run into millions and millions of pounds worth of debt.
 B risk falling into debt which they will find hard to get out of.
 C are unable to furnish their house without falling into debt.

`3`

4 The credit crunch began in the USA when the banks
 A would no longer lend money to each other.
 B started losing money over mortgage repayments.
 C wouldn't make any more company investments.

`4`

5 It is difficult to get credit in the UK if you
 A need to borrow a large sum of money.
 B already have a mortgage or loan to pay off.
 C are at any risk of not being able to repay a loan.

`5`

6 One couple's home is being repossessed by the bank because they
 A have millions of pounds worth of debts.
 B filed for bankruptcy.
 C they can no longer rely on their credit cards to pay off their debts.

`6`

7 Another couple have managed to keep their home
 A thanks to a debt management plan.
 B because they do not spend on non-essentials.
 C because they were able to pay back their creditors.

`7`

12 Listen to the recording again and answer the following questions.

1 Who according to the financial expert is responsible for the credit crash in Britain and the USA?
2 Why does the cost of credit have to be increased?
3 Why did the banks in America stop lending to each other?
4 Who will have difficulty getting credit in Britain?
5 What does a debt management plan enable people to do?

13 If you got into debt due to a financial economic crisis, would you seek the advice of a financial adviser to pay off all your debts over a period of time or would you declare yourself bankrupt? Tell your partner which alternative you would choose and why and what you think the consequences could be.

1 Read the text about the city of Berlin. For questions 1-15, choose from the sections (A-F). The sections may be chosen more than once.

Berlin

A - World Class Architecture

Berlin has taken off its cold-war coat and turned itself into a living, breathing open-air museum. The last two decades since the fall of the Berlin Wall have seen the German capital transformed into an architectural masterpiece. The success of this dramatic change has been due to a careful balancing of old and new, the past and the future.

The city is home to many buildings designed by the world's top architects. These buildings are daring and modern but have been designed to be in keeping with Berlin's distinctive character. The past and the future coexist in this city, reunited after the fall of the Berlin Wall in 1989. It is no coincidence that amongst the new constructions there are many bridges. These not only provide a link across the city's rivers, but are powerful symbols of a reunited Berlin. The first bridge built to reconnect East and West Berlin is the Kronprinzenbrucke, designed by Spanish architect Santiago Calatrava. It is constructed in white steel and is both functional and beautiful.

B - Potsdamer Platz

This square was completely destroyed during the Second World War, but that destruction has given the world's most respected architects the freedom and space to play with – and break – all the rules. They turned it into the world's biggest building site. Italian architect, Renzo Piano, designed the Damler-Benz, a dramatic construction in steel and glass. The Sony Center, designed by Helmut Jahn, is a complex of buildings linked by a central covered square, inspired by Mount Fuji, which changes colour depending on the weather conditions. The spectacular DB Tower, housing the headquarters of the German railway is over 100 metres tall. Today Potsdamer Platz is both the physical and metaphorical heart of Berlin. It epitomises how the city has changed to embrace the future.

C - Reichstag

The Reichstag shows how successfully the old can be joined with the ultramodern. The original Reighstag was built in 1871 and is the seat of the German government. It has been given a new purpose and character with the addition of a breathtaking glass cupola, the work of British architect Norman Foster, its transparency symbolically representing a new era of 'transparent' government. Inside the building, two spiral staircases allow public access to the heart of the government building.

D - Alexander Platz
This square at the heart of the old East Berlin is home of one of the city's most famous buildings, the Fernsehturm, the Television tower, which is the second tallest building in Europe. It is nearly 400 metres tall and can be seen from every part of the city. It sits on a platform shaped like an arrow. It also has a World clock which marks the different time zones of the Earth.

E - The Beautiful and the Bizarre
One of the most unusual buildings in the new Berlin is the Nordic Embassies, which houses the embassies of Sweden, Finland, Norway, Denmark and Iceland. They are linked by a spectacular central courtyard which is full of light. The DX Bank headquarters, designed by American architect Gehry, most famous for his Guggenheim Museum in Bilbao, has a central courtyard covered by a delicate metal lattice like a spider's web. In the courtyard is a moving structure in the shape of a horse's head, inside of which is a conference centre.

F - The Jewish Memorial
The new Jewish Museum by Daniel Libeskind is unlike most buildings in that it is not simply a functional space to put things in. The shape and structure of the rooms are designed to tell the story of the Jewish people. It is nicknamed 'Blitz', the German word for thunder bolt, because of its zig-zag design. Even before its official opening in 2001, while the building was still empty, it was visited by over 350,000 people. The entrance to the building has been made difficult and long, symbolising the difficulties faced by Jewish people throughout their history. One of the most important works in the museum is Shalechet, meaning fallen leaves. It is made of ten thousand open-mouthed faces printed on metal. The Holocaust Memorial, close to the Brandenburg Gate, was built in 2005. It is made up of 2711 pillars of different heights and leaning in different directions. It is designed to make you feel disoriented. It represents a regime apparently built on order but which has in fact lost all connection with human reason.

Which section

- describes how the material used for a part of a new building in Berlin is a metaphor for the concept of clarity? [1]
- mentions how there have been major architectural changes in Berlin in the past twenty years? [2]
- describes a very high building, visible from all over Berlin? [3]
- mentions how the inspiration for one of the new buildings in Berlin was a geographical feature in another part of the world? [4]
- describes an unconventional building with strong links to Scandinavia? [5]
- mentions how the design of the new buildings in Berlin is adventurous, but, at the same time, appropriate for the style of the city? [6]
- describes a building whose form represents a narrative of struggle? [7]
- talks about a part of Berlin that, with the extensive changes it has undergone, is a perfect example of the city's welcoming of what lies ahead? [8]
- describes a construction deliberately designed to make people feel uncomfortable, as part of its symbolism? [9]
- mentions the building where the country is run from? [10]
- mentions a good place to go if you want to know what the time is in another part of the world? [11]
- describes constructions that act as a metaphor for Berlin's reunification? [12]
- mentions a part of a building that doesn't keep still? [13]
- mentions how architects have been able to exploit the destructive consequences of an event in history? [14]
- mentions a building informally known by a name that also describes its shape? [15]

Vocabulary

Places we live in

2 Match the words below to a picture.

1 block of flats (B.E.) / apartment block (A.E.) ☐
2 detached house ☐
3 terraced house ☐
4 block ☐
5 cottage ☐
6 bungalow ☐
7 flat (B.E.) / apartment (A.E.) ☐
8 semi-detached house ☐

B.E. British English
A.E. American English

3 Choose a word or phrase from the box to complete the short texts opposite, putting it into the correct form as necessary.

| building (x 2)   design (noun)   design (verb)
| construction   build (x2)   build from scratch
| building materials   building site   plot   architect |

Honestly, my neighbours' garden looks like a
1 .... They're having their house done up and
there are **2** .... everywhere – bricks, bags of
cement, pots of paint.

There aren't so many new houses **3** .... now,
with the recession. Where I live, **4** .... that
had already been started has stopped, as people just
can't afford to buy a new house at the moment, so
there are lots of half-finished **5** .... that have
just been left.

I'm really excited! We've bought a **6** .... of
land and we' **7** .... a house .... by
ourselves. OK, so we got an **8** .... to help us
9 .... it, but we' **10** .... it on our own.
The **11** .... is quite unusual – pretty avante-
garde for a small village! **12** .... is going to
take at least three years, I think.

Grammar

Conditionals

4 Choose the correct option to complete the sentences.

1 If the party .... better, we would have stayed for longer.
A was   B had been   C is

2 What .... if you lost your job?
A would you have done   B would you do   C do you do

3 If I .... more money, I would move to a bigger flat.
A had   B had had   C have

4 If my son .... in the sun too long, he burns.
A stayed   B had stayed   C stays

5 She .... out with us tonight if she finishes work early enough.
A comes   B would have come   C 'll come

6 If he .... (break) his leg, he wouldn't be in hospital now!
A hadn't broken   B hasn't broken   C didn't break

7 Would you have moved to the UK, if you .... Richard?
A didn't meet   B won't meet   C hadn't met

8 If I .... (be) you, I'd talk to him about the problem.
A were   B am   C had been

5 Complete the sentences using the third conditional.

1 If I .... (not go) to that party,
I .... (never / met) her.

2 If Penny .... (think) more about
it, she .... (chose) to study
Maths at university.

3 If they .... (have) more time in
the U.S.A., they .... (go) to
Seattle, too.

4 You got on the train without a ticket? What
.... (you / do) if the inspector
.... (come round)?

5 You .... (have to pay) so much
in excess baggage if you ....
(bring) so much stuff back on the plane with you!

6 If she .... (ask) you to marry
her when you were on holiday, what
.... (you / say)?

7 We .... (go) there on holiday, if
we .... (know) that a civil war
was going to break out!

8 If I .... (not go) to see Veronica
when she was ill, I .... (not catch)
the flu!

6 Complete the second sentence so that it has a similar meaning to the first sentence.

1 Sally got to work late because the bus broke down.
If the bus .... ,
Sally .... to work late.

2 Maria went to live in Canada because she got a job there.
If Maria .... in Canada,
she .... there.

3 It's likely that I'll get a pay rise – then we can buy a bigger house.
If I .... a pay rise,
we .... a bigger house.

4 Too long spent in the sun, and I get burnt.
If I .... too long in the sun,
I .... burnt.

5 Greg didn't remember it was his wife's birthday, so he didn't get her a present.
If Greg .... ,
he .... a present.

6 She has to look after their children, so she can't work full-time.
If she .... their children,
she .... full-time.

7 Snow is likely this weekend - perhaps we can go skiing.
If it .... this weekend,
we .... skiing.

8 We got food poisoning because we chose the dish with the prawns.
If we .... the dish with the
prawns, we .... food poisoning.

7 For questions 1–12, read the text below and think of the word which best fits each gap. Use only one word in each gap.

Dubai's Big Bang

Dubai's incredible economic development is founded on two major business sectors: finance and tourism. The city started to take **1** .... around 1992, **2** .... plans to modernise the city began to **3** .... shape. Dubai's need to develop both the business and tourism sector of its economy has **4** .... to a large number of unique buildings and constructions – unique because of their design and their size.

It's difficult to know where the city ends and the desert begins nowadays, because there are so **5** .... building projects in progress on the outskirts of the city. Districts known **6** .... International City, Silicon City, Sport City and Dubailand, which will be the world's biggest theme park, are springing up right in the middle of the desert, whilst most of the tourist areas are **7** .... developed along the city's coast.

By 2015, Dubai's three, enormous 'Palm Islands' will be finished. These are artificial islands built in the stylised shape of a palm tree, destined to be exclusive residential areas with 500 apartments, 2,000 villas, 25 hotels, 200 high-class shops, several cinemas and an aquarium. The building materials **8** .... to construct just one of these islands would be enough to build a wall round the Earth three times! **9** .... door to the Palm Islands, another 300 islands are being built. **10** .... the air, these islands look **11** .... a gigantic map of the world. They're being **12** .... separately and prices range from 1 to 15 million dollars.

Listening Part 3

8 Liverpool and Stavanger were both elected European Capital of Culture in 2008. Read about Stavanger and discuss the answers to the questions with a partner.

Stavanger is a city and municipality in the county of Rogaland, Norway. It is located on a peninsula on the southwest coast of Norway and is the 4th largest city in Norway, with a population of 120,798. The city is commonly referred to as the *Petroleum Capital of Norway*. The city is a combination of new and old influences and it has several beautiful lakes, which are popular recreational areas. Situated in the city centre is *Stavanger Domkirke*, Norway's oldest cathedral. It was built between 1100 and 1150 by the English bishop, Reinald, in Anglo-Norman style and is the only Norwegian cathedral that is almost unchanged since the 1400-century. *Old Stavanger* is located right next to the city centre and has a collection of eighteenth and nineteenth century wooden structures as well as the *Stavanger Museum*, commemorating the city's past glory as the *Herring Capital of Norway*. Tourists can also visit the museum of Archaelogy and the *Norwegian Petroleum Museum* which is located at the harbour. This museum reflects the fact that *Stavanger* has been Norway's oil capital since oil drilling activities started in the North Sea in 1966. Every May, *Stavanger* is host to *MaiJazz*, the Stavanger International Jazz Festival, followed by the International Chamber Music Festival in August.

1 Why is Stavanger cited as the Petroleum Capital of Norway?
2 What other capital city is it referred to as?
3 What is particular about Stavanger Domkirke?
4 What can tourists enjoy in the spring and summer?

9 Match the words that you will hear in the recording to their definitions.

1 eyesore   4 berth
2 wipe out   5 gateway
3 liner   6 highlight

a a large luxurious passenger ship formerly used on a regular line ☐
b a place regarded as giving access to another place ☐
c a thing that is very ugly, especially a building ☐
d an outstanding part of an event or period of time ☐
e a ship's allotted place at a wharf or dock ☐
f remove or eliminate something completely ☐

CD 2 3

10 You will hear five different people talking about Liverpool being elected the European Capital of Culture. For questions 1–5, choose from the list (A–F), whether or not they approve of this decision. Use the letters only once. There is one extra letter which you do not need to use.

A This person was pleased to witness the remodernisation that has taken place.

Speaker ☐ 1

B This person feels that the money could have been invested more wisely.

Speaker ☐ 2

C This person thought more exhibitions should have been put on.

Speaker ☐ 3

D This person is ashamed of the fact that so many small shops were put out of business.

Speaker ☐ 4

E This person believes that commerce will thrive.

Speaker ☐ 5

F This person wasn't wholly satisfied with the exhibition.

11 Which European city do you think is worthy of being voted European Capital of Culture in the future? Discuss your ideas with a partner.

Speaking Part 3

12 Here are some pictures showing different types of places to live in. Which of the words and expressions in the box below would you use to describe them?

attractive	austere	charming	demolish	derelict	do up	damp	falling down	dilapidated
hideous	run down	unsafe	quaint	loud	lonely	stark	makeshift	homely

13 Read the dialogue about living in different places and try to guess the missing words.

Chris: If I had to choose a place to grow **1** .... in, I think out of all these, I would pick the lighthouse. Just imagine how exciting it would be!

Joy: Yes, it'd be fun but don't you think it'd get a bit lonely on a tiny little island like that? I would rather live in a place with a fairly large community like this village in the countryside. Think of all the home grown produce you could get, not to **2** .... all that fresh air!

Chris: If it's fresh air you're **3** .... , then this village built into the cliff edge couldn't be better! I wouldn't want to live there, **4** .... you. It's ok if you like skiing or mountaineering but I would find it too isolated.

Chris: Hmm. Maybe. **5** .... living on a circus? I don't think I would like that very much, but I don't suppose you have much choice if your parents happen to be a couple of trapeze artists!

Joy: It must be quite a hard life, all that packing up and moving around from town to town. I wonder what living in a camper van is like? I know they're **6** .... out with all sorts of mod cons and they're great if you want to go on a driving holiday, but I don't think they're suitable for permanent accommodation.

Chris: And what about the winter when it's cold and wet? I'd rather be in a nice warm house than a **7** .... cold camper van. I suppose a houseboat must be a bit like living in a camper van. It's okay in the summer but it must get very damp in the winter and then I would worry about **8** .... burgled.

Joy: You stand just as much **9** .... of being burgled in a houseboat as in a large city. I wouldn't live in a large noisy metropolitan city if you paid me and I wouldn't want my kids to be **10** .... in one either. But the worst place must be having to live in makeshift shacks and huts on the **11** .... of a large city like this one. What prospects of survival do children have there where they're cold, dirty and hungry.

Chris: Yes, **12** .... is better than there.

14 Now talk to a partner. Take it in turns to describe each place and say what it must be like to live there. Then decide which is the most unsuitable place for a child to grow up in and say why.

1 Read the text and decide if, in the experiment she carried out, the writer was:

1 100% successful. ☐
2 reasonably successful. ☐
3 a failure. ☐

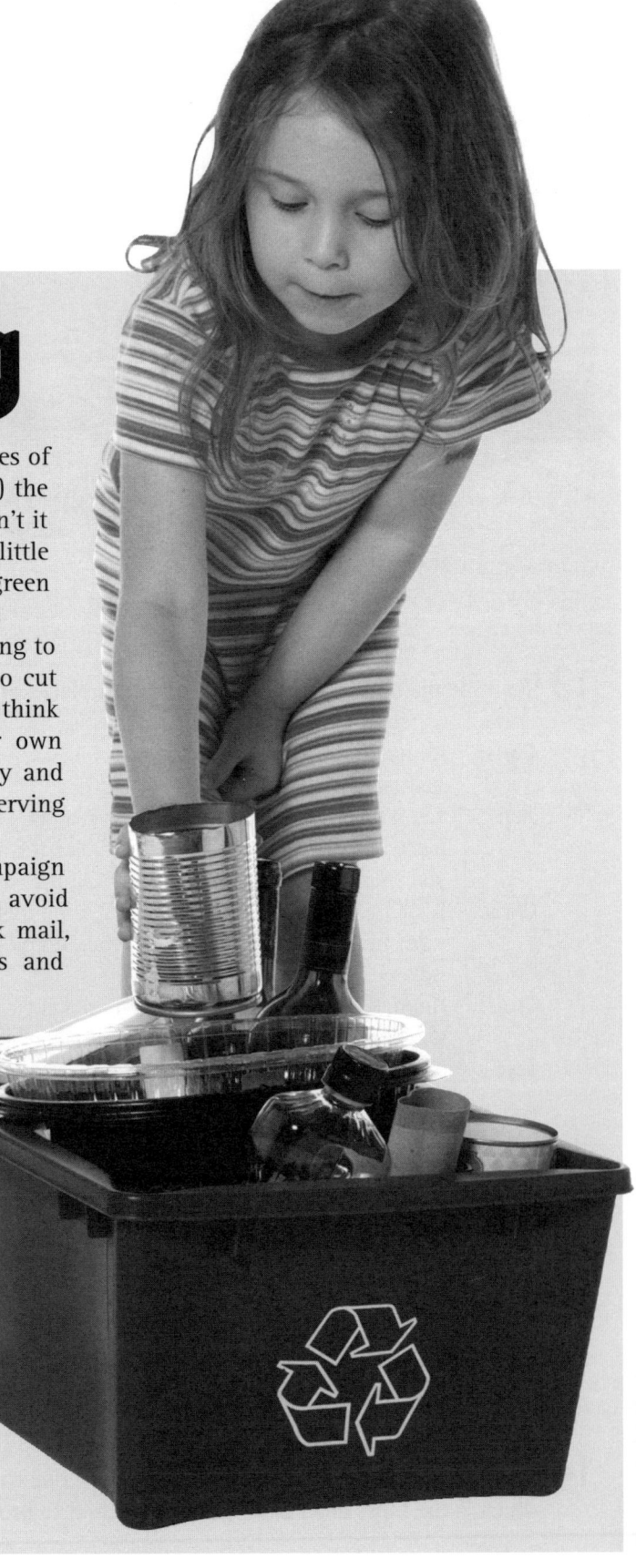

Precycling

Every Tuesday, as a house, we put out two big green boxes of recycling. I say green because a) they literally are and b) the presumption is that by using them, so are we. But wouldn't it be greener not to put out the recycling – to generate so little waste that, come Tuesday, there is nothing to put in the green box? **1** ☐ I decided to try it for a month to find out.

'Precycling' is the practice of reducing waste by attempting to avoid accumulating it in the first place. Precyclers try to cut out as much packaging as possible and, to this end, they think ahead, shop locally, buy things loose and bring their own containers. The benefits are various; from saving money and creating less landfill to reducing food miles and conserving natural resources.

The term was coined in 1988 for a waste awareness campaign in Berkeley, California. Residents were encouraged to avoid single-use items and to buy in bulk. They refused junk mail, carried precycling 'kits' (such as cloth sandwich bags and cutlery) and when the Internet came, they did their reading online to cut down on pulp. Today, precycling is generating interest among the eco-aware. **2** ☐

3 ☐ This I learn on day one of my trial when I forget to bring my lunch to work and am reduced to eating fruit and ice-cream (the cone being the ultimate in edible packaging). The following day, I get organised: daily sandwiches (in a washable sandwich wrap), a travel mug, cloth shopping bags and a water bottle are on hand at all times. Gone are the impulse, convenience shopping sprees of old times – to be replaced by an intentional, almost military approach to what I need to buy and from where.

I start doing the shopping at local markets, fishmongers, butchers and bakers and rediscover the joys of having bottles of milk delivered to my doorstep (milk and orange juice bottles can be reused 20 times before they are recycled). [4] It speaks of gentler times, a greater custody of care, and thoughtful, less hurried, consumption. It saves me money and encourages experimentation.

However, convenience food is aptly named. [5] Finding naked staple foods takes real tenacity, but they do exist. There are shops that sell dried goods in open bins, beside loose toilet rolls and a small line in refillable juices and cosmetics – and give you a discount when you bring your own container. Rural and city farms are alive and well, and great for eggs and dairy products, while farmers' markets and home delivery schemes can supply your fruit and vegetables.

So how did I do? During my month, the green halo slipped often. [6] (It is hard to find decanted wine.) But by the end of the month, my black bin was hardly being used and we were putting out one green bin, a quarter full.

Eventually, says Nimish Shah, a 35-year-old precycler from London, it will be empty. Shah hasn't been to a supermarket for years. He shops at small stores and always brings his own bags. [7] 'When I look at an item,' he says, 'the first thing I think is whether I could just do without the packaging or, failing that, reuse it somehow. Recycling a product should be the last option really'.

2
Read the article again. Seven sentences have been removed from the article. Choose from the sentences A-H the one which fits each gap (1-7). There is one extra sentence which you do not need to use.

A Buying unpackaged is, initially, hugely inconvenient.

B In the UK, financially concerned and environmentally aware consumers are turning to tap over bottled water and carrying canvas shopping bags.

C He cuts an eccentric figure at his local market, putting fish fillets in a cloth bag that he washes and reuses.

D There is a nostalgic pleasure that comes from carrying apples in a paper bag and using a handkerchief to blow my nose.

E Recyling is a greener option – saving between 25% and 90% of the energy it would take to create new products – but there is still an environmental cost.

F It is an idealistic notion, but is it practical?

G The key to being a good precycler is being prepared.

H I still bought my mayonnaise in bottles and tuna in cans and I never did find a solution to the wine issue.

Natural Disasters and the Environment

3 Put the words and phrases below into the correct category. Some may fit into more than one category.

1 natural disasters

....
....

2 geographical features

....
....

3 protecting the environment / 'being green'

....
....

4 manmade environmental problems

....
....
....

coastline	landscape
deforestation	pollution
drought	precycling
earthquake	recycling
eco-buildings	solar power
famine	toxic waste
flood	tsunami
forest fire	typhoon
global warming	volcanic eruption
hurricane	water contamination

4 Complete the sentences below with a word or phrase from Exercise 3, putting it into the correct form as necessary.

1 Millions of people in Africa are affected by .... Drinking affected supplies is the cause of many diseases.

2 .... is a sustainable source of energy and perfect for countries that get a lot of sunlight.

3 I think it's shocking that .... are sometimes started deliberately. Why would anyone want to set alight and destroy whole areas of land?

4 Cornwall in the UK is a county that has miles and miles of dramatic .... - the land meets the sea on three sides of the county.

5 San Francisco is prone to .... because it's built on a faultline in the Earth.

6 In a city such as Athens, in Greece, the air .... is a real problem. The number of cars in the city doesn't help.

7 I don't understand why some people won't accept that .... is really happening. I mean, it's clear from all the figures that scientists have produced that the Earth is getting hotter.

8 .... is quite a new term: it means trying to buy stuff when you go shopping that doesn't have packaging.

9 Getting rid of .... is a major problem for governments. Finding somewhere to put lethal rubbish like this must be a nightmare.

10 How is it possible that there are still .... in the world, when, in so many countries, obesity is a problem because people have too much to eat?

11 OK, so .... and .... mean pretty much the same thing. They're both a very, very strong wind that blows in circles.

12 It hasn't rained properly for two years. Water is being rationed and the government has declared an official ....

Wish, If only, I'd rather

5 Choose the correct option to complete the sentences. For some, there is more than one possibility.

1 I wish my parents .... me stay out later at night - I have to be home by 10.30 p.m., even on Saturdays!
A would let   **B** let   **C** would have let

2 If only I .... that patch of ice, I wouldn't have crashed my car.
A didn't hit   **B** hadn't hit   **C** wouldn't hit

3 I'd rather you .... anything to anyone about the problem.
A didn't say   **B** don't say   **C** wouldn't say

4 I'd rather .... to the cinema than the theatre tonight, I think.
A went   **B** go   **C** hadn't gone

5 I wish I .... so much for lunch – I've got stomachache now.
A didn't eat   **B** don't eat   **C** hadn't eaten

6 If only people .... trains more, instead of flying, we wouldn't have such a problem with global warming.
A use   **B** would use   **C** used

7 I wish Christmas .... over! It's my favourite time of year.
A wouldn't be   **B** wasn't   **C** isn't

6 Rewrite the sentences using *I'd rather.*

1 I want to go for a Chinese meal tonight, not Italian.

....

2 I want to phone him now.

....

3 Do you want to go to see them play on Friday or Saturday night?

.... ?

4 They want you to arrive on 31st.

....

5 I'm not happy that you borrowed my car without asking.

....

6 Would you mind turning the music down?

.... ?

7 Complete what these people say about how they would like things to be different by putting the verb in brackets into the correct form.

1 When I was at school, boys couldn't do subjects like Cookery. We had to do Metalwork and Woodwork instead. I wish .... (can / do) Cookery, as I .... (love / become a chef).

2 Honestly, he just doesn't listen when I'm trying to tell him something. I wish he .... (listen) a bit more!

3 My brother's been so bad-tempered lately. I know he's really upset about his girlfriend, but I do wish he .... (not / be) so grumpy.

4 Something I regret is not learning to play the guitar or rather, giving up lessons after only a few months. I liked playing it, but I was just too lazy. I wish I .... (carry on) with it, then, who knows? I .... (become) a professional guitarist!

5 When my children were younger, I was always wishing that they .... (be) older, that they .... (can/do) more things for themselves. But now that they're teenagers, I find myself wishing that they .... (be) younger again, and .... (need) me more!

8 For questions 1-10, read the text below. Use the word given in capitals at the end of some of the lines to form a word that fits in the gap in the same line.

Eco Solutions

The *Worldwatch Institute*, which publishes an annual state-of-the-world report, has said that **1** .... problems are a direct cause of human social and economic problems. Changes in weather patterns and the **2** .... of our planet's natural resources are already having serious effects in many of the **3** .... areas of the world. We are seeing increased rates of desertification and **4** .... of water, but, at the same time, flooding. These disasters are causing famine in countries such as Malawi, Madagascar and Senegal.

ECOLOGY

DESTROY

POOR

SHORT

More positively, many countries are waking up to the problems facing our planet and some effort is being made to cut down on our use of natural resources. The *Worldwatch Institute* says that the use of **5** .... energy like wind and **6** .... energy has increased by 30% over the last five years in Germany, Japan and Spain. In many cities throughout the world the first **7** .... eco-buildings are being built. The largest of these is the David L. Lawrence Convention Center in Pittsburgh, in the United States, which was built using recycled materials and uses no toxic materials. In Melbourne, Australia, 80% of the city's electricity comes from the sun and 70% of the **8** .... water is taken from collected rain water.

RENEW

SUN

SUSTAIN

DRINK

What can we as individuals do? **9** .... makes up 50% of all urban waste. Help reduce this by choosing products that come in recyclable containers, like glass bottles. Avoid **10** .... products you only use once then throw away. Look out for refill services, where you take your used containers to the shop and have them filled up again with the same product. Avoid buying products in small packs - try to buy them in bigger containers. And recycle whenever and whatever you can.

PACKAGE

DISPOSE

9 Have you ever visited a place where a natural disaster has occurred? If so, what was it like? If not, what do you think it would be like? Now describe the photograph in pairs.

10 Read the definitions of several words that you will come across in the recording and complete the crossword.

Across

2 move something from its proper or usual position

5 a sudden violent shaking of the ground

6 of little depth

7 the outermost layer of rock of which a planet consists

9 a large rock that has been worn smooth by erosion

12 the tract of country which drains into a lake or sea

Down

1 a potential danger or risk

3 increase or cause to increase in quantity

4 relating to earthquakes or other vibrations of the earth

8 open out something so as to extend its surface area, width, or length

10 a collapse of a mass of earth or rock from a mountain or cliff

11 have a specified place within a grading system

 11 You will hear an expert talking about the phenomena of the Tsunami.
For questions 1-10, complete the sentences.

Tsunamis

A tsunami is a succession of huge waves caused by an [____ **1**] disruption.

Tsunami waves are sometimes described as [____ **2**] which is incorrect.

Scientists have been able to produce successful [____ **3**] systems thanks to extensive documentation.

Seismic sea waves are more commonly generated by [____ **4**] occurring underneath the ocean.

All it takes is a [____ **5**] for tsunami waves to cross an entire ocean.

The speed of the tsunami depends on the [____ **6**] of the ocean.

A tsunami can have [____ **7**] over 60 miles which produce devastating effects.

The first tsunami ever to be registered took place in [____ **8**] off the coast of Syria.

The most destructive tsunami on [____ **9**] happened in 2004 in the Indian Ocean.

A network of [____ **10**] which monitors the ocean is to be implemented in the Indian Ocean.

12 Discuss in pairs what tsunamis are, how they are formed, the worst cases that have occurred to date and what can be done to prepare for natural hazards such as these.

Speaking Part 2

13 Look at the photographs of the two places below. Which of the words in the box would you use to describe them.

> hazardous   precarious   unstable   threatening   dreadful   terrifying
> menacing   vast   colossal   petrifying   hanging   astonishing

14 Compare the photographs and say what sort of dangers you think people living in places like these face and what reasons they may have for choosing to live there.

15 Now read this description of the two photographs and fill the blanks with a suitable word.

Both photographs show places built on the edge of a natural **1** .... The first is *Diamond Head Crater* in Oahu, Hawaii. Diamond Head Crater is the most famous volcanic crater in the world. It was occupied by a major defence fort, *Fort Ruger* in 1898 and an observation deck was constructed at its summit in 1910. The volcano has been extinct for over 150,000 years, however, if it were to erupt again, the city would be **2** .... in lava and many lives would be lost. The city, which has developed around the crater over the centuries, looks **3** .... and has even spread to the foot of the crater and up onto its left hand side.

The second photograph is of the *Hanging Houses*, in Cuenca, in Spain. This city has been designated a UNESCO World Heritage site for its wealth of monuments which date **4** .... to the 15th century. Only three of these amazing examples of Gothic architecture remain today thanks to their thorough **5** .... at the beginning of the century. In the part of the building that houses the *Spanish Museum of Abstract Art* some original elements can still be **6** .... The exterior entrance is in Renaissance style and comes from an old palace in *Villarejo de la Penuela*.

I can't imagine why anyone would actually choose to live near the **7** .... of a volcano or on the edge of a cliff, but perhaps they were guaranteed that no **8** .... will come to them. They might have been informed that the volcano is **9** .... or that there will never be a landslide but personally I wouldn't take any **10** .... !

16 Imagine you are going to move to *La Cuenca or Oahu*. Discuss the questions with a partner and give a reason for each answer.

1 How different would your lifestyle be?
2 What do you think you would find most difficult to adapt to?
3 What would you miss most about where you live now?

Myths and Legends the World over

1 You are going to read four texts about Prehistoric sites in Britain. For questions 1-15, choose from sites A-D. The sites may be chosen more than once.

Britain's Heritage

A - Maiden Castle

Situated two miles outside the Dorset town of Corchester is Maiden Castle, the biggest and most complex Iron Age hill fort in Europe. It is so massive that you need to see it from the air to understand the scale of it. It is the size of 50 football pitches and was home to hundreds of Anglo-Saxons until the Romans arrived in 43 AD. The main site was started in 3000 BC and what we see today dates from about 800 BC, but people were living there for over 6000 years. The name Maiden comes from the Celtic 'Mai Dun', which means great hill. Maiden Castle was probably used as a semi-fortified settlement by the people who lived there and farmed nearby.

B - The White Horse of Uffington and The Ridgeway

For at least five thousand years, people have walked the Ridgeway path and you can really feel all that history when you walk along it. The Ridgeway originally started as a trade route from the South coast in Dorset and ended in Norfolk on the East coast. Much of it lies along the top of a range of hills with stunning views over the countryside. Since 1973, it has been a National Trail. Walking along the Ridgeway near Uffington in Oxfordshire, you will be startled by the sight of an enormous, stylised chalk horse carved into the hillside, just beside an Iron Age hill fort. The horse and fort are over 3000 years old and are thought to have marked the territory of the powerful horse tribes who controlled the area. Local people, however, say that the 'horse' is in fact a depiction of the dragon killed by Saint George.

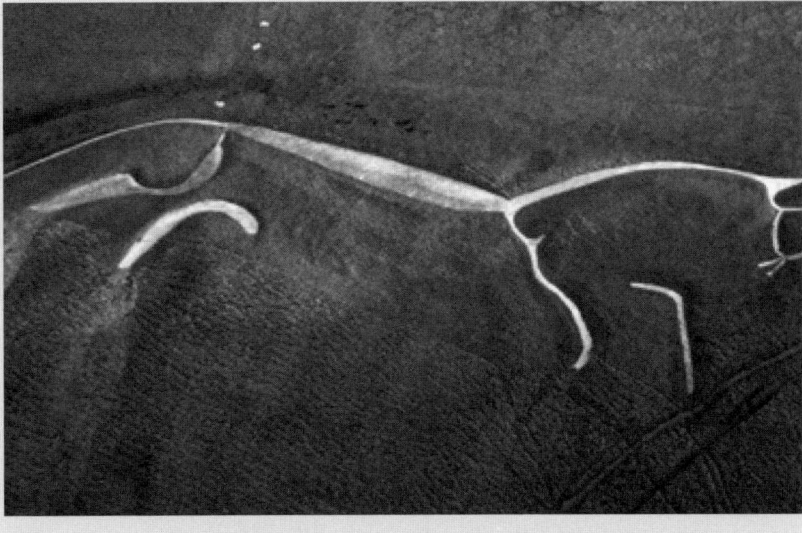

C - Stonehenge

This World Heritage site near the town of Salisbury, in Wiltshire, is five thousand years old. It took an estimated thirty million hours of human labour to construct and theories about its use range from human sacrifice to the worship of the sun and the moon. Stonehenge is an amazing example of engineering from any age, but it is an astonishing achievement by our ancestors in an age before machinery. The largest stone in the circle weighs over 50 tonnes and was transported for many miles using rollers and ropes. Modern scientists think it would have taken 500 men to pull one stone, with another 100 men laying the huge rollers in front of it. Stonehenge is perhaps the most mysterious of all ancient sites in the UK.

D - Wayland's Smithy

Not far from the hill fort of Uffington in Oxfordshire is an ancient burial chamber, Wayland's Smithy. The original site dates back many thousands of years, but the construction of the tomb as we see it today is likely to have been started around 3500 BC. It is one of many prehistoric sites associated with Wayland or *Wolund*, the Norse and Saxon god of blacksmithing. It is thought that the name was given to the site by Saxon invaders, who reached the area some four thousand years after Wayland's Smithy was first built. According to legend, a traveller whose horse has lost a shoe can leave the animal, along with a silver coin, at Wayland's Smithy and when he returns next morning he will find that his horse has been re-shod and the money gone.

Which site

- was once the home of an entire community of people? `1`
- has been the subject of calculations about how much time and effort it took to build? `2`
- will surprise people when they come across it? `3`
- would be better seen from a plane or helicopter, if you want to get an idea of its size? `4`
- was built for someone who was no longer alive? `5`
- has a myth attached to it involving the magical replacement of an item? `6`
- has two different opinions about what it was designed to represent? `7`
- is considered to be an incredible feat for its time? `8`
- has been internationally recognised as being of great historical value? `9`
- is linked with a prehistoric mythical metal worker? `10`
- is the largest of its type in Europe? `11`
- gives people a sense of the past as they're exploring it. `12`
- runs across a part of Britain, from one county to another? `13`
- got its current name from people who were coming to the area to take it over? `14`
- has varying opinions about what it was originally used for? `15`

Unit 20

Vocabulary

Myths and Legends

2 Complete the sentences below by choosing the correct option. In one of the sentences, two options are possible.

1 In lots of fairy stories, there's a wicked witch who .... a spell on the protagonist to make something bad happen, like in the story of the Sleeping Beauty, where the princess falls asleep for a hundred years.

A casts   B gets   C puts

2 Leprechauns are the little people in Irish myths that secretly do things to annoy humans, like turning the milk sour or hiding things. In other words, they .... mischief.

A get through   B get over   C get up to

3 My children are always .... tricks on me, like putting plastic spiders in my bed!

A casting   B playing   C having

4 Jim .... his children a fairy tale every night, before they go to sleep. He's run out of all the traditional ones, so now he invents the stories himself!

A tells   B says   C puts

5 For lots of people nowadays, the heroes they .... – that they admire, respect, even love in some extreme cases – are celebrities who they don't even know!

A mythologise   B worship   C reckon

6 If someone were to .... you a wish – anything you wanted – what would you ask for?

A cast   B tell   C grant

7 Legend .... it that, on this hill, a queen from prehistoric times fought off twenty dragons singlehandedly.

A tells   B puts   C has

3 Use the words in the box to complete the sentences below.

> ancestors   ancestral   ancestry   goddess
> legendary   mythical   mythological   mythology

1 In Greek .... , there are so many gods, I can never remember them all.

2 Aphrodite was the Greek .... of love, wasn't she?

3 The .... sword of King Aurthur has a special name. It was called Excalibur.

4 He's very proud of his Irish .... , even though his family hasn't lived there for generations!

5 They're Canadian Inuits, so have .... rights to land in Canada.

6 My .... migrated from Scotland to England in the 17th Century.

7 Terrifying, imaginary animals such as dragons still appear in fairy tales today. Children love hearing about these .... creatures.

8 When we're talking about the ancient past, it's sometimes difficult to separate out historical facts from .... inventions because there's so little surviving evidence from those times.

Grammar

Say, tell, ask

4 Decide which of the sentences below have mistakes in the use of the reporting verbs *say*, *tell* and *ask*, and make the necessary corrections.

1 She said me she was in her last year at school.

2 Alison told me that she'd met another man and that she was leaving me!

3 They said they were lost and asked to me which way they should go.

4 What did she tell *you*? She said to *me* that she would come out tonight.

5 The doctor told Thomas take the antibiotics for seven days.

6 I said to he that we could meet at the café in the High Street.

7 Mrs Jones told to them that the trip had been cancelled, due to bad weather.

8 I asked Shirley whether she had to work next Saturday, but she doesn't know yet.

5 Complete the reported speech version of the sentences in direct speech below, using a reporting verb from the box in the correct form, plus any other words that you need.

> explain   suggest   tell sb to do sth
> threaten to do sth   warn sb   wonder

1 'Let's go to the cinema, shall we?'
She .... to the cinema.

2 'If you don't do more work, you won't pass your exams.' (*Your teacher to you*)
She .... if .... more work, I .... my exams.

3 'I'll tell the teacher that you cheated in the exam if you don't let me play football with you!'
(*Jane to Geoff*)
.... the teacher that Geoff
.... in the exam if he .... football with him.

4 'Why didn't any of my students come to class?'
(*Mrs Jenkins*)
Mrs Jenkins .... none of her students
.... to class.

5 'Look, first you load it, then you press this button here, then that one there, and that's it!'
(*Lucy to James*)
Lucy .... to work the DVD player.

6 'You've been very naughty. Go to your room right now.' (*Liz to her son*)
.... to his room.

6 Reorder the words to make a more polite form of the following questions.

1 What will the salary be?
the / Would / be / you / telling / mind / me / what / salary / will?
.... ?

2 Where do I have to go?
you go have you tell me think Do where I to could?
.... ?

3 Have you got time to help us with our homework?
homework help you whether We had time to us wondered with our?
.... ?

4 What's the time?
is tell me what Could time the, please you?
.... ?

5 What's this?
this know what Do is you?
.... ?

6 Will you cook the dinner tonight?
would I whether you dinner cook the wondering tonight was.
....

7 Give me a hand with the shopping, will you?
hand you shopping giving me Would a with the mind?
.... ?

8 Explain how this works.
how wondering if you explain could this I was works.
....

7 Report the questions in 6 in the most natural-sounding way. Use *me* where it's necessary to mention who was asked the question.

1 *I asked what the salary would be.*
2 She ....
3 They ....

4 A man on the street ....
5 She ....
6 He ....
7 My mother ....
8 Jim ....

Use of English Part 1

8 For questions 1–10, read the text below about Australian myths and legends and decide which answer (A, B, C or D) best fits each gap.

Myths and Legends from Australia

For the Aboriginal people, Australia is criss-crossed with a **1** .... of sacred paths or 'songlines' linking the spiritual sites of their **2** .... The Walpa (meaning winds) Gorge near Uluru – also **3** .... as Ayers Rock – is the home of Wanambi, the Rainbow Serpent, who helped shape Uluru with his breath. Each path, each crevice in the rock has a spiritual **4** .... given to it by Wanambi. The British writer, Bruce Chatwin, wrote *The songlines*, **5** .... describes the Aborigine's sacred paths and their creation stories. Aborigines are not allowed to tell their myths and stories to outsiders, but many of their paintings, some of which are thousands of years old, tell these stories in picture form.

A more modern-day Australian myth is that of the Sneaky Hoop Snake. Legend has it that in the early nineteen hundreds, children would stay **6** .... school and ride around all day on their bikes, so the parents, in an effort to get the children home before dark, made **7** .... the story of the Hoop Snake. This terrible creature, they said, would lie on the sides of the dirt roads waiting for the sounds of the children on their bikes. Just as the **8** .... cyclist passed, the snake **9** .... coil up and bite its own tail to make the shape of a hoop, before rolling down the road, trying to catch the cyclist. If it caught one, it would bite **10** .... into the heels of its victim.

1 **A** net	**B** network	**C** string	**D** thread
2 **A** ancestors	**B** relatives	**C** descendents	**D** relations
3 **A** said	**B** known	**C** called	**D** told
4 **A** interpretation	**B** prominence	**C** greatness	**D** significance
5 **A** that	**B** what	**C** which	**D** whose
6 **A** at	**B** off	**C** out	**D** in
7 **A** over	**B** about	**C** up	**D** out
8 **A** unsuspecting	**B** unexpecting	**C** disbelieving	**D** unaware
9 **A** will	**B** would	**C** used	**D** had
10 **A** hardly	**B** harden	**C** hardness	**D** hard

Listening Part 4

9 The boy in the photograph below is holding a four-leafed clover which is supposed to bring good luck. What do you think? Do you believe in good or back luck? Are you superstitious? Would you walk under a ladder, put a pair of newly bought shoes on the table or open an umbrella indoors? Tell your partner about the superstitions you are familiar with and whether or not you believe in them.

10 Now say what the items in each photo are and whether they are supposed to bring good or bad luck.

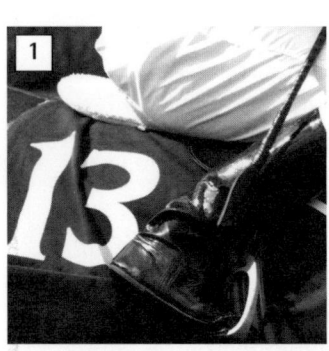
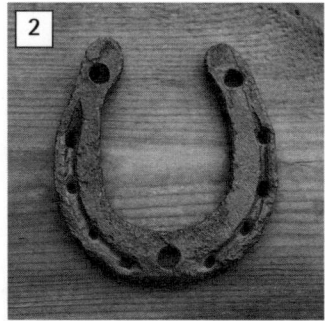
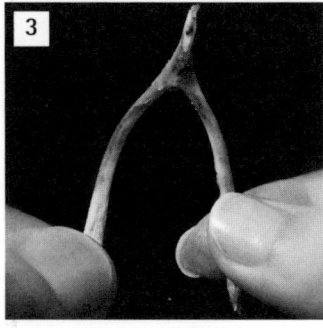

11 The definitions below are for words that you will hear in the recording. Read each sentence and find the corresponding word in the wordsquare.

1 deep respect for someone or something
2 originating or occurring naturally in a particular place
3 a god or goddess in a polytheistic religion
4 adopt a more steady or secure style of life
5 attempt to find something
6 subject someone to hostility because of their race or political or religious beliefs
7 a religious or other solemn ceremony or act
8 an ancestor
9 the practice of black magic with the use of spells and the invocation of spirits
10 deriving ideas, style, or taste from a broad and diverse range of sources
11 a group or meeting of witches.
12 The spiritual or immaterial part of a human being or animal, regarded as immortal

```
P  K  R  N  D  E  I  T  Y  W  I  C
A  E  Y  A  L  R  L  X  I  Q  N  I
K  O  R  T  E  I  I  T  K  E  D  T
D  A  T  S  Y  B  C  T  O  E  I  C
S  E  Q  S  E  H  E  N  E  L  G  E
S  Q  E  Y  C  C  R  R  A  S  E  L
D  E  E  R  O  F  U  A  O  I  N  C
K  G  A  J  V  S  B  T  Y  F  O  E
W  F  R  C  E  G  V  K  I  P  U  A
T  U  Y  W  N  L  U  O  S  O  S  V
E  C  N  E  R  E  V  E  R  C  N  C
C  B  N  O  X  N  Y  K  M  U  M  Y
```

12 Now complete the sentences below with one of the words found in the wordsquare.

1 Rituals showed honour and .... for the deceased.
2 Coriander is .... to southern Europe.
3 Can you name a .... of ancient Greece?
4 In 1963 the Robertsons .... in London.
5 They came here to .... shelter from biting winter winds.
6 Hilda was .... by some of the other girls.
7 The British family Christmas ....
8 You shouldn't be ashamed of your ....
9 Do you practice .... ?
10 Most universities offer an .... mix of courses.
11 Is it true that witches meet in .... ?
12 I'm starting to believe you've got no .... whatsoever!

CD 2 5

13 You will hear an expert on mythology talking about Paganism. For questions 1-7, choose the best answer (A, B or C).

1 The word 'Paganism' refers to
A several religions which worship nature.
B the traditional way of life of indigenous peoples.
C different religious beliefs.

`1`

2 Tribes
A wouldn't accept the beliefs of the country they had settled in.
B left their beliefs behind when they settled in Britain.
C settled in Britain from countries across Northern Europe.

`2`

3 To many pagans, paganism is
A nothing more than a religion.
B a manner in which lives should be led.
C living above and beyond nature.

`3`

4 Something is known about druidry today
A thanks to the papers left behind by the Romans
B due to the Roman conquests.
C the honour and respect shown to the druids by the Romans.

`4`

5 Heathens have great respect for
A Norse mythology.
B pre-Christian people.
C people who have given them some sort of inspiration.

`5`

6 Some of the English days of the week get their names from
A Heathen ancestors.
B Heathen deities.
C Heathen spirits.

`6`

7 Wiccans work with
A no more than four people at a time.
B earth, water, air and fire.
C groups of people standing in circles outside caverns.

`7`

14 Now listen again and write the answers to the following questions.

1 What does Paganism draw upon? ....
2 How do Pagans believe you can get closer to deity? ....
3 What should be made clearer? ....
4 Where did the original Heathens come from? ....
5 What are some of the English days of the week named after? ....
6 What do Wiccans believe in and how do they perform their ceremonies? ....
7 What are the main characteristics of Shamanism? ....

15 Are you familiar with any myths, legends or stories of witchcraft? Share them with your partner and say which one you like the most.

Informal letter

Task

You have recently seen this leaflet advertising a sports holiday. You would like to go with a friend and have made some notes about the holiday. Read the leaflet and the notes. Write an email to a friend to see if they are interested in going with you.

Write your **letter** in **120–150** words in an appropriate style.

Active Holidays

Enjoy an exciting activity holiday designed with teenagers in mind. Our purpose built centre is located in the midst of the Pyrenees in the province of Huesca, in northern Spain.

Like to go?

We offer a range of different packages:

- The Pyrenees Experience: including mountaineering, white water rafting and abseiling.
- Goal: a football coaching holiday. Qualified coaches will help you improve your all round game.

Football?

- Picasso: an arts and crafts holiday that will liberate your creative spirit.

Comfortable accommodation.

Which date best?

Dates available 3rd - 10th July, 12th - 19th July or 28th July - 4th August.

The price of **£350** includes all meals, accommodation and activities as well as airport transfers and an outing to either a local theatre or cinema.

Reasonable price?

You'll have the time of your life!

Theatre or cinema?

Model answer

Hi Chris,

State why you are writing.

Great to hear from you. I'm glad to hear your exams are almost over - mine too! I think we both deserve a fun holiday afterwards.
I saw this leaflet for a sports holiday and I was wondering if you would be interested in going with me. The Football holiday looked the most exciting to me. It'd be a wonderful opportunity to get a little bit better. I think we both need it ;)
I'm not very interested in theatre and I think it would be difficult to understand in Spanish, so the cinema visit would be best. How about you?
Any of those dates are fine with me. Which would suit you best? And what do you think of the cost? It seems quite good value to me.

Make sure all points from the rubric are covered.

Sign off.
Write back soon and let me know what you think.

All the best,

Dani

Use appropriate closing formulas.

1 Answer the following questions.

1 Has Dani included all the points mentioned in the question?
2 Is the letter written in the appropriate style (formal or informal)? Find examples in the letter.
3 How does Dani begin and end the letter?
4 Does the letter have an appropriate greeting and ending?
5 How does Dani rephrase:
   a Like to go?
   b Improve your all round game
   c Which date best?
   d Reasonable price?
   Underline the expressions in the model answer.

Useful phrases

Beginning:	• Thanks a lot for your last email / letter...
	• Sorry I haven't been in touch for so long
	• Lovely to hear from you (again).
	• Sorry / Great to hear about...
Asking for opinions / Making suggestions:	• What do you think of (+noun)... about (+gerund)?
	• How about (+gerund)?
	• Why don't we (infinitive without "*to*")... ?
Ending the letter:	• Looking forward to hearing from you.
	• Write back soon (and let me know how it goes / what you think).
	• Can't wait to see you again soon,
	• Say hello to... / Give my regards to... / All the best to...

---

2 Read the leaflet and the notes. Write an email to a friend to see if they are interested in going with you. Write your answer in 120–150 words in an appropriate style.

Korsa Fun!

Interested?

Korsa Fun have been organising winter sports holidays for over 10 years.

We can offer a tailor made package to suit your needs exactly.

Beginners?

From beginner's snow boarding and skiing instruction, to advanced techniques taught by our team of Olympic competitors.

Andorra?

Choose from 3 locations: France, Andorra or Northern Italy. We offer 4 day mini breaks, as well as 7 day and 10 day programmes.

Self catering?

Accommodation in self catering cottages or 3* hotels.

7 days?

Prices start from €400 and include ski passes, rental of equipment, all instruction and airport pick-up service (breakfast and evening meal included in hotel option).

Article

Task

You see this advertisement in a local English language newspaper.

Weekly Dispatch
is looking for articles about inventions

What do you think has been the most important invention of modern times? The computer? The car? The internet? And why has it had such an important effect? The winning article wins a year's subscription to The Weekly Dispatch and a brand new MP3 player. How does that sound?

Write your **article** in **120–180** words.

Model answer

> Give the article a title.

> Engage the reader's interest in the topic.

> Using personal anecdotes can make the article more interesting to the reader.

> Sum up your feelings and leave the reader with something to think about.

Man's greatest invention: The washing machine?

Could you live without your computer? Could you live without the Internet or your mobile phone? I think we all could easily. But can you imagine life without a washing machine?

Have you thought about what people did before the washing machine? My grandmother remembers her mother with a block of soap, a large tub and scrubbing for hours, then squeezing every item as dry as possible before hanging them to dry in the garden. It was difficult enough to find the time to do everything that needed to be done at home, let alone spend time studying or having a career.

The washing machine was the first and most important of these labour saving devices and I believe it has played an important part in allowing women to leave the home and play a more important role in society. Which would you prefer: spending 8 hours scrubbing clothes in the river, or spending your day studying something you're interested in, or having a rewarding job?

1 Read the text and answer these questions.

1 Does the title of the article relate to the content?
2 How does the writer engage the reader?
3 Does the main paragraph link in with the title?
4 Does the writer express their opinion?
5 Does the composition use formal or informal language?
6 How does the writer leave the reader with something to think about?
7 How does the writer personalise the article?

2 Look at the following sentences. Decide where they have to be included.

- The Introductory Paragraph (*Int*)
- The Main paragraph (*Main*)
- The Ending (*End*)

1 What would you consider the most important invention?   *Int*

2 All this makes me think that the washing machine must surely
be considered as the most important invention.   ....

3 Some of the women in the village even used to have to take
their laundry down to the river.   ....

4 All of these jobs were virtually always done by women.   ....

5 The washing machine has helped emancipate women.   ....

6 Now, you can load your washing machine before you go
to work or college, and it's clean when you return home.   ....

7 So, next time you turn on your washing machine, spare a thought
for what you would be doing without it.   ....

Useful phrases

Introductory Paragraph	• Have you ever thought / considered / wondered about… ?
	• What would you say if someone suggested… ?
	• The topic of… is fascinating, don't you think?
	• What can be said about… ? What can we say about… ?
Main Paragraph	• Beginning with…
	• On top of that…
	• Leading on from that…
	• Another advantage is, of course,…
	• What I particularly admire / like / love / respect…is / are
Ending	• All in all, I believe…
	• It seems that…
	• In my opinion…
	• Looking at all these factors, I have to conclude that…

---

3 You see this announcement in an English language magazine. Write your article in 120-180 words.

Whizz-kids Magazine

We are hoping to publish articles
about the effect of technology on our daily lives.
We would like our readers to submit articles
about how important a role technology plays in your life.

The writer of the best article will win a new laptop.

Essay

Task

Your local high school is thinking about introducing a school uniform. The headmaster and the governors of the school have asked local people to send in essays giving their opinion about the following statement:

State schools should be able to insist their students wear uniforms.

Write your **essay** in **120–180** words.

Model answer

Introduce the topic without giving your opinion.

The debate over the benefits and disadvantages of school uniforms is still going on after many years. People on both sides of the argument have strong views.

Some people feel that uniforms save families money because parents don't have to buy fashionable clothes they cannot afford. Furthermore they aren't judged by their classmates because of their outfits. Many people also believe that a school uniform promotes discipline.

2 or 3 arguments in favour.

2 or 3 arguments against (don't forget to use phrases of contrast. See the useful phrases box).

However, while it is true that parents may not have to buy expensive designer clothing, school uniforms themselves are not cheap and manufacturers exploit the need for uniforms and charge too much for them. Some people also claim uniforms suppress young people's freedom of expression.

In my opinion the economic arguments in favour of uniforms are mistaken. Uniforms are expensive and if students want to follow fashions they will with shoes, watches, bags etc. and will also want designer labels for their weekend outfits. I believe parents will have to spend much more on clothes.

State your own opinion.

1 Answer the following questions.

1 How many different expressions does the writer use for "clothes"?
2 What are the main points the writer gives in favour of uniforms?
3 What are the main points against uniforms?
4 In which paragraph does the writer state their own opinion?
5 Does the writer give an opinion in the first paragraph?

2 You have had a class discussion about piercings in schools. Your teacher has asked you to write an essay giving your opinion on the following statement:

Piercings should be banned in schools.

Write your answer in 120-180 words in an appropriate style. Before you start write down some of your ideas in the box below.

Paragraph 1: Why is this issue important? Why is the issue being discussed?	
Paragraph 2: Think of some arguments in favour of banning piercings in school (if you can't think of any, imagine what your parents or grandparents might think)	
Paragraph 3: Think of some arguments that support piercings in schools (if you can think of any, imagine, what people with piercings might think)	
Paragraph 4: What is your opinion? Do you think piercings should be banned? Why / Why not?	

Useful phrases

Giving people's points of view	• Some / Many people say / claim / believe • It is believed / often said • Many / Some people hold the view that • It is widely thought that / It has been suggested that
Contrasting opinions	• On the other hand, many / some people hold the opposite view • While others argue that... • Whereas there are those that believe... • However
Conclusion: Giving your opinion	• In conclusion / To sum up • Looking at both sides of the argument, I have to say that... • In my personal opinion... • I think the evidence suggests that...

Letter of application

Task

You have seen this advertisement in a local English language magazine. Read the advertisement and the notes you have made. Write a letter of application.

Write your answer in **120–180** words in an appropriate style.

TOUR GUIDES REQUIRED

Friday and Saturday?

We are looking for young people to spend two days a week showing groups of North American students around this region. We would like to hear from anyone who has:

- a good knowledge of local history
- a reasonable level of spoken English
- an outgoing friendly personality

Member of local history society

Studying for First Certificate

Send us a letter of application explaining why you would be suitable for the job.

Like meeting new people

---

1 Read Bruno's letter and put it into the correct order. The first one is done for you.

Model answer

	I was wondering if it would be possible to work on Fridays and Saturdays as these are the only days I don't have any English classes in the evening.
	Bruno Corradi.
	Yours faithfully,
	I am available for an interview at your convenience. I can be contacted at 950 67 46 56 09 every evening after 7p.m
	With regards to my level of English, I am currently studying for the Cambridge First Certificate Exam and my teachers are confident I will do very well in the oral part of this exam. Furthermore, I am a sociable person and I have always enjoyed talking to native English speakers and making new friends.
	I am an active member of the local history society and often attend talks given by prominent local historians, so I believe I have an above average knowledge of the region and its history and would be very suitable for this position.
	I am writing in response to your request for Tour Guides which appeared in this month's edition of "Go English."
1	Dear Sir/Madam,

2 Read the letter in the correct order, then answer the questions.

    1 What is the purpose of the first paragraph?
    2 Does he use all the notes from the task?
    3 Is the register formal or informal? Find some examples.
    4 How can Bruno be contacted?
    5 When is he available for an interview?
    6 List the reasons Bruno thinks he is suitable for the job?

3 Match the opening formulas in the box with the appropriate closing formulas.

Dear Sir,	Dear Ms Jane Jones,	Dear Miss Smith,	To Whom It May Concern:	Dear Sirs,	Dear Sir or Madam,	Dear Madam,

Yours faithfully,	Yours sincerely,

Useful phrases

Stating your reason for writing	• I am writing in response to your advertisement (+ say when and where it appeared and what it is for)
	• I am writing to apply for the post / position of (+ say which job and where and when you saw the announcement)
Stating your experience and suitability	• One of the main reasons I am applying for this post is...
	• I have a lot of experience of... (+ noun / gerund)
	• I have a wealth of experience with (+ noun / gerund)
	• I believe I would be the ideal candidate for this position because...
Ending the letter	• Thank you for considering me for this position.
	• Thank you in advance for considering my application.
	• I look forward to hearing from you (soon / in the near future)

4 You have seen this advertisement in an English language newspaper. Read the advertisement and the notes you have made. Write a letter of application. Write your answer in 120-180 words in an appropriate style.

Weekends only

Professional manner

Currently studying for FCE

FashionBags Co.

We are looking for students of English with retail experience to work part time in our City Airport outlet.

The right applicants will receive a good wage and conditions.

Write to us giving information about your level of English and your suitability for this post.

3 years experience as a sales assistant

Available for interview any evening after 4 p.m.

Report

Task

Your school canteen has decided to make some changes to the school cafeteria. You have been asked to write a report to the governors of the school suggesting what changes should be made. In your report you should also explain the benefits of these changes.

Write your **report** in **120–180** words.

Model answer

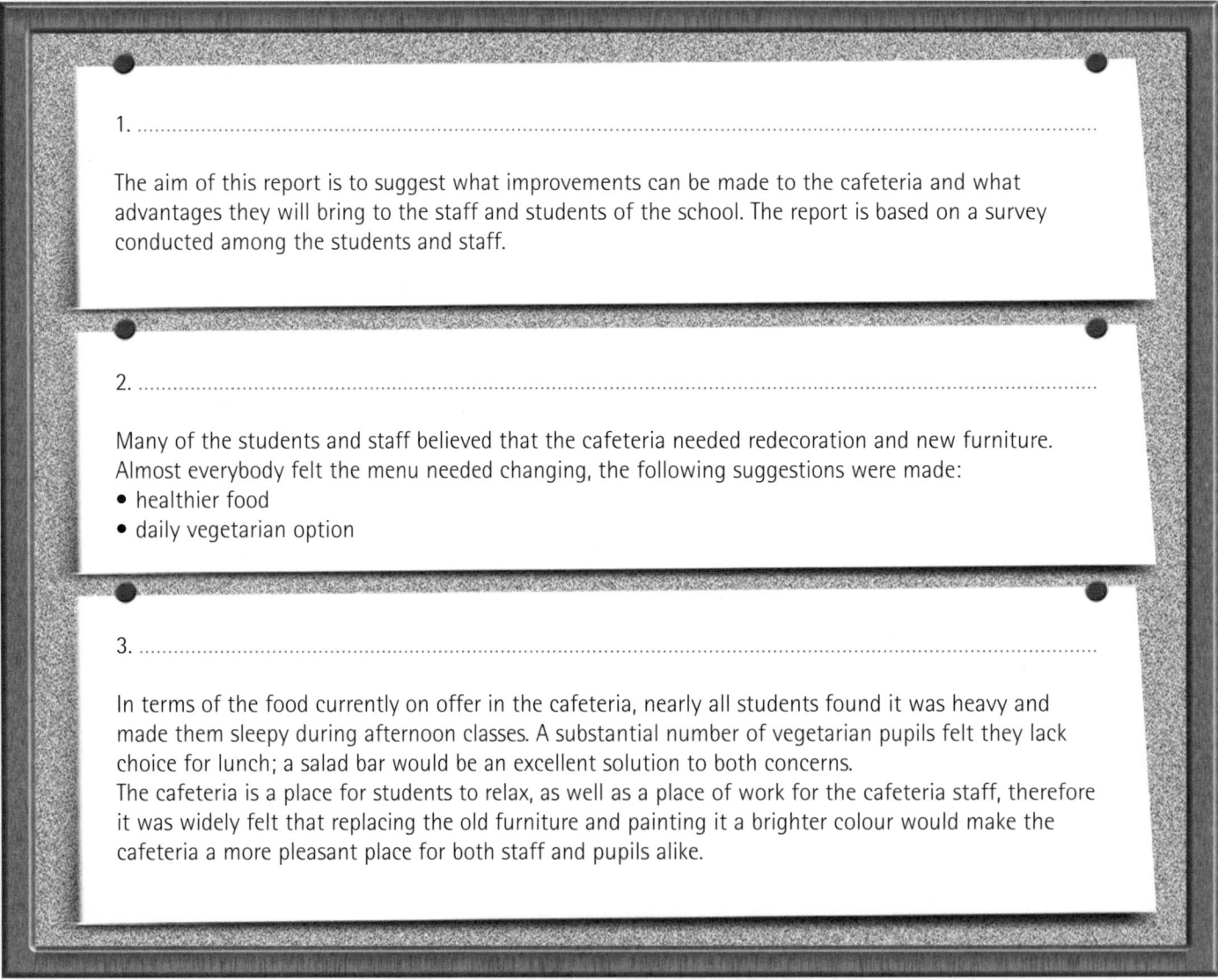

1. ....

The aim of this report is to suggest what improvements can be made to the cafeteria and what advantages they will bring to the staff and students of the school. The report is based on a survey conducted among the students and staff.

2. ....

Many of the students and staff believed that the cafeteria needed redecoration and new furniture. Almost everybody felt the menu needed changing, the following suggestions were made:
• healthier food
• daily vegetarian option

3. ....

In terms of the food currently on offer in the cafeteria, nearly all students found it was heavy and made them sleepy during afternoon classes. A substantial number of vegetarian pupils felt they lack choice for lunch; a salad bar would be an excellent solution to both concerns.
The cafeteria is a place for students to relax, as well as a place of work for the cafeteria staff, therefore it was widely felt that replacing the old furniture and painting it a brighter colour would make the cafeteria a more pleasant place for both staff and pupils alike.

1 Write the headings to the paragraphs in the model answer.

Recommendations   Introduction   Suggestions

2 Look at the checklist and decide which are good ideas for reports (✓) and which aren't (✗).

1 Use headings and bullet points	✓
2 Write your address in the top right-hand corner	✗
3 Use informal language	
4 Give the report a title	
5 Use formal language	
6 Begin "*Dear Sir / Madam*"	
7 Divide the text into three parts	
8 Use "*for*" and "*against*" arguments	
9 Provide an introduction and conclusion	

3 Match the phrases in the box to the appropriate part of the report.

The aim of this report is to examine...	I would strongly recommend...	Many people felt...
I feel it would be to our advantage if...	Many people surveyed said...	The report is based on a survey conducted among...
In conclusion...	It was widely believed that...	The report will also consider...

Introduction	
Suggestions	
Recommendations	

Useful phrases

Introduction
- The purpose of this report is to evaluate / look at / describe / look into / examine / assess / appraise / analyse / investigate...
- This report has been carried out with the intention of (+gerund)
- ...were surveyed / interviewed / polled / asked.

Suggestions
- Most / many / some of those surveyed felt / believed / thought / considered / were convinced that...
- The following suggestions were made / Among the suggestions voiced were...
- A number / few suggestions were made, namely...

Recommendations
- To sum up...
- In the light of / Considering the results of the survey...
- I would, therefore, recommend... (+gerund or noun)
- ...would benefit from... (+gerund / noun) to...

---

4 Your school has decided to organise an end of term party for students and teachers. You have been asked to write a report for the school principal suggesting food and catering arrangements for the party. In your report you should also explain the advantages of your suggestions. Write your report in 120-180 words.

Story

Task

You have decided to enter an international short story competition. The competition rules say that the story must begin with the words:

John looked down at what he held in his hands but couldn't believe it.

Write your **story** in **120–180** words.

Model answer

> John looked down at what he held in his hands but couldn't believe it. His heart was beating faster.
>
> As he turned the pages, he heard footsteps above. John knew he should leave, but he couldn't stop looking at this beautiful scrapbook. Inside were photographs of him, and a picture had been cut from the local newspaper. Somebody was coming down the stairs.
>
> John had been playing football. He had gone to collect the ball when he noticed the old man. As soon as John saw the man, he started to walk away. John decided to follow. After a while the old man went into a small garden next to an equally small house. John opened the door and went in.
>
> Suddenly John was facing the old man, who looked strangely familiar. The old man smiled and told John he was his grandfather's brother, they had had a fight many years ago and had never spoken again. John and the old man spent hours talking, laughing and telling stories.
>
> Finally, as John left the house he turned, waved goodbye and decided to talk to his grandfather as soon as possible.

Generate some suspense.

Use a range of narrative tenses.

Give the story a conclusion.

1 Answer the questions below.

1 What did John have in his hands?
2 Why was it interesting to John?
3 What had John been doing before he noticed the man?
4 Who was the old man?
5 Why didn't John know the man before?
6 How did John and the old man spend the rest of the afternoon?
7 What did John decide to do after he left the house?
8 Why do you think he decided to do this?

2 Using the text find an example of different tenses and complete the box.

Past continuous	*His heart was beating faster.*
Past simple	
Past perfect simple	
Past perfect continuous	
The passive	

Useful Time Expressions

- as soon as...
- before / after
- after a while
- later
- then
- everyday

- at last
- when
- finally
- while
- immediately
- in the end

- suddenly
- all of a sudden
- unexpectedly
- straight away
- without warning
- in an instant

3 Your teacher has asked you to write a short story for the school's English language magazine. Write your story in 120-180 words. Your story must begin with the following words:

They had no choice, they had to do what the man told them.

Before you begin writing think about the following questions.

1 Who were they?
2 Where were they?
3 What did they look like?
4 How did they get there?
5 Who was the man?

6 What did he look like?
7 What did he tell them to do?
8 Why did he tell them to do it?
9 What happened next?
10 What happened in the end?

- Remember you only have less than 200 words, so you can't build complex characters or tell us much about the people in it. The story has to be very simple and there has to be an ending.
- Try and use interesting adjectives, adverbs and expressions
- Follow the following plan:

Paragraph 1: Set up the scene and create atmosphere
Paragraph 2: Describe the plot
Paragraph 3: Reach a solution
Paragraph 4: Express final outcome

Review

Task

An English language magazine for students has asked readers to contribute reviews for its forthcoming "film special" issue. Readers are invited to send in reviews of films they have enjoyed.

Write your **review** in **120–180** words.

Model answer

Groundhog Day

Groundhog Day is a comedy starring Bill Murray and Andie MacDowell. It was directed by Harold Ramis, and won Best Film in the 1993 British Comedy Awards.

The film takes place in a small village where egocentric TV weatherman Phil Connors (Bill Murray) is forced to cover the annual Groundhog Day festivities for the fifth year in a row. After the event, Phil, his Cameraman and the producer, can't leave because the main road is closed due to a blizzard. The next morning Phil awakes to find he is reliving the previous day. This happens over and over again.

Both Bill Murray and Andie MacDowell, who plays Phil's love interest, perform brilliantly, and she received the Saturn Award for Best Actress. They represent opposites; Phil is selfish and childish, whereas Rita is kind and generous. However, I do think that this leads to a predictable ending, when opposites attract as they do in so many romantic comedies.

To sum up, it's well worth seeing this film if you enjoy comedies. I have loved it since I was a child. I've already seen it 5 times and I'll never get fed up watching it and I think it's Bill Murray's best performance.

A basic introduction to the film.
What sort of film is it?
Who is the director?
Who are the stars?
When was it made?
Did it win any awards?

A basic summary of the plot.
What happens?
This is often done in the present simple.

The strong points of the film, or the weak points, or both (remember to use contrasting expressions: *however, on the other hand, in contrast*). It's a good idea to try and think of one negative aspect of a good film or one positive aspect of a bad film, if you can. It makes your review look more balanced.

Sum up, give your final opinion. Would you recommend the film to people? What sort of people? How does it compare with similar films, films by the same director, the sequel or prequel, etc?

Useful phrases

Describing 1ˢᵗ paragraph

Films
- ...was filmed in (+ year)
- The first in a trilogy...
- Starring (+ actors)
- Directed by...
- Featuring... (+ character / s)
- Set in (+ time and / or place)

Books
- Written in (+ year)
- ...'s first / debut novel...
- Originally written in (+language)
- The first in a series of 5 books...
- Featuring... (+ character / s)
- Set in (+ time and / or place)

Plays
- First performed in (+ where and when)
- Directed by...
- ...relates the story of...
- A powerful drama...
- A hilarious comedy...
- Written by...
- With... in the starring role...

Albums
- ...'s first / debut album
- Featuring (+ name of successful singles / other musicians)
- Produced by...
- The follow up to (+ previous album)

Paragraph 2: Critical comments
- What stands out most is...
- The acting / main characters are very convincing
- One particular strength / weakness is...
- The plot / story / ending was exciting / predictable / gripping / clichéd
- What stands out most is...
- One particular strength / weakness is...
- The use of (+ instrument / musical style) is particularly impressive / misconceived

Paragraph 3:

Linking:
- Furthermore, moreover, in addition, besides, above all, as for..., in particular..., especially

Contrasting:
- In contrast, However, Even though, Yet, While, Despite, Although

Paragraph 4: Final opinion
- I would highly recommend it to anybody who likes... / is interested in...
- I strongly advise people (not) to see / read / go to / listen to / buy
- All in all I found it...
- ...is well worth seeing / reading / watching / buying / listening to

1 An international website for students has asked its readers to contribute reviews of films / books / plays or albums from their country. Write your review in 120-180 words.

Set text

1 Read the descriptions of characters from *Great Expectations* and decide who they describe. Complete the chart below with the names from the box. The first one is done for you.

Joe Gargery		Mr. Pumblechook		Miss Haversham		Phillip Pirrip ('Pip')	*1*
Bentley Drummle		Estella		Herbert Pocket		Magwitch	
Biddy		Mrs. Joe Gargery		Mr. Jaggers		Compeyson	

1 The principal character of the story and the narrator. An apprentice blacksmith, he attempts to rise above his social class after meeting Miss Haversham.

2 Pip's rival for Estella. A rude and stupid boy from a wealthy aristocratic family. He later marries Estella.

3 Pip's bad tempered sister who brings him up after the death of their parents.

4 Joe Gargery's pompous uncle. A wealthy merchant, he introduces Pip to Miss Haversham.

5 A wealthy spinster. She lives in a mansion which is falling down and wears her old wedding dress every day.

6 Miss Haversham's adopted daughter. Although she is beautiful and wins the heart of Pip, she is cruel, cynical and manipulative.

7 Pip's friend in London, they share an apartment. He teaches Pip 'gentlemanly ways'.

8 A convict who escapes and is helped by Pip as a young boy. He later becomes Pip's benefactor.

9 A London lawyer. He represents Pip's benefactor and also acts for Miss Haversham.

10 Pip's brother in law. He acts like a father to Pip and is an honest, working man.

11 She is kind and intelligent but very poor. She teaches Pip and is obviously in love with him. She later marries Joe Gargery and they have a child they name Pip.

12 The main villain of the book. A professional cheat, he is the man that was supposed to marry Miss Haversham and later betrays Magwitch.

This is part of a letter from an English speaking friend, Mary. It deals with *Great Expectations* by Charles Dickens.

We've just started studying *Great Expectations* at school. I know you've read it, so I was wondering who you thought was the most interesting character. Write and tell me what you think.

Model answer

SET TEXT
questions
may be articles,
essays, letters,
reports or
reviews.
Use the
appropriate
style.

Dear Mary,

I hope you like studying *Great Expectations*, I really enjoyed reading it. The book is full of interesting characters, but I think the most interesting must be Pip because not only is he the main character of the book, but he's also the narrator of the story many years after the events.

At the beginning of the book Pip is a kind and sympathetic young orphan who has a humble life with his difficult sister and her kindly husband. The two most important things that happen to the young Pip are that he helps an escaped convict and later meets Miss Haversham and her adopted daughter, Estella, who Pip falls in love with. After this meeting with Estella, Pip becomes quite selfish and cruel to the people around that love him. In the end though, I think Pip realises his mistakes and tries to make up for them. All in all, I think it's because Pip is the narrator and you see the events unfold through his self-critical analysis that makes him the most interesting character.

What do you think? Write back and tell me your opinion when you've finished reading it.

All the best,

Stefan

Refer to the question. Avoid just writing the plot of the book.

Demonstrate you know the plot and the characters of the book well.

2 Answer the following questions.

1 How does Pip have two different roles in the novel?
2 What sort of background does Pip come from?
3 What event does the writer think changes Pip's character?
4 Is this a positive or a negative change?
5 What reason does the writer give for Pip to be the most interesting character?

3 Think about these questions about this set text (*Great Expectations*).

1 Would you recommend this book to somebody? Why / Why no?
2 Describe a memorable part of the book.
3 Is the ending of the book good? Why / Why not?
4 Would the book make a good film? Why / Why not?
5 How does the title relate to the book?
6 What are the relationships between the characters?
7 What's the main story of the book?
8 Describe some of the places the book is set.
9 Who is your least favourite character?
10 What makes the book interesting, in your opinion?

4 Pip and Estella are very different characters. Write an essay discussing their differences and any similarities they might have.

PAPER 1: READING Part 1 (Questions 1-8)

Part 1

You are going to read an extract from a novel. For questions **1-8**, choose the answer (**A,B,C**, or **D**) which you think fits best according to the text.

Mark your answers **on the separate answer sheet**.

One morning, about ten days after Mrs Churchill's decease, Emma was called downstairs to Mr Weston, who could not stay five minutes, and wanted particularly to speak with her. He met her at the parlour-door, and hardly asking her how she did, in the natural key of his voice, sunk it immediately, to say, unheard by her father:

'Can you come to Randalls at any time this morning? Do, if it be possible. Mrs Weston wants to see you. She must see you.'

'Is she unwell?'

'No, no, not at all – only a little agitated. She would have ordered the carriage, and come to you, but she must see you alone, and that you know,' nodding towards her father, 'Humph! – Can you come?'

'Certainly. This moment, if you please. It is impossible to refuse what you ask in such a way. But what can be the matter? Is she really not ill?'

'Depend upon me – but ask no more questions. You will know it all in time. The most unaccountable business! But hush, hush!'

To guess what all this meant, was impossible even for Emma. Something really important seemed announced by his looks; but, as her friend was well, she endeavoured not to be uneasy, and settling it with her father, that she would take her walk now, she and Mr Weston were soon out of the house together and on their way at a quick pace for Randalls.

'Now,' said Emma, when they were fairly beyond the sweep gates, 'now Mr Weston, do let me know what has happened.'

'No, no,' he gravely replied. 'Don't ask me. I promised my wife to leave it all to her. She will break it to you better than I can. Do not be impatient, Emma; it will all come out too soon.'

'Break it to me,' cried Emma, standing still with terror. 'Good God! Mr Weston, tell me at once. Something has happened in Brunswick Square. I know it has. Tell me, I charge you tell me this moment what it is.'

'No, indeed you are mistaken.'

'Mr Weston do not trifle with me. Consider how many of my dearest friends are now in Brunswick Square. Which of them is it? I charge you by all that is sacred, not to attempt concealment.'

'Upon my word, Emma.'

'Your word! Why not your honour! Why not say upon your honour, that it has nothing to do with any of them? Good Heavens! What can be to be broke to me, that does not relate to one of that family?'

'Upon my honour,' said he very seriously, 'it does not. It is not in the smallest degree connected with any human being of the name of Knightley.'

Emma's courage returned, and she walked on.

'I was wrong,' he continued, 'in talking of its being broke to you. I should not have used the expression. In fact, it does not concern you – it concerns only myself, that is, we hope. Humph! In short, my dear Emma, there is no occasion to be so uneasy about it. I don't say that it is not a disagreeable business – but things might be much worse. If we walk fast, we shall soon be at Randalls.'

Emma found that she must wait; and now it required little effort. She asked no more questions therefore, merely employed her own fancy, and that soon pointed out to her the probability of its being some money concern, something just come to light, of a disagreeable nature in the circumstances of the family, something which the late event at Richmond had brought forward. Her fancy was very active. Half a dozen natural children, perhaps – and poor Frank cut off! This, though very undesirable, would be no matter of agony to her. It inspired little more than an animating curiosity.

'Who is that gentleman on horseback?' said she, as they proceeded speaking more to assist Mr Weston in keeping his secret, than with any other view.

'I do not know. One of the Otways. Not Frank; it is not Frank, I assure you. You will not see him. He is half way to Windsor by this time.'

'Has your son been with you, then?'

'Oh! yes – did not you know? Well, well, never mind.'

For a moment he was silent; and then added, in a tone much more guarded and demure:

'Yes, Frank came over this morning, just to ask us how we did.'

They hurried on, and were speedily at Randalls. 'Well, my dear,' said he, as they entered the room, 'I have brought her, and now I hope you will soon be better. I shall leave you together. There is no use in delay. I shall not be far off, if you want me.'

line 49 And Emma distinctly heard him add, in a lower tone, before he quitted the room, 'I have been as good as my word. She has not the least idea.'

Emma by Jane Austen **1775-1817**

PAPER 1: READING Part 1 (Questions 1-8)

1   When Mr Western first spoke to Emma

   A   he whispered.
   B   he coughed.
   C   he murmured.
   D   he stuttered.

2   Despite Emma's insistence, Mr Western refuses to

   A   mind his own business.
   B   accompany Emma in the carriage.
   C   take Emma's father with them.
   D   say what is the matter.

3   When Mr Western says his wife will break the news to her, Emma is

   A   annoyed.
   B   relieved.
   C   alarmed.
   D   amused.

4   How does Mr Western manage to calm Emma down?

   A   By taking her back to the house in Brunswick Square.
   B   By explaining that he isn't directly involved.
   C   By giving her his word that no harm has come to anyone.
   D   By promising to tell her as soon as they arrive at Randalls.

5   Emma walks on in silence and comes to the conclusion that

   A   Mr Western has disinherited his son.
   B   Mr Western must have fallen out with someone.
   C   Mrs Western is expecting a baby.
   D   the family must be having financial problems.

6   Emma enquires after the man on horseback

   A   to distract herself.
   B   out of curiosity.
   C   to take Mr Western's mind off the matter.
   D   because she thought she recognized him.

7   When Mr Western mentions his son's visit he seems

   A   ill at ease.
   B   angered.
   C   saddened.
   D   pleased.

8   What does Mr Western mean by the expression 'I have been as good as my word' in line 49?

   A   That he will leave them alone to talk in private.
   B   That he has kept his promise.
   C   That he has spoken quietly.
   D   That he has behaved like a gentleman.

PAPER 1: READING Part 2 (Questions 9-15)

Part 2

You are going to read an article about the discovery of DNA. Seven sentences have been removed from the article. Choose from the sentences **A-H** the one which fits each gap (**9-15**). There is one extra sentence which you do not need to use.

Mark your answers **on the separate answer sheet**.

Crick and Watson and the Discovery of DNA

In 1953, Francis Crick walked into a pub in Cambridge, England and told everyone that he and his colleague, Watson, had found 'the secret of life'. **9**

The 'Double Helix'
In 1951, Francis Crick was working at the Cavendish Laboratory in the physics department of the University of Cambridge. He was joined there by an American scientist, James Dewey Watson. They had similar scientific interests and started working on the project to uncover the structure of DNA, or deoxyribonucleic acid. **10** From this new knowledge they then worked out that DNA was the main way that inherited information was passed from parent to offspring in all animals and plants – this was the true 'secret of life'.

The Nobel Prize
It was one of the most significant and important scientific breakthroughs of the last century. The men who first described it, and Maurice Wilkins from the University of London, were awarded the Nobel Prize for Physiology or Medicine in 1962. There are many people who say that these three men would not have been able to make their discovery without the work of Rosalind Franklin also of London University. **11** However, she died in 1958 and Nobel Prizes are not given posthumously.

What is DNA?
DNA is the chemical substance which chromosomes and genes are made up of. DNA has a structure which looks like a twisting ladder and is made up of pairs of four 'building blocks', called adenine (A), thymine (T), guanine (G) and cytosine (C). **12**

What is the importance of this discovery today?
Forensic scientists working on a crime use a process called DNA profiling. They use human samples taken from the place where a crime has happened and look at the pattern of pairs A, T, G and C from the DNA. Each of us has a unique pattern, and this means that it is a very reliable way of proving who the criminal is. **13** This information can be used to match a sample, and hopefully a crime can be solved.

Another important, and sometimes controversial, use of DNA (or rather rDNA which is artificial, or man-made, DNA) is in the areas of biology and biochemistry to produce genetically modified organisms (GMO). **14**

The Future
The technology based on our understanding of DNA keeps on improving and developing. **15** We are so used to seeing that double helix structure and the astonishing things that science is doing with Crick and Watson's discovery, that it is hard to remember that it was only just over fifty years ago that Crick walked into a Cambridge pub and told everyone he had discovered the 'secret of life'.

PAPER 1: READING Part 2 (Questions 9-15)

A She had developed sophisticated X-ray imaging techniques to 'photograph' DNA.

B In the UK there is a growing national collection of DNA profiles taken from thousands of people.

C It will change our lives forever, whether we like it or not, and in ways we can only begin to imagine.

D That dramatic statement must have had quite an effect on the pub's customers that day, and what's more, it was true, and it was going to change completely the way we look at life.

E The forensic scientists were not able to process the scene of the crime.

F DNA can make copies of itself, a process called self-replication.

G DNA-based technology can also be used in anthropology to discover your distant ancestors and how population groups are related across the planet.

H Using a combination of new mathematical theories, the latest X-ray imaging techniques and some blinding inspiration, they uncovered the now-familiar double helix structure of DNA.

PAPER 1: READING Part 3 (Questions 16-30)

Part 3

You are going to read a magazine article about four different celebrities. For questions **16-30**, choose from the people (**A-D**). The people may be chosen more than once.

Mark your answers **on the separate answer sheet**.

Which person

stumbled upon their career by chance? | 16 |

got some of their work stolen? | 17 |

had a relative who conducted a choir? | 18 |

got their first contract when they were still at school? | 19 | | 20 |

longed to make a success of their career despite their background? | 21 |

takes their work along with them wherever they may go? | 22 |

received formal training? | 23 | | 24 |

had a relative who taught the members of a famous band to play a musical instrument? | 25 |

was chosen for a unique role? | 26 |

didn't follow in their father's footsteps? | 27 |

had to wait a long time before their talent was recognised? | 28 |

was asked to perform at a very important occasion? | 29 |

has won many awards but never an Oscar? | 30 |

PAPER 1: READING Part 3 (Questions 16-30)

Star Quality

A **Clive Owen**

Clive is the son of a Country and Western singer, Jess Owen. He is the fourth of five brothers, two of whom are musicians. His family were poor and as a child he was not encouraged in this acting talent. Clive didn't let that put him off, he was determined to be a success. He had his first acting role at 13 and then went on to study at the prestigious Royal Academy of Dramatic Art (RADA) in London. Clive eventually became a Hollywood star at the age of forty, after decades as an actor on British TV series and films. George Clooney describes him as 'the greatest discovery of recent times.' Although Clive says no one spoke to him about it, many people thought he would be the next James Bond after Pierce Brosnan, in the end, of course, that job went to Daniel Craig. Clive was nominated for an Oscar and has won a number of awards, including the BAFTA and Golden Globe awards.

B **Cate Blanchett**

As a child, Cate studies dance and piano. At the age of 18 she goes on holiday to Egypt and gets a walk-on part in an Egyptian film about a boxer. It is this experience that makes her fall in love with acting and she decides that this is the career she wants to follow. She studies at the National Institute of Dramatic Arts in Sydney and starts working in the theatre and in TV serials. She gets her first film role in 1997 and the following year she stars in Shekhar Kapur's *Elizabeth* for which she receives an Oscar nomination. Over the next few years Cate Blanchett stars in some of the most successful films of all time and then in 2004 she appears in Martin Scorsese's *The Aviator* with Leonardo DiCaprio and is awarded an Oscar for Best Supporting Actress. In 2007 she is the only woman chosen to interpret one of six aspects of the life and work of Bob Dylan in the film *I'm Not There* and is awarded the Volpi Cup for Best Actress at the 64th Venice Film Festival.

C **Usher**

Usher discovers his talent for singing at an early age. He joins his local gospel choir in his home town in Tennessee, where his mother is the conductor. He signs a record deal while he is still at high school. His debut album *Usher* is released in 1994 and one of the singles from the album does so well in the charts that he is asked to sing for the Olympics held in Atlanta in 1996. The release of Usher's album *All About U* is planned for 2001, but the songs are illegally uploaded onto the web which millions of people are able to download for free! His record label abandons the release of that album and Usher begins work on some new tracks. The new album is called *8701* (because that is the album's release date) and is a huge hit. Usher is one of the most successful R&B artists in the world. To date he has sold over 30 million albums and has received 5 Grammy Awards.

D **Norah Jones**

Norah Jones has music in her genes! Her father is Ravi Shankar, the Indian maestro who taught the Beatles how to play the sitar. Her mother, Sue Jones, was a dancer and singer of soul music. Her grandmother adores country music and Norah's sister is also a singer. At an early age, Norah joined the school choir, where she learnt how to sing. She began playing the piano at the age of five and briefly played the alto saxophone. She won the Down Beat Student Music Award (SMA) for Best Original Composition in 1996 and for two years running was awarded the SMA for Best Jazz Vocalist. In 2000, a music producer heard some of Norah's work and recognised her great talent. The director of Blue Note, the most important record label in jazz, signed her up that year. When she was 23, she released *Come away with me* which won her 8 Grammy Awards and sold 18 million copies. In 2004, after releasing *Feels like home*, she went on a world tour, taking her guitar and notebooks with her so she could write the songs for her next album *Not too late*, which was released in 2007.

PAPER 2: WRITING Part 1 (Question 1)

Part 1

You **must** answer this question. Write your answer in **120-150** words in an appropriate style on the opposite page.

1   You have received an email from your English-speaking friend, Lucy, who is planning on accepting a summer job she has been offered. Read Lucy's email and the notes you have made. Then write an email to Lucy, using **all** your notes.

---

e-mail

From: Lucy Rogers
Sent: 30th January 2009
Subject: Summer Job

Do you remember me telling you about that summer job I saw advertised in the local paper just before Christmas? Well, I applied and they've just written back offering me the job!

It's from the beginning of June to the end of September. I'll be working in the reception and it'll be my job to greet tourists when they arrive and check them into their rooms. It's a small hotel which means I'd be responsible for the guests for the whole of their stay, making sure it's as comfortable as possible. Do you think that means working from early in the morning to late at night?

Say what you think.

I'm a bit worried about my Italian. It's really quite rusty as I haven't been to Italy for a couple of years now and I'm afraid I won't be able to understand anything! So, I'll need to brush up on my Italian before I leave. Can you recommend any good schools?

Yes, give details.

Four months is a long time and I'm afraid I'll get homesick. Would you be able to come out and stay for a while? I could arrange for you to stay in my room and I would take you round in my free time.

Say when and for how long.

One last thing, I was wondering if you could lend me your video camera. Mine's broken and I can't afford a new one at the moment. I promise I'll treasure it with my life!

Write soon,

Say no and explain why.

Lucy

Write your **email**. You must use grammatically correct sentences with accurate spelling and punctuation in a style appropriate for the situation.

PAPER 2: WRITING Part 1 (Question 1)

Question 1

e-mail

To: Lucy Rogers
Sent: 31st January 2009
Subject: Summer Job

PAPER 2: WRITING Part 2 (Questions 2-5)

Part 2

Write an answer to **one** of the questions **2–5** in this part. Write your answer in **120–180** words in an appropriate style on the opposite page. Put the question number in the box at the top of the page.

2 Your teacher has asked you to write a story for an international magazine. The story must **begin** with the following words:

As Jennifer fasten her seat belt, a feeling of dread came over her and she began to wonder why she'd ever agreed to meet Mr Finch at all.

Write your **story**.

3 You have seen this announcement in a magazine.

THE MOST IMPORTANT PERSON IN MY LIFE

Tell us about a person who has greatly influenced your life. Say how he or she influenced you and the effect it has had on your life.

We will publish the most interesting articles in our next issue.

Write your **article**.

4 You recently saw this notice in a magazine called *The Theatre Goer*.

When did you last go to the theatre? What did you see and what was it like?
Write a review and tell us what you thought of the acting and the scenery.
The most entertaining reviews will win two free tickets to next month's show!

Write your **review**.

5 Answer **one** of the following two questions based on **one** of the titles below. Write the letter **(a)** or **(b)** as well as the number 5 in the question box on the opposite page.

(a) *Great Expectations* by Charles Dickens
This is part of a letter from your English-speaking penfriend.

I'm reading Great Expectations by Charles Dickens. Did you say you've read it, too? Who is your favourite character and why?

Write a **letter** to your penfriend, giving your opinion. Do not write any postal addresses.

Write your **letter**.

(b) *The Phantom of the Opera* by Gaston Leroux
Which character do you feel most sympathy for? Write an **essay** giving your opinion and explaining why.

Write your **essay**.

PAPER 2: WRITING Part 2 (Questions 2-5)

Question

....
....
....
....
....
....
....
....
....
....
....
....
....
....
....
....
....
....
....
....
....
....
....
....
....
....
....
....
....

PAPER 3: USE OF ENGLISH Part 1 (Questions 1-12)

Part 1

For questions **1-12**, read the text below and decide which answer (**A, B, C** or **D**) best fits each gap. There is an example at the beginning **(0)**.

Mark your answers **on the separate answer sheet**.

Example:

| 0 | **A** firstly | **B** greatly | **C** widely | **D** not mostly |

| 0 | A B **C** D |

When Graffiti Becomes Art

Banksy is **(0)** .... believed to be one of the most exciting artists of our time. His art is funny, political and thought- **(1)** .... It is often made with cans of spray paint and stencils and can be found on the side of buildings in the streets of London, Bristol and **(2)** .... the world.

Banksy has managed to maintain complete **(3)** .... But in the UK, where the mainstream culture is obsessed with fame and celebrity, his desire to remain unknown seems a political **(4)** .... It is difficult to see how he is going to stay anonymous when newspapers and magazines often have articles about him, he was recently voted as an 'arts hero' in a **(5)** .... of young people, and some of the most famous people in the world have bought his work.

Banksy's work is about questioning authority, the status quo, consumerism and the way we **(6)** .... our planet. Some of it is quite shocking, some looks simply funny and then stays with you, making you question your **(7)** .... In one short film Banksy is seen, his back to the camera, spay painting a message on a blank **(8)** .... in London. The message says 'The Joy of Not Being Sold Anything.'

Banksy works quickly, often in **(9)** .... daylight, and often disguised as a council worker. He has even managed to smuggle some of his work into London's top museums. Most **(10)** .... a piece of 'neolithic art' painted on a stone with a hunter pushing a supermarket shopping trolley. This 'neolithic art' was **(11)** .... signed by the artist 'Banksyus Maximus' and the British Museum took eight days to **(12)** .... it shouldn't be there!

PAPER 3: USE OF ENGLISH Part 1 (Questions 1-12)

1 **A** evoking **B** producing **C** arousing **D** provoking

2 **A** throughout **B** through **C** everywhere **D** over

3 **A** unanimity **B** familiarity **C** anonymity **D** similarity

4 **A** disclosure **B** statement **C** utterance **D** relevation

5 **A** vote **B** election **C** referendum **D** poll

6 **A** treat **B** deal **C** handle **D** manage

7 **A** reasons **B** beliefs **C** ideas **D** dreams

8 **A** pamphlet **B** leaflet **C** billboard **D** flier

9 **A** bright **B** broad **C** wide **D** complete

10 **A** lately **B** early **C** shortly **D** recently

11 **A** even **B** still **C** yet **D** ever

12 **A** recognise **B** recover **C** realise **D** register

PAPER 3: USE OF ENGLISH Part 2 (Questions 13-24)

Part 2

For questions **13-24**, read the text below and think of the word which best fits each gap. Use only **one** word in each gap. There is an example at the beginning **(0)**.

Write your answers **IN CAPITAL LETTERS on the separate answer sheet.**

Example: 0   O N ⬚⬚⬚⬚⬚⬚⬚⬚⬚⬚⬚⬚⬚⬚⬚⬚

Into the Dragon's Den

The Dragon's Den is the name of a popular TV show on the BBC which is having an effect
(0) .... the wider business world and encouraging a whole new generation of entrepreneurs
and inventors to follow their dreams.

The show is hosted by five of the UK's top business people, all of **(13)** .... are very
successful, very rich and very scary. Dragons in human form! In order to get **(14)** .... the
show you have to submit your idea for a new business or your new invention to the BBC. The
thousands of applications are then sorted **(15)** .... and if you are lucky you will be chosen to
present your idea on the show. Then comes the really terrifying bit. You have to stand up in front of
the Dragons and sell them your idea while you are **(16)** .... filmed for a national TV show
with millions of **(17)** .... If the Dragons like your idea then they will invest some of
(18) .... own money in your business. Often the Dragons give the thumbs **(19)** .... ,
but other times they are prepared to invest tens **(20)** .... thousands of pounds.

The Dragons Den has inspired many people to follow their business dreams. It has given them
insights into **(21)** .... to get financial investment and a deeper understanding of how the
world of business and finance works.
It is not **(22)** .... simply to have a good idea, you have to know how to sell your idea and the
investors are your first customers. Success is rare and there are no **(23)** .... for failure, but
the rewards, both personal and financial, can **(24)** .... life changing.

PAPER 3: USE OF ENGLISH Part 3 (Questions 25-34)

Part 3

For questions **25-34**, read the text below. Use the word given in capitals at the end of some of the lines to form a word that fits in the gap **in the same line**. There is an example at the beginning **(0)**.

Write your answers **IN CAPITAL LETTERS on the separate answer sheet**.

Example: | 0 | S | P | I | R | I | T | U | A | L | | | | | | | | |

The Pilgrimage to Santiago de Compostela

Every year, two hundred thousand pilgrims walk for hundreds of
kilometres to the Sanctuary at Santiago de Compostela. The journey
they make is **(0)** .... , rich in tradition, and passes through   **SPIRIT**
(25) .... landscape.   **PHENOMENON**

The most **(26)** .... pilgrims' route is the one which starts in   **LEGEND**
France, leaving from Roncevaux (Navarre) and arriving in Santiago.
It is 800 kilometres long and crosses the Pyrenees mountains.
The oldest path is the **(27)** .... route which follows the   **NORTH**
(28) .... coast of Spain with its rias, or drowned river   **SPECTACLE**
valleys, unique to this part of the world. To show the way, the path is
(29) .... with pictures of yellow scallop shells on blue   **MARK**
backgrounds which **(30)** .... the Pilgrims.   **SYMBOL**

In the past, pilgrims **(31)** .... to Santiago followed a route   **WALK**
marked by the Milky Way. These **(32)** .... pilgrims included   **EARLY**
Saint Frances of Assisi (1182-1226), the Patron saint of Italy. In 1989,
Pope John Paul II went to Santiago to meet a **(33)** .... of   **CONGREGATE**
over half a million young people who had gathered there from all over
the world. Today, pilgrims who make the journey receive a credencial,
a certificate stating that they are making the pilgrimage. Once they
reach Santiago they are **(34)** .... the compostela,   **AWARD**
a certificate in Latin which declares that they have completed the
pilgrimage. Just like passing an exam!

PAPER 3: USE OF ENGLISH Part 4 (Questions 35-42)

Part 4

For questions **35-42**, complete the second sentence so that it has a similar meaning to the first sentence, using the word given. **Do not change the word given**. You must use between **two** and **five** words, including the word given. Here is an example **(0)**.

Example:

0   Our neighbour took us into town.

     TAKEN

     We …………………………………………… our neighbour.

The gap can be filled by the words 'were taken into town by', so you write

Example: **0** | W | E | R | E | | T | A | K | E | N | | I | N | T | O | | T | O | W | N | | B | Y |

Write **only** the missing words **IN CAPITAL LETTERS on the separate answer sheet**.

---

35   I'll never go to that restaurant again.

     LAST

     That's …………………………………………….. I will ever go to that restaurant.

36   This is our last stop.

     FAR

     This is ……………………………………………. go.

37   I really don't care anymore.

     PAST

     I ………………………………………….. anymore.

38   I'm really looking forward to my holidays.

     WAIT

     I ………………………………………….. my holidays to come.

PAPER 3: USE OF ENGLISH Part 4 (Questions 35-42)

39 I regret saying such nasty things.

WISH

I ………………………………………………….. such nasty things.

40 It was a mistake to invest in property that year.

SHOULD

John ………………………………………………….. in property that year.

41 They are collecting money to build a children's hospital.

BEING

Money ………………………………………………….. to build a children's hospital.

42 We repaired the roof to stop it from leaking.

SO

We repaired the roof ………………………………………………….. leak.

PAPER 4: LISTENING Part 1 (Questions 1-8)

CD 2 6

Part 1

You will hear people talking in eight different situations. For questions **1-8**, choose the best answer (**A**, **B** or **C**).

---

1   You overhear a woman talking to her son on the phone.

What would she like him to do?

A   stop getting into debt
B   buy better quality clothes
C   get a better paid job

| 1 |

2   You hear a man talking about city life.

What is he complaining about?

A   that he finds it difficult to breath when he goes out
B   that he has to wear a mask when he rides to and from the office
C   that he can't afford to live in the countryside

| 2 |

3   You overhear a man and a woman talking.

What is the woman upset about most?

A   that nobody raised the alarm
B   that her husband could be so forgetful
C   that she had to wait outside in her night wear

| 3 |

4   You hear a teacher reciting the myth of Jason and the Golden Fleece.
How was the Golden Fleece stolen?

A   Hercules and Orpheus gave the dragon a potion to send it to sleep.
B   The Argonauts got it out of the wood and took it back to Greece in the Arno.
C   Jason managed to steal the fleece while the dragon was sleeping.

| 4 |

PAPER 4: LISTENING Part 1 (Questions 1-8)

5   You hear part of a talk on the radio.

What is the man talking about?

   A   a short trip
   B   an expert on Shakespeare
   C   a play

   [5]

6   You hear a woman talking about a diet.

What does she say about the diet?

   A   It made her feel weak.
   B   It left an awful taste in her mouth.
   C   She couldn't stick to it.

   [6]

7   You overhear a man talking about his new job.

What does he do?

   A   a doctor
   B   a psychologist
   C   a salesman

   [7]

8   You overhear a woman talking to a friend.

What is she doing?

   A   complaining about something
   B   giving him advice
   C   warning him

   [8]

PAPER 4: LISTENING Part 2 (Questions 9-18)

CD 2
7

Part 2

You will hear an expert talking about the mystery surrounding the origins of Stonehenge.
For questions **9-18**, complete the sentences.

STONEHENGE

Archaeologists have been attempting to find out why Stonehenge was

| | 9 | for centuries.

They have pondered over whether it could have been an area dedicated to

| | 10 |

A team of experts believe that the | | 11 | circle of stones originated
from as far away as Wales.

A geomorphologist thought it highly improbable that Bronze Age man had

| | 12 | the stones to Stonehenge.

The Oxford Journal of Archaeology made the assumption that the bluestones had been torn away by

| | 13 |

The Cursus are avenues of long ago which | | 14 | the area encircling
the stones.

A team of archeologists discovered a particle of an | | 15 | while
excavating an ancient burial site.

The theory that the Cursus might have been a chariot | | 16 | in
Roman times was abandoned when it was found out it dated much further back.

It is thought that the stones were transferred to the middle of the site from the

| | 17 | in 2300 BC.

When Stonehenge was first built, the number of | | 18 | from Wales
may have been as many as fifty-six.

PAPER 4: LISTENING Part 3 (Questions 19-23)

Part 3

You will hear five different people talking about various holiday experiences. For questions **19–23**, choose from the list **(A–F)**, what each person says about the holidays. Use the letters only once. There is one extra letter which you do not need to use.

A	An important event might have to be postponed.		
		Speaker 1	19
B	The tourists were taken in by the travel agency.		
		Speaker 2	20
C	One of the holiday makers couldn't muster any enthusiasm.		
		Speaker 3	21
D	The flier was to prevent people from being swindled.		
		Speaker 4	22
E	Neither insurance company was willing to cover costs incurred.		
		Speaker 5	23
F	The customers were unaware that they could get their money back.		

PAPER 4: LISTENING Part 4 (Questions 24-30)

CD 2 9

Part 4

You will hear an interview with a musician about teaching children to play a musical instrument. For questions **24-30**, choose the best answer (**A, B** or **C**).

24 Music can be taken up

  A   only by people with good physical coordination.

  B   people looking for a rewarding pastime.

  C   anyone wishing to do so.

24

25 A sure sign of enthusiasm is when children

  A   don't have to be reminded to practise.

  B   choose their favourite instrument to learn to play on.

  C   stop playing around with their instrument and take it more seriously.

25

26 The recorder is a suitable instrument to start with because

  A   children find it less difficult to blow once they've got their second set of teeth.

  B   it doesn't require as much strength to blow as other woodwind instruments.

  C   children feel more at ease with this instrument than a violin or cello.

26

27 Starting lessons before the age of eight

  A   can give a child the chance to acquire a taste for music.

  B   can allow a child to learn about different musical instruments.

  C   can be too demanding for a child.

27

28 Music therapy

  A   is particularly suitable for children who have been ill-treated.

  B   stimulates children and enhances their social skills.

  C   and its impact have been heavily remarked upon.

28

 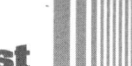

PAPER 4: LISTENING Part 4 (Questions 24-30)

29   State registered therapists

    A   work in health centres administered by the Government.

    B   are qualified professionals who have successfully completed a training course. | 29 |

    C   provide training courses at APMT.

30   The ability to express oneself through music

    A   depends on musical expertise.

    B   relies on spoken language. | 30 |

    C   is an inborn competence.

PAPER 5: SPEAKING Part 1

Part 1
3 minutes (5 minutes for groups of three)

Good morning/afternoon/evening. My name is .... and this is my colleague ....

And your names are?

Can I have your mark sheets, please?

Thank you.

First of all we'd like to know something about you.

- Where are you from *(Candidate A)*?
- And you *(Candidate B)*?

- What do you like about living *(here / name of candidate's home town)*?
- And what about you *(Candidate A/B)*?

Select one or more questions from any of the following categories, as appropriate.

Homelife

- **Tell me something about your home town? ...... (What do you like about it?)**
- **What do you do when you're at home? ...... (Who do you spend time with?)**
- **Do you come from a large family? ...... (How many brothers and sisters have you got?)**
- **Which is your favourite room in the house? ...... (Can you describe it to me?)**
- **Have you ever thought about moving? ...... (Where would you move to?)**

Likes and dislikes

- **What do you like doing in your spare time? ...... (Why?)**
- **Do you have any hobbies? ...... (How much time do you dedicate to your hobby?)**
- **What's your favourite TV programme? ...... (What do you like about it?)**
- **Do you like going to the cinema? ...... (Tell us about a film you saw recently.)**
- **Tell us about a holiday you really enjoyed recently.**

PAPER 5: SPEAKING Part 1

Part 1
3 minutes (5 minutes for groups of three)

Education and Work

- Are there any universities or colleges where you live? ...... (What are they like?)
- Have you ever taken part in an evening course? .... (What did you study?)
- Are you good at team work? ...... (Why? Why not?)
- Can you remember your first day at school? ...... (What was it like?)
- Did you get on well with your classmates at primary school? ...... (Why? Why not?)
- Would you rather work for a company or for yourself? ...... (What would you like to do?)

Media

- Would you rather watch the news on TV or listen to the radio? ...... (Why?)
- How much TV do you watch each day? ...... (Do you think you watch too much?)
- Do you subscribe to any online newspapers? ...... (Which ones?)
- Do you buy a newspaper everyday? ...... (What do you do if you can't get hold of one?)
- Tell us about the worst programme you've ever seen.
- Who's your favourite newsreader? ...... (Why?)

Holidays and Travel

- What's the most tiring journey you've ever been on? ...... (Tell us about it.)
- Is public transport reliable where you live? ...... (Do you ever use it?)
- Have you planned your next holiday yet? ...... (Where would you like to go?)
- Have you ever lost your passport? ...... (How did it happen and what did you do?)
- What's the most beautiful place you've ever visited? ...... (Can you describe it to us?)
- Do you have lots of holiday snaps? ...... (Where do you keep them?)

PAPER 5: SPEAKING Part 2 (pages 170-171)

1 Friendship 2 Hobbies	**Part 2** 4 minutes (6 minutes for groups of three)

Interlocutor	In this part of the test, I'm going to give each of you two photographs. I'd like you to talk about your photographs on your own for about a minute, and also to answer a short question about your partner's photographs. (*Candidate A*), it's your turn first. Here are your photographs. They show **different people enjoying themselves outdoors.** *Place **Photo 1** in front of Candidate A.* I'd like you to compare the photographs, and say **how important friendship is to each child.** All right?
Candidate A 🕐 *1 minute*	....
Interlocutor	Thank you. (*Candidate B*), **did you use to have lots of friends when you were a child?**
Candidate B 🕐 *approximately 20 seconds*	....
	Thank you. Now, (*Candidate B*), here are your photographs. They show **people dedicating time to their hobbies.** *Place **Photo 2** in front of Candidate B.* I'd like you to compare the photographs, and say **why you think these hobbies are important to the different people.** All right?
Candidate B 🕐 *1 minute*	....
Interlocutor	Thank you. (*Candidate A*), **which hobby would you rather have and why?**
Candidate A 🕐 *approximately 20 seconds*	....
Interlocutor	Thank you.

PAPER 5: SPEAKING Parts 3 and 4 (page 172)

3 Careers	Parts 3 and 4
	7 minutes (9 minutes for groups of three)

Part 3

Interlocutor Now, I'd like you to talk about something together for about three minutes. *(4 minutes for groups of three)*

I'd like you to imagine that a friend of yours needs some advice in choosing a career. Here are some suggestions for you to consider.

*Place **Picture 3** in front of the candidates.*

First, talk to each other about **how challenging each job might be.** Then decide **which one would provide better job satisfaction in the long term.**

All right?

Candidates
🕐 *3 minutes (4 minutes for groups of three)*

....

Interlocutor Thank you.

Part 4

Interlocutor *Select any of the following questions, as appropriate:*

- **Which career would you rather choose?**
  ...... (Why?)

- **Is there any job you would never consider doing?**
  ...... (Why?)

- **Which jobs are the most highly qualified?**
  ...... (What sort of skills and qualifications would you need?)

- **Which is one of the most highly paid jobs nowadays?**
  ...... (Do you think the salary is fair?)

- **What should people think carefully about when choosing a career?**

Thank you. That is the end of the test.

PAPER 5: SPEAKING Part 2

| How important is friendship to each of these children? | 1 |

PAPER 5: SPEAKING Part 2

Why are these hobbies important to the different people?

PAPER 5: SPEAKING Parts 3 and 4

3

- How challenging might these jobs be?
- Which one would provide better job satisfaction in the long term?

Multi-part Verbs

a) Verbs + particle

There are verbs that are **always followed by the same particle / particles.** Verbs + particle are generally followed by an object (if the object is a verb, it is in the -ing form).

apologize for	*He apologized for his delay / for being late.*
believe in	*She still believes in fairies.*
comment on	*Would you like to comment on his decision?*
complain about / of	*He complained about the way he had been treated.*
depend on	*She depends too much on her boyfriend. / The quality of the items depends on the fabric.*
insist on	*They insisted on going to the new restaurant.*
listen to	*She always listens to my advice.*
look at	*Have you looked at the newspaper yet?*
succeed in	*I'm sure she will succeed in breaking the world record.*
suffer from	*She has suffered from headaches for years.*
take care of	*Can you take care of my cats while I'm on holiday?*
take part in	*Is Julie going to take part in the race?*
thank someone for	*I'd like to thank you for your help.*
think of / about	*I don't want to think of / about him now!*
wait for	*We are still waiting for their reply.*

b) Phrasal Verbs

Phrasal verbs **are verbs followed by one or more particles. The meaning of the verb changes depending on the particle** / particles.

look for = try to find   *look after* = take care of   *look forward to* = wait for something pleasant

Phrasal verb verbs can be followed by an object or not. Sometimes the object can be placed both before or after the particle.
If the object is a pronoun, it always comes before the particle.
bring up = educate a child → *Mrs Sway brought up her children / brought her children up very strictly.*
Mrs Sway brought them up very strictly.

phrasal verb	meaning	
break down	stop working or functioning	*The telephone system broke down during the storm.*
break in / into	enter a building by force	
break out	a) start suddenly b) escape	*A fire broke out while we were having lunch.* *The prisoner broke out of prison two days ago.*
break up		*bring a relationship to an end*
bring back	make somebody remember something	*That song brought back a very painful day.*
bring out	produce or publish something	*The writer brought out his second novel.*
bring up	care for and educate a child	*Caroline brought up four children by herself.*
call off	cancel	*The match was called off because of heavy rain.*
carry on	continue	*Even though he was tired, he carried on studying.*

phrasal verb	meaning	
come across	meet somebody by chance	*I came across him while I was touring the USA.*
come round / around	visit somebody for a short time	*You really must come round and see us next year.*
come up with	find a solution or have a brilliant idea	*She came up with a great idea for the new ad.*
do without	succeed in living without something	*I can't understand how they can do without TV!*
drop out	quit school or a course	*She dropped out of university after only a year.*
fall out	quarrel with somebody	*Lisa and Dave have fallen out again!*
fill in	complete a form by writing information	*To make an order fill in this form.*
get off	a) leave a train, bus, plane b) start a journey	*Can you tell me where I have to get off?* *I think it's better to get off early in the morning.*
get on / along with	like each other and have a good relation	*She gets on very well with her sister.*
get over	overcome a problem and start feeling well	*I'm sure she will get over the shock she had.*
get through to	contact somebody by telephone	*I tried many times, but I couldn't get through to him.*
give in	admit you have been defeated	*The police forced the rebels to give in.*
give out	distribute	*Why are you giving out these leaflets?*
give up	stop doing or having something	*You should give up working and relax a bit more.*
go off	a) explode b) become bad (about food)	*The bomb went off in the market square.* *What a terrible smell! The milk must have gone off.*
go on	continue	*I don't want to go on talking about the same things!*
go out	stop burning	*Suddenly the lights went out.*
go out with	have a romantic relationship	*Cindy is going out with an Italian boy.*
go over	revise or examine carefully	*Go over the test before you hand it in.*
hold on	wait to talk to somebody (on the phone)	*Can you hold on? Let me see if Tim is here.*
keep away	avoid going near somebody or something	*Keep away from the pier! It's dangerous.*
keep in	restrain	*Don't keep your anger in!*
keep on	continue	*The snow kept on falling for three days.*
keep up with	learn about the latest news or events	*She always keeps up with the latest fashion trends.*
live through	survive after an unpleasant situation	*Mr Sword has lived through the Second World War.*
look after	take care of	*Laurie, can you look after my daughter tomorrow?*
look forward to	wait for something pleasant	*I'm looking forward to seeing her again.*
look into	examine deeply and carefully	*A special committee will look into the matter.*
look out	be careful	*Look out! A bee is flying around you.*
look up	look for information in a reference book	*I had to look these words up in the dictionary.*
make into	change into something or somebody else	*This poem was made into a song after many years.*
make off	hurry away to escap	*The pickpockets made off on foot.*
make out	manage to see or hear clearly	*She could make out a person in the darkness.*
make up	invent a story	*I often make up funny stories for my niece.*
make up with	become friendly again after an argument	*Don't worry, he'll make up with her by tonight.*
pick up	go and collect someone in a car	*I'll pick you up at 8 p.m, OK?*

phrasal verb	meaning	
put off	postpone	*The match will be put off if it rains.*
put on	a) gain (usually weight) b) wear clothes	*I think he has put on about three kilos. It's very cold.* *Why don't you put your coat on?*
put out	stop something from burning	*Excuse me, can you put your cigarette out, please?*
put through	connect by telephone	*Could you put me through to the headmaster, please?*
put up	let somebody stay at your home	*I'm sorry, but I can't put you up for the night.*
run across / into	meet somebody by chance	*I've just run across Dave! He's here for few days.*
run out of	finish a supply of something	*The car stopped because it had run out of fuel.*
run over	a) knock somebody down (with a vehicle) b) read something quickly	*An old lady was run over by a truck yesterday.* *You had better run over your notes again.*
set off	begin a journey	*What time are you going to set off for Madrid?*
talk over	discuss a problem	*You should talk your problem over with an expert.*
take after	look like a member of your family	*Your niece really takes after you.*
take down	write something down	*The secretary quickly took the message down.*
take off	leave the ground and fly (plane)	*The plane couldn't take off due to thick fog.*
take up	start doing something regularly	*He decided to take up playing the guitar.*
throw out / away	get rid of something you no longer need	*Why don't you throw out / away that old sweater?*
try on	put on clothes to see how they fit	*Try these trousers on before buying them.*
turn down	refuse an offer or a proposal	*I think he'll turn your invitation down.*
turn down / up	reduce / increase (volume or heating)	*an you turn the volume of the radio down / up?*
turn on / off	start / stop a machine (pressing a button)	*He didn't want to turn the TV on / off.*
turn out	a) happen in a particular way b) prove to be	*The party turned out very well.* *The book turned out to be really exciting.*
turn up	arrive	*Your friends haven't turned up yet.*
work out	find a solution or an answer	*The President is trying to work out a compromise.*

Answer Key

Unit 1

Our Society Pages 8 – 13

1 2
2 1 B 2 C 3 A 4 B 5 D 6 C 7 A 8 C
3 1 poverty 2 harmonious 3 harmoniously 4 refugee
   5 immigration 6 immigrant 7 immigrant 8 citizenship
   9 conflict 10 conflicting / conflictive 11 conflictively
   12 tolerance 13 tolerant 14 tolerantly 15 negotiation
   16 negotiator 17 negotiable 18 cultural 19 culturally
   20 integration 21 integrated 22 emigrate 23 emigrant
   24 emigrant
4 a integrate b poverty c poor d emigrate e conflict
   f immigrant g intolerant
5 1 off 2 over to 3 after 4 for 5 out 6 into 7 up
   8 off with 9 up
6 a 3 b 1 c 5 d 6 e 4 f 2
7 a 3 b 10 c 1 d 6 e 5 f 7 g 2 h 9 i 8 j 4
8 1 B 2 A 3 C 4 A 5 C 6 B 7 C 8 B
9 1 look forward to 2 couldn't make out 3 have lived
   4 has gone 5 made up of 6 have been writing 7 made into
   8 not been to Paris since
10 Students' own answers
11 9 50% 10 inter-ethnic 11 surface 12 waiting list
   13 troublemakers 14 relationships 15 together 16 medium
   17 artwork 18 implement
12 a 4 b 3 c 2 d 1
13 Students' own answers

Unit 2

Food for Thought! Pages 14 – 19

1 1 H 2 C 3 A 4 E 5 B 6 F 7 G
2 1 9 2 14 3 11 4 4 5 2 6 10 7 12 8 5 9 1 10 7 11 3
   12 13 13 6 14 8
3 good for you milk cereal juice pasta bread tuna fruit
   vegetables olive oil low-fat cheese rice a little bit's OK
   coffee soft drinks butter red meat eggs bad for you
   chocolate crisps cake biscuits
4 1 a lot of, a lot of 2 any, lots of 3 many 4 much, some
   5 a few, too many 6 many, much 7 a large number of
   8 a great deal of
5 1 thoughtless 2 misunderstood 3 disagree 4 unbelievable
   5 recycling 6 wonderful 7 kindness 8 thoughtful
   9 preview 10 rewrite
6 1 piece / slice 2 cups 3 going 4 few 5 who 6 meal 7 out
   8 so / that 9 off 10 won't 11 such 12 whatever
7 Students' own answers
8 1 C 2 F 3 A 4 E 5 D
9 Speaker 1 Peanuts Speaker 2 Shellfish Speaker 3 Lactose
   Speaker 4 Soya Speaker 5 The protein in cow's milk
10 1 Peanuts 2 Shellfish 3 lactose intolerance
11 1 1 2 3 3 6 4 7 5 4 6 2 7 5
12 Students' own answers

Unit 3

Be a Sport! Pages 20 -25

1 1 C 2 C 3 B 4 D 5 B 6 C 7 A 8 C 9 B 10 D 11 A
   12 D 13 C 14 A
2 1 5 2 4 3 1 4 2 5 6 6 3
3 1 amazing 2 astonishing 3 thrilled 4 shocked
   5 exhilarated 6 frightened
4 1 est 2 r 3 st 4 double 5 er 6 double 7 est 8 i 9 er
   10 i 11 est 12 more 13 the 14 most
5 a better b the best c worse d the worst e more f the most
   g better h the best
6 1 the best / the greatest, of 2 the best / the greatest 3 more
   important, than 4 the largest, in 5 better at, than 6 nicer
   than 7 most challenging, ever 8 better than
7 1 I mean, there's isn't any difference between the two of them
   in speed 2 - it was less expensive then than it had been before
   Christmas 3 considering she didn't revise for it al all! 4 - we're
   late 5 from people as far away as Iceland 6 in no fewer than
   20 minutes 7 - he must have missed at least four matches due
   to injury 8 - she's obviously trained a lot in the past few
   months
8 1 as good as 2 less expensive than 3 far better (mark in the
   exam) than 4 a bit faster 5 as far away as 6 in no fewer
   than 7 on more than one occasion 8 a lot better than
9 1 fastest 2 athlete 3 Championships 4 medalist 5 weighs
   6 best 7 visitors 8 special 9 signed 10 sportswear
10 Photo 1 Peking 2008, Photo 2 Athens 2004
11 a 3 b 5 c 7 d 8 e 1 f 9 g 10 h 4 i 6 j 2
12 1 B 2 A 3 C 4 A 5 B 6 B 7 C
13 Students' own answers

Unit 4

Music and the Internet Revolution Pages 26 - 31

1 B
2 1 D 2 D 3 A 4 B 5 D 6 C 7 B 8 A
3 Across 1 burn 3 gig 4 deal 7 upload 8 clip 10 network
   11 rip 12 piracy 13 demo Down 2 unsigned 5 laptop
   6 non-mainstream 9 download
4 a 6 b 3 c 5 d 2 e 1 4 is the extra one; 1 unsigned 2 clips
   3 laptop 4 upload 5 deal 6 gig 7 non-mainstream
   8 download 9 burn 10 rip
5 1 the 2 the, the 3 the 4 the, X 5 X 6 the 7 X 8 X, the
   9 The, the 10 X, X
6 1 X - young people, MP3 players, the - The Chinese 2 X - Italy
   3 the - the USA, the UK 4 X - Monday 5 the - the guitar
   6 the - the film 7 the - the north of Europe, the sun, the
   Internet, the radio, the state 8 X - English lessons 9 X - on
   holiday
7 1 The music industry is facing a new challenge 2 In the early
   1990s, email was still a new phenomenon 3 Every day, a
   hundred million video clips are viewed on the site 4 Anyone
   with access to the Internet can decide if a band is good 5 One
   of the songs was recorded using a home-made amplifier
   6 In the business world, an increasing number of people are
   addicted to email
8 1 B 2 B 3 C 4 D 5 C 6 C 7 B 8 A 9 B 10 B 11 A
   12 D
9 Students' own answers

10 1 online community 2 upload 3 two 4 keep track 5 server
6 fan base 7 rapport 8 deduce 9 scouting 10 home based
11 1 T 2 F 3 F 4 T 5 T 6 F
12 C
13 1 ancient 2 string 3 sleeveless 4 braces 5 back 6 elderly
7 crossed 8 make out 9 taken 10 headdresses 11 sale
12 sign
14 Students' own answers

Unit 5

Read on... Pages 32 - 37

1 2
2 1 B 2 A 3 D 4 B 5 B 6 C 7 D 8 A 9 D 10 C 11 D
12 A 13 B 14 C 15 A
3 1 dictionary 2 biography 3 encyclopaedia 4 manual
5 albums 6 guidebook 7 novel 8 atlas 9 logbook 10 diary
4 1 C, D 2 A, E 3 B 4 A, C, D 5 E
5 a 7 b 8 c 5 d 3 e 4 g 1 f 6 h 2
6 a When I was at University, I played football every Saturday
b The alarm clock went off. She woke up and realized it was
very late c The protesters were demonstrating loudly in the
street, the police were guarding the embassy, the Saturday
afternoon shoppers were wandering in and out of the shops...
d I was sitting in the sun when I heard somebody ring the door
bell. e When I got off the bus, I realised that somebody had
stolen my purse f I'd been working very hard for weeks and
not sleeping much when I went down with 'flu g She was
doing her homework at 7p.m. yesterday h While I was living in
Canada, my brother was working in Sweden
7 1 'd / had (already) been living 2 met 3 was rushing 4 ' / had
overslept 5 stopped 6 realised 7 was going on 8 ran
9 opened 10 jumped 11 slammed 12 was 13 pulled
14 asked 15 was doing 16 didn't apologise 17 asked
18 was going 19 invited 20 was 21 couldn't 22 agreed
23 got 24 turned out 25 'd / had seemed 26 led
8 1 As 2 on 3 the 4 as 5 instead 6 up 7 that / which
8 the 9 where 10 most 11 to 12 which
9 Students' own answers
10 1 D 2 E 3 F 4 B 5 A
11 1 Speaker 3 2 Speaker 5 3 Speaker 2 4 Speaker 4 5 Speaker 1
12 1 tedious 2 sequel 3 drearily 4 disdain 5 snippet
13 1 drearily 2 disdain 3 snippets 4 tedious 5 sequel
14 Students' own answers
15 1 12 2 4 3 1 4 6 5 13 6 3 7 11 8 7 9 9 10 2 11 10
12 5 13 8 They chose 'Cooking with me' and 'Art &
Photography'
16 Students' own answers
17 Students' own answers

Unit 6

Tomorrow's World Pages 38 - 43

1 1 D 2 B 3 A 4 C 5 F 6 E
2 1 D 2 C 3 B 4 A 5 B 6 B 7 C 8 A
3 1 g 2 a 3 e 4 d 5 k 6 c 7 i 8 b 9 h 10 f 11 j

4 1 resigned 2 retiring 3 state pension 4 interview
5 promotion 6 salary 7 application form 8 got the sack
9 redundant 10 on the dole 11 unemployed
5 1 correct 2 incorrect ... we'll have been living... 3 correct
4 correct 5 incorrect ... we will be lying... 6 incorrect ... I'll
pick you up... 7 incorrect ... I'm sure he'll phone... 8 correct
9 correct 10 incorrect ... it's going to snow, I'm sure!
6 Answers with alternative future forms could be possible, but the
following are the most natural-sounding ones. 1 're getting
married 2 're you going 3 'll be relaxing 4 'm looking
forward to that (this is an example of the Present Continuous
for something in progress at the moment, rather than a
reference to the future) 5 's 6 's going to be taking off / 's
going to take off / 's taking off 7 is it going to be 8 are you
going to do 9 'll last 10 'll take 11 're going to do
12 're you going to live / will you live 13 won't be / "s not
going to be 14 's going to be / 'll be 15 'll be living 16 won't
have 17 's going to come up with 18 'll just have to
19 won't they 20 'll share (Whilst uncontracted forms wouldn't
be wrong grammatically, in informal conversations like these,
contracted forms would always be used.)
7 1 succeed 2 reality 3 imaginative 4 ethical 5 emotions
6 adaptable 7 contributions 8 resourceful 9 communicator
10 reliable
8 1 a human cannonball 2 two flying trapeze artists 3 an
acrobat on the tight rope or high wire 4 a clown with a puppet
5 performing acrobats 6 artists walking on stilts in a parade
7 a clown waving to the public 8 a juggler performing on the
street to passersby
9 1 C 2 B 3 B 4 A 5 A 6 C 7 A
10 1 nervous 2 bungee jumping 3 turn 4 dummy model
5 knees 6 propelled
11 Students' own answers

Unit 7

What a Brainwave! Pages 44 – 49

1 1 E 2 A 3 D 4 H 5 G 6 C 7 B
2 1 come across 2 come down with 3 come into 4 come up
against 5 come round/over 6 come round 7 come out
8 come up with
3 a 8 b 4 c 6 d 3 e 1 f 5 g 2 h 7
4 1 e 2 extra invention 3 f 4 g 5 c 6 d 7 b 8 a; a being
used b were ever invented c had never been invented d have
been made e will have been persuaded f 're not turned off
g have been / be invented
5 1 get used to working such 2 coming up against / up against
3 won't come with you unless 4 didn't let him 5 as soon as
6 doesn't / does not have to / need to 7 not keen on
8 came up with
6 1 a lawn mower 2 tea maker
7 1 chocolate dispenser 2 convinced 3 cheques 4 dangerous
5 Pin number 6 withdraw 7 vandalised 8 figure 9 plaque
10 cash
8 1 1967 2 Barclays Bank, Enfield, North London 3 an actor
4 in the bath 5 the Chief Executive of Barclays Bank
6 cheques soaked in carbon 14 7 the machine detected the
carbon 14 and matched the cheque to a pin number 8 the
inventor's wife 9 about 1.6 million 10 mobile phones
9 Students' own answers
10 Students' own answers

Unit 8

Happy Holidays! Pages 50 - 55

1 2
2 1 C 2 B 3 D 4 A 5 D 6 A 7 B 8 C
3 (Over, Down, Direction) 1 CAMPING (6, 9, E) 2 CRUISE (9, 3, S)
   3 TREKKING (12, 8, N) 4 SAFARI (6, 3, NW) 5 SIGHTSEEING (11, 2,W) 6 TOUR (11, 5,W) 7 TRIP (8, 6, NW) 8 VOYAGE (1, 5, SE)
4 1 B 2 C 3 B 4 A 5 C 6 B 7 A 8 B
5 1 Who drove 2 What's happened 3 When did you get back
   4 Who did you go 5 Whose (house) did you stay 6 What was
   7 Where did you go 8 Which (country) do you like 9 How
   many (people) went 10 How much did (the holiday) cost
6 1 7 2 6 3 3 4 5 5 8 6 2 7 4 8 1 9 9 10 10
7 1 do you 2 can't it 3 are we 4 am I 5 would you 6 were
   you 7 did he 8 will you
8 1 travel 2 best 3 detailed 4 characteristic 5 hygiene
   6 medication 7 comfortable 8 flight 9 securely 10 better
9 **Across** 3 opt 6 burglar 7 rim 8 dawn 10 surge
   Down 1 decibel 2 stall 4 prejudice 5 ailment 9 dusk
10 1 B 2 B 3 B 4 C 5 A 6 C 7 C 8 B
11 1 F 2 F 3 F 4 F 5 T 6 F 7 T 8 F
12 a 8 b 4 c 10 d 5 e 9 f 7 g h 2 i 6 j 3

Unit 9

Man's Best Friend Pages 56 - 61

1 1 3 2 6 3 4 4 2 5 1 6 5
2 1 A 2 C 3 H 4 F 5 E 6 B 7 G
3 a 5 b 7 c 6 d 3 e 2 f 1 g 8 h 4
4 1 wolf in sheep's clothing 2 catch / kill two birds with one
   stone 3 running around like a headless chicken 4 curiosity
   killed the cat 5 like a lamb to the slaughter 6 can't teach an
   old dog new tricks 7 can lead a horse to water, but you can't
   make it drink 8 like a bear with a sore head
5 1 either 2 both 3 neither 4 enough 5 most of 6 each of
   7 each 8 none 9 most 10 every 11 none of 12 several
6 1 Come and see me whenever you like 2 (You can) bring
   whoever you like to the party 3 Whichever dress you choose...
   it'll look good on you 4 However you do it, just get the work
   done! 5 Wherever we go skiing, it's going to be expensive
   6 He won't change his mind, whatever we say
7 1 D 2 A 3 B 4 B 5 C 6 A 7 D 8 D 9 A 10 B 11 C
   12 A
8 (Over, Down, Direction) 1 DEVICE (7, 1, SW) 2 HARNESS (8, 4,
   SW) 3 BORDERCOLLIE (12,1,S) 4 UNRULY (4, 11, E) 5 BORDER
   (13, 8, N) 6 DEBRIEFING (2, 3, SE) 7 DISTRAUGHT (11, 13, W)
   8 COUNSELLING (11, 3, SW)
9 1 counselling 2 unruly 3 harness 4 border collies
   5 distraught 6 device 7 border 8 debriefing
10 Students' own answers
11 1 C 2 B 3 A 4 B 5 B 6 C 7 A
12 1 feeding bowl 2 Londonderry 3 changes 4 unruly
   5 background 6 misunderstood 7 harness 8 psyche 9 orders
   10 debriefing 11 distraught 12 chasing
13 Students' own answers

Unit 10

Are you a Fashion Fanatic? Pages 62 - 67

1 1 D 2 A 3 C 5 B
2 1 A 2 B 3 D 4 B 5 B 6 D 7 C 8 A 9 D 10 C 11 A
   12 B 13 D 14 B 15 C
3 1 smart-casual 2 loose-fitting 3 above the knee 4 timeless
   5 broke all the rules 6 outrageous 7 accessories 8 match
4 a 5 b 6 c 2 d 4 e 3 f 7 g 1
5 1 turned (his talents) into 2 started off 3 set up 4 paid off
   5 turned (her) back on 6 coming up with 7 looked back
6 1 used to dress 2 did (you) use to wear 3 used to wear
   4 used to wear 5 used to have 6 used to take / would take
   7 used to help / would help 8 Did (they) use to let 9 was
   (always) getting 10 used to / would send 11 didn't use to like
7 1 What I hated about punks was the safety pins through the
   face 2 What I love about fashion is how it's constantly
   changing 3 What you should do is write to your newspaper
   4 What he told us was a lie 5 What most annoys me about him
   is his arrogance OR What annoys me most about him is his
   arrogance 6 What we used to do when we were punks was
   spray our (hair green)!
8 1 were 2 One 3 from 4 which 5 century 6 have 7 to
   8 The 9 is 10 are 11 but 12 the
9 Students' own answers
10 1 tights 2 vest 3 blazer 4 cords 5 tracksuit 6 belt 7 boot
   8 cardigan 9 tie 10 suit
11 1 D 2 F 3 A 4 E 5 C
12 1 T 2 T 3 F 4 T 5 F
13 Students' own answers
14 Students' own answers
15 Students' own answers

Unit 11

Keep Up Appearances Pages 68 - 73

1 1 B 2 A 3 D 4 B 5 D 6 C 7 A 8 C
2 **Across** 2 cheerful 4 stubborn 5 considerate 6 big-headed
   7 sociable 10 aggressive 12 reliable 13 funny
   Down 1 self-conscious 3 optimistic 4 sensible 8 ambitious
   9 lazy 11 generous
3 1 stubborn 2 big-headed 3 funny 4 sociable 5 considerate /
   generous 6 optimistic (cheerful also possible) 7 lazy
   8 ambitious 9 sensible 10 reliable 11 generous
4 Possible answers 1 her brother 2 a classmate, a boy she likes
   3 her mother 4 a close friend
5 Students' own answers
6 1 affectionate 2 careful, careless 3 cheerful 4 enjoyable
   5 grateful 6 hopeful, hopeless 7 miserable 8 passionate
   9 reliable 10 skillful 11 thoughtful, thoughtless 12 useful,
   useless
7 1 affectionate 2 miserable 3 useful 4 hopeless / useless
   5 grateful 6 passionate 7 enjoyable 8 careless
8 1 A 2 C 3 C 4 D 5 B 6 D 7 A 8 D 9 B 10 C 11 A
   12 C
9 Students' own answers
10 1 dress sense 2 gaudy 3 traits 4 fuss 5 laid back 6 at ease
11 1 dress 2 personality 3 birth 4 according 5 self-confidence
   6 change 7 modify 8 fussy 9 traits 10 determined

12 1 It affects our dress sense 2 No, they can behave quite differently 3 By doing an online survey or fill in a questionnaire 4 Because we have to adapt our personality to the situations and people we share our lives with 5 People don't worry about things as much as they did when they were younger

13 Students' own answers

14 Students' own answers

15 1 He is clenching his degree 2 He is wearing a broad grin on his face 3 No, he wasn't. It was his hard work that paid off in the end 4 No, there aren't 5 A mortar board is an academic cap and a gown is a long dark cloak typically worn at university 6 It was the photographer's idea to go on the beach 7 The girl is draping the train of her wedding gown over her arm to protect it from the sea water and sand 8 The breeze is lifting the bride's veil

16 Students' own answers

Unit 12

It all Ads up! Pages 74 - 79

1 1 C 2 E 3 A 4 G 5 D 6 B 7 H

2 1 freedom of the press 2 keeping up-to-date with the news 3 breaking news 4 presenter 5 bombarded with news 6 quiz programme 7 on the air 8 the headlines 9 Press coverage 10 switches channel 11 soap operas 12 weather forecast

3 1 British Broadcasting Corporation 2 Central Intelligence Agency 3 Cable News Network 4 Food and Agriculture Organisation 5 Master of Arts 6 Central Intelligence Agency 7 North Atlantic Treaty Organisation 8 United Nations Children's Fund 9 World health Organisation 10 World Wide Web

4 1 A, B 2 A, B 3 A, B 4 A, B 5 C 6 B 7 B 8 C

5 1 1 the people 2 The experts 3 the person or people 4 an organisation 5 Advertising really started to develop 6 the producer 7 This is the moment we've all been waiting for 8 the village 2 sentences 1, 2, 3, 4, 5, 6, 8 3 sentence 3 4 sentence 3

6 1 that / who 2 whose 3 which 4 who 5 that / which 6 that / which 7 when 8 which

7 1 on their own 2 even though 3 came up with 4 suggested going 5 prevent the children watching 6 take into account 7 We'd better switch over 8 ought to have done

8 It is a printing press which was invented by goldsmith Johann Gutenberg in Germany and dates back to 1439

9 1 papyrus 2 hoarding / billboard 3 handbill 4 printing press 5 prop 6 trust 7 target 8 billboard/hoarding 9 newspaper 10 advert

10 1 hoardings 2 emerged 3 seventeen 4 sponsors 5 flourish 6 successful 7 archive 8 ban 9 immoral 10 advice

11 a F b T c F d T e T f F

12 Students' own answers

13 Students' own answers

14 Students' own answers

15 Students' own answers

Unit 13

Break a Leg! Pages 80 - 85

1 1 C 2 B 3 A 4 B 5 B 6 D 7 A 8 C

2 1 audience - this is a group of people, all the others are individuals 2 cast - this is name for the group of actors in a play, all the others are reactions from the audience 3 box - this is a place to sit inside a theatre, concert hall, etc, all the others are venues for artistic events 4 review - this is something that a critic writes giving her opinions about a production, all the others are places inside a theatre, concert hall, etc. 5 choreographer - this is the person who plans and directs dance routines, all the others are to do with theatre productions 6 play - this is a theatre production, all the others are linked with musical productions 7 dress rehearsal - this is the final practice of a play, opera or ballet, before it opens to the public - all the others are artistic events 8 curtain - this is the large piece of fabric that is put across the stage to hide it from the audience - all the others are groups of people connected with artistic events

3 1 theatre 2 dress rehearsal 3 play 4 cast 5 opera 6 opera house 7 curtain 8 gallery 9 audience 10 booing 11 vocalist 12 standing ovation 13 ballet 14 review 15 choreographer 16 stalls

4 1 insist on 2 approve of 3 apologise for 4 believe in 5 fantastic at 6 terrified of 7 awful at 8 interested in 9 capable of 10 proud of 11 keen on 12 worried about

5 1 terrified of travelling 2 apologise for keeping 3 keen on / interested in (the idea of) trying 4 approve of (people) living 5 believe in saving up 6 proud of getting 7 awful at drawing 8 insisted on leaving 9 worried about / terrified of not passing 10 fantastic at playing 11 capable of having 12 interested in going

6 1 to play 2 working 3 to see 4 listening 5 not to see 6 to come 7 go out 8 to work 9 have 10 eat 11 to buy 12 going

7 1 correct 2 incorrect - tried so many times to take 3 incorrect - stopped work for ten minutes to have 4 correct 5 incorrect - stop making 6 incorrect - remember to turn off 7 correct

8 1 affectionately 2 prestigious 3 presenters 4 acceptance 5 achievement 6 nomination 7 performer 8 marketing 9 popularity 10 successful

9 Students' own answers

10 1 D 2 F 3 E 4 B 5 C

11 1 C 2 B 3 C 4 A 5 A

12 Students' own answers

13 Students' own answers

Unit 14

Get yourself an Education! Pages 86 - 91

1 1

2 1 C 2 H 3 D 4 E 5 F 6 G 7 A

3 1 grades 2 degree 3 lecture 4 lecturer 5 dropped out 6 failing 7 academic 8 state school 9 boarding school 10 scholarship 11 fees 12 academic 13 playing field 14 expelled

4 1 A / C 2 A / C 3 D / E 4 C 5 B 6 D 7 D 8 C

5 1 should / ought to 2 should / ought to 3 may / might
4 may / might 5 may / might / could 6 Should 7 should have
done 8 may / might / could 9 may / might 10 may / might /
could have

6 1 correct 2 I haven't been able to 3 correct 4 correct
5 I was finally able to get in touch 6 Will you be able to come
to dinner OR Can you come to dinner 7 correct 8 Being able
to speak

7 1 who takes care of 2 succeeded in passing 3 hadn't (not)
overslept, he would 4 In spite of going 5 haven't (not) studied
anything since 6 looking forward to finishing 7 think it's
worth paying 8 from Janice, nobody has

8 Students' own answers

9 a 4 b 6 c 7 d 5 e 1 f 2 g 3

10 1 dropped out 2 fit in 3 deter 4 outreach 5 tuition
6 foundation 7 entrants

11 a 4 b 5 c 6 d 1 e 2 f 3

12 1 fit / in 2 drop back 3 fit / into 4 dropping into
5 dropping off 6 fitted out 7 drop in on

13 1 B 2 A 3 A 4 C 5 B 6 A 7 B

14 1 To encourage students to apply to universities regardless of
their background or social status 2 No, they are autonomous
institutions 3 Yes, they are given a target or benchmark which
they have to adhere to 4 It is spent on recruiting and
supporting students from outreach schools 5 They are courses
provided to students whose grades do not meet university
entrance requirements which will enable them to gain access to
colleges 6 It has increased by over 12% 7 Changes have been
made to the application policy and applicants no longer have to
have a language at GCSE level 8 Yes, there has been a general
increase in the last decade

Unit 15

Sweet Dreams! Pages 92 – 97

1 1 A 2 F 3 G 4 D 5 H 6 C 7 B

2 1 B 2 A 3 A 4 B 5 C 6 B 7 C 8 A

3 1 a nightmare 2 be asleep 3 daydreaming about 4 in my
wildest dreams 5 sleepy 6 Dream on 7 did you get to sleep
8 a vivid dream

4 1 correct 2 Do your parents let you 3 correct 4 Please don't
make me 5 We need to 6 I'm not allowed 7 correct
8 correct

5 1 are not allowed to 2 make him do his 3 get her to come
4 Are we allowed to take 5 let her stay out 6 need to eat
7 didn't let him borrow 8 didn't make me 9 don't need to
have / you don't need (without 'to have' also possible)
10 Get her to come round

6 1 get / have (the house) painted 2 got / had (the boiler)
serviced 3 get / have (it) repaired 4 had (my car windows)
smashed 5 gets / has (paperwork) sent 6 got / had (his house)
broken into 7 get / have (my wedding dress) made 8 get /
have (it) cut 9 had (my handbag) stolen 10 get / have (it)
cleaned

7 It's not possible to use *get* with sentences 4 and 9 because, in
their use of the present perfect to talk about an unpleasant
event that wasn't arranged, using *get* would mean that the form
would be *I've / She's got*, etc., which would seem like *have got*
for possession

8 1 its 2 when 3 never 4 out 5 by 6 Rather 7 such
8 catch 9 off 10 out 11 that 12 worse

9 Students' own answers

10 1 trigger 2 issue 3 tummy 4 at stake 5 rumbling
6 cognitive 7 disorder

11 1 brain 2 conditions 3 sleep 4 hormones 5 nuisance
6 memory 7 sleepless 8 stimulants 9 triggers 10 seek

12 1 T 2 F 3 F 4 T 5 T 6 T 7 F 8 T 9 T

13 Students' own answers

14 Students' own answers

15 **Photo 1** The man is slumped on the end of the bench and not
the edge of the bench; The bags are beside him and not
underneath him; The bicycle is propped up against the bench
and not a wall; The ground looks wet and not dry; He is leaning
on a blanket and not a tent **Photo 2** It could be some sort of
outdoor gym not indoor gym; The people are lying on the mats
not standing; Some people are walking between the rows of
people on the ground and not over them; It might be close to
the sea and not far from the sea; It could be a 'lie-in' and not a
'sit-in'

16 Students' own answers

Unit 16

The Sounds of Music Pages 98 - 103

1 1 A 2 A 3 B 4 C 5 A 6 B 7 D 8 B 9 A 10 C 11 A
12 D 13 C 14 A 15 B

2 **strings** cello double-bass guitar harp viola violin **wind**
clarinet didgeridoo flute harmonica recorder saxaphone
trumpet **percussion** cymbals drums maracas xylophone
keyboards harpsichord organ piano synthesizer

3 a 5 b 1 c 10 d 13 e 14 f 2 g 4 h 9 i 12 j 7 k 8 l 3
m 11 n 6

4 1 A B C 2 B 3 A D 4 A C 5 C 6 A 7 B C 8 A C 9 D
10 B C

5 1 with - f 2 on - b 3 with - k 4 with - a 5 of - e 6 to - l
7 on - i 8 to - g 9 to - j 10 with - c 11 of - h 12 of - d

6 1 get rid of 2 take care of 3 put up with 4 got away with
5 has caught up with 6 cut down on 7 looking forward to
8 ran out of

7 1 I'd rather go / I'd rather we went 2 's / is in charge of 3 got
rid of 4 might not be working 5 didn't run out of 6 has been
given 7 came up with 8 should have carried on with

8 (Over, Down, Direction) 1 PRICY (1, 10, N) 2 SUIT (8, 4, NE)
3 SCRUFFY (13, 1, S) 4 RESORT (7, 15, NW) 5 POINTLESS (10,
11, N) 6 FORCEFUL (3, 13, NE) 7 DEBATE (10, 12, W)
8 FLATTERING (15, 10, NW) 9 AMATEUR (1, 1, SE) 10 NAG (7,
14, E) 11 TACTLESS (1, 4, E) 12 BEWARE (8, 7, SW)

9 1 forceful 2 tactless 3 suit 4 scruffy 5 flattering
6 nagging 7 pointless 8 amateurs 9 pricy 10 beware
11 debate 12 resorting

10 1 B 2 C 3 A 4 A 5 C 6 A 7 B 8 A

11 a 7 b 10 c 4 d 9 e 6 f 2 g 8 h 1 i 5 j 3

Unit 17

Big Spender! Pages 104 - 109

1 1 B 2 C 3 C 4 B 5 A 6 C 7 B 8 D

2 1 florist's 2 baker's / bakery 3 stationer's 4 butcher's
5 chemist's 6 greengrocer's 7 pet shop 8 antiques dealer
9 newsagent's 10 jeweller's 11 sweetshop 12 hardware store
13 fishmonger's 14 grocer's 15 tobacconist's

3 1 sales 2 selling off 3 cheap 4 reduced 5 bargain
6 expensive 7 quid 8 knocked off 9 value 10 bargain

4 a 4 b 8 c 9 d 1 e 10 f 13 g 6 h 5 i 2 j 14 k 7 l 11
m 3 n 12

5 1 don't get... I'm always 2 would you buy... won 3 snows...
won't be able to... We'll have to 4 were... I'd try 5 would you
do... never had to 6 usually get... eat 7 are not going / won't /
can't go... promise 8 don't start... won't have 9 I'll let... help
10 might / may / will come... invite 11 go... didn't live 12 will
we / are we going to manage... lose

6 1 B 2 C 3 C 4 D 5 B 6 B 7 A 8 D 9 B 10 D

7 Students' own answers

8 a 10 b 6 c 9 d 3 e 1 f 4 g 2 h 7 i 5 j 8

9 loan 4 owing 7 debt 8 reckless 10 outcome 6 repossess 9
recession 2 mortgage 4 weakness 1 default 5

10 1 default 2 mortgage 3 loan 4 debt 5 repossessed
6 owing 7 reckless 8 outcome 9 weaknesses 10 recession

11 1 A 2 C 3 B 4 A 5 C 6 B 7 A

12 1 According to the financial expert both the clients and the
banks are responsible for the credit crash 2 The cost of credit
has to be increased because consumer debt runs into millions of
pounds 3 Banks in America stopped lending to each other
because they feared being exposed to losses from mortgages
4 Anyone who has had problems with credit in the past will
have difficulty getting credit in Britain 5 A debt management
plan enables people to pay all their bills each month including
their creditors

13 Students' own answers

Unit 18

City Life Pages 110 - 115

1 1 C 2 A 3 D 4 B 5 E 6 A 7 F 8 B 9 F 10 C 11 D
12 A 13 E 14 B 15 F

2 1 2 2 8 3 5 4 7 5 3 6 4 7 1 8 6

3 1 building site 2 building materials 3 being built
4 construction / building 5 buildings 6 plot 7 're going to
build (a house) from scratch 8 architect 9 design
10 're going to build 11 design 12 Building / Construction

4 1 B 2 B 3 A 4 C 5 C 6 A 7 C 8 A

5 1 hadn't gone... would never have met 2 had thought...
wouldn't have chosen 3 had had... would have gone 4 would
you have done... had come 5 wouldn't have had to pay... hadn't
brought 6 had asked you to marry... would you have said
7 wouldn't have gone... had known 8 hadn't gone... wouldn't
have caught

6 1 hadn't broken down... wouldn't have got 2 hadn't got a
job... wouldn't have gone to live 3 get... can / will be able to
buy 4 spend... get 5 had remembered it was his wife's
birthday, would have got her 6 didn't have to look after...
would be able to work 7 snows... can / could go 8 hadn't
chosen... wouldn't have got

7 1 off 2 when 3 take 4 led 5 many 6 as 7 being 8 used
9 Next 10 From 11 like 12 sold

8 1 Stavanger is cited as the Petroleum Capital of Norway due to
its museum which reflects the fact that oil drilling activities first
started in the North Sea in 1966 2 Stavanger is also referred to
as the Herring Capital of Norway 3 Stavenger domkirke is
Norway's oldest cathedral which is almost unchanged since the
14th century 4 Tourists can enjoy the Stavanger International
Jazz Festival, MaiJazz, in May and the International Chamber
Music Festival in August.

9 a 3 b 5 c 1 d 6 e 4 f 2

10 1 D 2 A 3 F 4 B 5 E

11 Students' own answers

12 Students' own answers

13 1 up 2 mention 3 after 4 mind 5 Fancy 6 fitted
7 freezing 8 being 9 chance 10 raised 11 outskirts
12 anywhere

14 Students' own answers

Unit 19

Man and Nature Pages 116 - 121

1 1 B

2 1 F 2 B 3 G 4 D 5 A 6 H 7 C

3 **natural disasters** drought earthquake famine flood
hurricane tsunami typhoon volcanic eruption forest fire
geographical features coastline landscape **protecting the
environment / being green** eco-buildings precycling
recycling solar power **manmade environmental problems**
famine forest fire global warming pollution toxic waste
water contamination

4 1 water contamination 2 solar power 3 forest fires
4 coastline 5 earthquakes 6 pollution 7 global warming
8 precycling 9 toxic waste 10 famines 11 typhoons and
hurricanes (or the other way round) 12 drought

5 1 A B 2 B 3 A 4 B 5 C 6 B C 7 A

6 1 I'd rather go for a Chinese meal tonight than Italian
2 I'd rather phone him now 3 Would you rather go to see them
play on Friday or Saturday night? 4 They'd rather you arrived
on 31st 5 I'd rather you hadn't borrowed my car without asking
6 I'd rather you turned the music down

7 1 could have done... would have loved to (have) become
2 would listen / listened 3 wouldn't be / wasn't 4 'd / had
carried on... could / might have become 5 were... could do...
were... needed

8 1 ecological 2 destruction 3 poorest 4 shortages
5 renewable 6 solar 7 sustainable 8 drinking 9 Packaging
10 disposable

9 Students' own answers

10 **Across** 2 displace 5 earthquake 6 shallow 7 crust
9 boulder 12 basin **Down** 1 hazard 3 pile up 4 seismic
8 spread 10 landslide 11 rank

11 1 impulsive 2 tidal 3 warning 4 earthquakes 5 day 6 depth
7 wavelengths 8 2000 BC 9 record 10 technology

12 Students' own answers

13 Students' own answers

14 Students' own answers

15 1 hazard 2 submerged 3 immense 4 back 5 restoration
6 found 7 foot 8 harm 9 inactive 10 chances

16 Students' own answers

Unit 20

Myths and Legends the World over Pages 122 - 127

Reading

1 1 A 2 C 3 B 4 A 5 D 6 D 7 B 8 C 9 C 10 D 11 A
12 B 13 B 14 D 15 C

2 1 A / C 2 C 3 B 4 A 5 B 6 C 7 C

3 1 mythology 2 goddess 3 legendary 4 ancestry 5 ancestral
6 ancestors 7 mythical 8 mythological

4 **1** incorrect - She said to me (that) / She said (that) she was in her last year at school **2** correct **3** incorrect - They said they were lost and asked me which way they should go **4** correct **5** incorrect - The doctor told Thomas to take the antibiotics for seven days **6** incorrect - I said to him that we could meet at the café in the High Street **7** incorrect - Mrs Jones told them that the trip had been cancelled, due to bad weather **8** correct

5 **1** She suggested going to the cinema **2** She warned me (that) if I didn't do more work, I wouldn't pass my exams **3** Jane threatened to tell the teacher that Geoff had cheated in the exam if he didn't let her play football with him **4** Mrs Jenkins wondered why none of her students had come to class **5** Lucy explained to James how to work the DVD player **6** Liz told her son to go to his room

6 **1** Would you mind telling me what the salary will be? **2** Do you think you could tell me where I have to go? **3** I wondered whether you had time to help me with my homework? **4** Could you tell me what time it is, please? **5** Do you know what this is? **6** I was wondering whether you would cook the dinner tonight **7** Would you mind giving me a hand with the shopping? **8** I was wondering if you could explain how this works

7 **1** I asked what the salary would be **2** She asked where she had to go **3** They asked if I had time to help them with their homework **4** A man on the street asked me what the time was **5** She asked me what it was **6** He asked whether I would cook the dinner tonight/that night **7** My mother asked me to help her with the shopping **8** Jim asked me to explain how it worked

8 **1** B **2** A **3** B **4** D **5** C **6** B **7** C **8** A **9** B **10** D

9 Students' own answers

10 **1** number 13 - bad luck **2** horseshoe - good luck **3** wishbone - good luck **4** crossed cutlery - bad luck **5** fortune cookie - good luck **6** dandelion - good luck

11 (Over, Down, Direction) **1** REVERENCE (9,11 SE) **2** INDIGENOUS (11,1 NE) **3** DEITY (5,1 N) **4** SETTLE (1,6 W) **5** SEEK (4,5 NW) **6** PERSECUTION (1,1 NW) **7** RITES (6,2 N) **8** FOREBEAR (10,8 E) **9** WITCHCRAFT (10,1 NE) **10** ECLECTIC (12,8 E) **11** COVEN (5,6 W) **12** SOUL (9,10 SE)

12 **1** reverence **2** indigenous **3** deity **4** settled **5** seek **6** persecuted **7** rites **8** forebears **9** witchcraft **10** eclectic **11** covens **12** soul

13 **1** A **2** C **3** B **4** A **5** C **6** B **7** B

14 **1** Paganism draws upon the traditional religions of indigenous peoples **2** They get closer to deity by getting closer to nature **3** It should be made clearer that Paganism isn't evil or witchcraft **4** They came from areas surrounding the North Sea **5** They are named after the Heathen Gods **6** They believe in Gods and Goddesses and they perform their ceremonies standing in small circles **7** Shamanism focuses on an ecstatic trance state in which the soul is believed to leave the body and ascend to the sky or heavens or descend into the earth or underworld

15 Students' own answers

Writing Reference Pages 128 - 143

Informal letter

1 **1** Yes **2** Yes, informal – 'how about you' and contractions: 'I'm' 'it'd' 'you'd' **3** Hi Chris. All the best **4** Yes **5 a** I was wondering if you'd be interested in going **b** Get (a little bit) better **c** Which would suit you best? **d** Good value

Hi Chris,

Great to hear from you. I'm glad to hear your exams are almost over - mine too! I think we both deserve a fun holiday afterwards.

I saw this leaflet for a sports holiday and <u>I was wondering if you would be interested in going</u> with me. The Football holiday looked the most exciting to me. It'd be a wonderful opportunity to <u>get a little bit better</u>.

I think we both need it ;)

I'm not very interested in theatre and I think it would be difficult to understand in Spanish, so the cinema visit would be best. How about you?

Any of those dates are fine with me. <u>Which would suit you best</u>? And what do you think of the cost? It seems quite <u>good value</u> to me.

Write back soon and let me know what you think.

All the best,
Dani

2 Hi Brian,

Lovely to hear from you again and that you're on school holidays at the same time as me. I saw an advert for a skiing holiday recently, how about coming with me?

The company offers coaching to various levels, and I think you're probably the same level as me, a beginner, aren't you?

There are also different places to choose from. I was thinking Andorra would be a good choice as neither of us has been there. What do you think? I think a week would be long enough as I suppose we'd get bored of skiing if we stayed any longer. We could save some money by choosing the self-catering option. Can't wait to see you again soon and give my love to your mum and dad.

Love,

John

Article

1 **1** yes **2** asks questions **3** yes. It talks about washing machines. Also the 'man's greatest invention' relates to the content... women tended to do the washing **4** yes, in the final paragraph very clearly **5** Neutral to informal **6** leaves them with a question to consider **7** relates the topic to someone they know, in this case, their grandmother

2 **1** Int **2** End **3** Main **4** Main **5** End **6** Main **7** End

3 Has technology killed peace and quiet?

Have you ever stopped to consider the impact of technology on your everyday life? Have you ever thought how technology is making us slaves to our work?

Imagine this scene: a business person is in a café, they are analysing data on their laptops, at the same time they are using a palm pilot to check appointments, a client calls them on their mobile phone, and meanwhile they receive an email. It doesn't sound too unusual nowadays, does it? When do they take a break? The temptation to stay in contact with people using the technology available to us is sometimes hard to resist.

I know that when I take a break from studying and lie on the sofa, you can guarantee that's the moment a classmate will send me an sms asking a question about the next exam.

In my opinion we have to recognise that all these methods of communication have their usefulness, but they do need to be turned off occasionally, to give us time to ourselves. When was the last time you turned everything off and just had a rest?

Essay

1 **1** 3: outfits, clothing, fashion **2** save money / discourage students from judging others / promotes discipline **3** uniforms expensive / suppress freedom **4** in the last paragraph **5** no

2 The question of whether facial or body piercings should be allowed in schools has been a hot topic of debate recently. While many teenagers argue that it is a fashion and no different to earrings or cosmetics, teaching staff and parents believe they should not be allowed in schools.

Opponents of piercings hold the view they are potential health risks. Piercings could be dangerous during a P.E lesson, for example. Moreover, as the piercing of under-18's is illegal, schools should not approve of them by allowing them to be worn at school.

On the other hand, there are many who believe that the current fashion for piercings is just an extension of earrings, which have been allowed in schools for as long as anybody can remember, so banning facial piercings would be hypocritical. Also the art of piercing has been practiced for hundreds, if not thousands, of years.

In my personal opinion, piercings are just a fashion and soon nobody will be wearing them. Where there is a risk of injury, due to the nature of the piercing or the activity, students with piercings should be forced to remove them.

Letter of application

1 5 8 7 6 4 3 2 1

2 **1** say why you are writing **2** yes **3** formal - I was wondering if it would be possible / furthermore / no contractions **4** by phone (number included) **5** whenever they like **6** he has a good knowledge of English / local history. He likes meeting new people

3 Dear Ms Jones and Dear Miss Smith go with 'Yours sincerely', the others with 'Yours faithfully'

4 Dear Sir or Madam,

I am writing in response to your advertisement for retail assistants which appeared in Friday's edition of The English Times. I believe I would be an ideal candidate for this position as I was employed as a salesperson by SuperShoes between September 2005 and October 2008. In that time I gained a lot of experience of the retail industry and was often praised by the manager of the store for my professionalism and efficiency.

Regarding my level of English, I shall soon be sitting the First Certificate exam and am expecting to get an A or a B grade. The advertisement stated the position was part-time, which would be perfect for me if the working hours were on Saturday and Sunday, as

I have a full time school timetable.

I can attend an interview from 4pm onwards on any day of the week.

I look forward to hearing from you soon,

Yours faithfully,

Alex Fontana

Report

1 **1** introduction **2** suggestions **3** recommendations

2 **1** ✓ **2** ✗ **3** ✗ **4** ✓ **5** ✓ **6** ✗ **7** ✓ **8** ✗ **9** ✓

3

Introduction	Suggestions	Reccomendations
Reccomendations	Suggestions	Introduction
Reccomendations	Suggestions	Introduction

A number of suggestions were made:
- A cold buffet
- A 2 course meal of pasta followed by meat or fish
- A barbecue

Considering the results of the survey and bearing in mind the budget on offer for the party, I would recommend the cold buffet option. Many of the students were keen on this and it would be much easier and cheaper to provide. In the light of information from the catering staff, a two course meal is difficult to arrange for such a large number and would require everybody to be served at the same time, and does not seem a practical option. Also, at this time of year a barbecue is not very practical, as it could start raining at anytime. Therefore it seems that the cold buffet would be the most practical and popular choice.

Story

1 **1** a scrapbook **2** there were pictures of him in it **3** playing football **4** his grandfather's brother **5** his grandfather didn't speak to his brother **6** talking **7** speak to his grandfather **8** to resolve their argument

2 **Past Simple** john looked down / he turned the pages / he heard footsteps / john knew he should leave / he couldn't stop **Past Perfect Simple** he had gone to collect the ball / they had had a fight / had never spoken **Past Perfect Continuous** had been playing football **The Passive** a picture had been cut out

3 They had no choice, they had to do what the man told them. James looked at his trembling wife, Caroline, and tried to put on a brave face. They had been shopping in the new hypermarket which was twenty minutes drive from the city. Once the car had been loaded, they got in and fastened their seatbelts. Caroline had looked across at James, smiled at him and squeezed his hand. Her smile faded when she saw the man lying in the back seat, who yelled at them to start the car. 'Drive!' shouted the man. James with shaking hands put the key in the ignition and pulled out of the car park. As soon as they had reached the outskirts of the town, the man told them to stop the car. James and Caroline looked at each other wondering what was going to happen next when the man said 'Thanks' and got out of the car. They stared at each other in disbelief. They had no idea who the man was, but they both knew they had been very lucky and decided to drive to the nearest police station.

Review

1 The Shadow of the Wind

The Shadow of the Wind was written in 2001 by Carlos Ruiz Zafón.

It was a bestseller in Spain, and when it was translated into English it became a global blockbuster. It's hard to say exactly what kind of book it is, it is a thriller, mystery and romance. It tells the story of Daniel whose father takes him to a secret library and says he can choose any book. He chooses a book called "The Shadow of the Wind" and becomes fascinated by it.

Daniel tries to find other books by the same author but cannot. Later he is approached by a man called Laín Coubert, the name of the devil in Daniel's book. This man has been finding copies of the book for years and burning them. So the mystery begins. The book is full of drama and it is excellently written and above all the story is gripping. However, I found the ending slightly obvious.

I would highly recommend The Shadow of the Wind to anybody, it is a book with something for everybody. When I read it I could not put my copy down.

Set text

1

Joe Gargery	10	Mr. Pumblechook	4	Miss Haversham	5	Phillip Pirrip ("Pip)	1
Bentley Drummle	2	Estella	6	Herbert Pocket	7	Magwitch	8
Biddy	11	Mrs. Joe Gargery	3	Mrs. Jaggers	9	Compeyson	12

2 **1** he is the narrator and the main character **2** humble / working class / lower class / modest **3** meeting Miss Haversham and Estella **4** negative **5** because you see the story through his eyes

3 Student's own answers

4 Perhaps the most important storyline in Great Expectations is the relationship between Pip and Estella. Pip's affection for Estella is the motivation for many of his later actions.

Pip begins the novel as a kind, working class boy. What is more he is illiterate and destined for life as an apprentice blacksmith. On the other hand, Estella is brought up by the aristocratic Miss Haversham to be cruel and to break men's hearts. Pip's is the first heart she will break. Pip falls in love with Estella despite her cruel treatment.

However, at the end of the book we learn a few things about Estella which show she and Pip are more alike than we had thought. Estella is really the daughter of the convict Magwitch and so from the lowest section of society. Also Estella reveals that she always loved Pip and that her unkindness was just the result of her upbringing.

To sum up, although Pip and Estella appear to be from different worlds, their behaviour and character are reflections of their education and experience. Really, they are just two young people who fall in love with each other.

Practice Test Pages 144 - 172

Reading Part 1
1 A 2 D 3 C 4 C 5 D 6 C 7 A 8 B

Reading Part 2
9 D 10 H 11 A 12 F 13 B 14 G 15 C

Reading Part 3
16 B 17 C 18 C 19 A/C 20 A/C 21 A 22 D 23 A/B 24 A/B 25 D 26 B 27 A 28 A 29 C 30 A

Writing Part 1
Question 1 Email

Hi Lucy,

You must have been very pleased to be offered a summer job. It might be fun to work in a hotel for the summer season and you will have the chance to meet quite lot of people. You will be pretty busy but I doubt you will have to work from morning till late at night.

As for your Italian, I took a course at the language school in the city, close to the library and found it very helpful. Thanks for inviting me over. I'd love to come and stay for a while but it would have to be a couple of weeks at the end of July.

I'm sorry, but I can't lend to you my video camera as I have already promised to my sister for her holiday and I use it quite a lot myself.

Let me know how things go,

Emma

4 marks

All points covered. Good realization of task. Effectively organized with appropriate paragraphing and linking. A wide range of structures and vocabulary. Well developed language with occasional, non-distracting errors (e.g. 'quite lot of people', 'lend to', 'promised to my sister'). Register and format fully appropriate to the task.

Writing Part 2
Question 2 Story

As Jennifer fastened her seatbelt a feeling of dread came over her and she began to wonder why she had ever agreed to meet Mr Finch at all. She turned the key in the ignition, put the car in gear and moved out into the traffic.
"I must concentrate," she thought, but found difficult to do so. What if it went wrong, if she could not remember the details she had been given? What if he became angry, if she couldn't give answers to all the questions he would ask?
Sitting at the traffic lights, Jennifer drummed her fingers on the steering wheel waiting for the green light. At last she moved off and turned into a tree-lined road. Suddenly she saw him, Mr Finch, waiting for her. Mouth dry and heart thudding, she stopped the car. How could she face him? After all, she'd only started working at the Estate Agents last week and Mr Finch was the first client she had to show around property!

5 marks

Excellent realisation of task. All content points included. Clearly organised with appropriate paragraphing and suitable linking. A good range of structures and vocabulary. Generally accurate with one or two non-distracting errors. Register generally appropriate to the task.

Question 3 Article

I suppose the person which has influenced my life more than everyone else would have been my grandmother. As a child, I saw her as a funny and generous and kind person, someone with who I love to spend time. We passed many hours in front the fire or in her garden.
As I grew up and understood things better, I began to realize how much strong and brave was this old lady and probably had always been. Her patience and fortitude had helped her through many difficulty and tragedies and now that I am older, I realize that she shown me the importance of family life and the will to share what you have with others in difficult times. This had an effect on all the family and I hope
I live my life as she would like.

3 marks
Adequate realization of task. Quite well organized, with generally appropriate linking. Adequate range of structures and vocabulary. Generally accurate with some awkwardness of expression that does not impede communication. Register and format generally appropriate to the task.

Question 4 Review

I last went to the theatre a couple of months ago to see a drama set in the seventies.

The story involves a young man turning over uninvited at a party held in the country home of a wealthy young couple. After a while, the husband starts to suspect that the young man is a thief and that he is intent to steal the painting on the wall above the fireplace.

The cast was made up of well-known actors so the acting was of a high standard and the play was very well written. As the whole play was set in the living room I don't think the scenery would have been too much of a problem and it certainly looked very elegant and appropriate to a large country house.

4 marks
All points covered. Good realization of task. Effectively organized with appropriate paragraphing and linking. A wide range of structures and vocabulary. Well developed language with occasional, non-distracting errors. Register and format fully appropriate to the task.

Question 5a Set Text - Letter

Dear Sally,

I'm glad you're enjoying Great Expectations. My favourite character is Pip who seems like a bit of a dreamer at the beginning.

When he was first invited to visit Estella how hard did he tried to please her and her stepmother, Miss Haversham. He believed he was born for better things and probably saw this as a chance to change his life. Then he begins to fall in love for Estella and it was a blow when Miss Haversham told him he was no longer needed.

Then when he helped an escaped convict by stealing food, little did he realise that he would be rewarded by that same person, Magwitch, who turns out Estella's father.

In the end Pip proves his loyalty and bravery when he rescues Miss Havesham and also when he tries to help Magwitch to leave the country, so he wasn't such dreamer after all!

Is Pip your favourite character, too?

Take care,

James

5 marks
All points covered. Good realization of task. Effectively organized with appropriate paragraphing and linking. A wide range of structures and vocabulary. Well developed language with occasional, non-distracting errors. Register and format fully appropriate to the task.

Question 5b Set Text - Essay

The character I feel most sympathy for is Erik, the Phantom, because he has no choose but to let the woman, he loves, Christine a singer with the Paris Opera, free. One day, while working, Christine hears a voice from behind a wall which she believes to be the spirit of music her dying father had told her about but it is really Erik, who, hidden from view, teaches her to sing so beautifully that she becomes a successful.
Christine meets the man she had fallen in love with years ago and they both realise they love each other yet. Eric, is insanely jealous and tries to make her stay with him but in the end he is so moved by her love for Raol that he lets her go and saves Raol from drowning, a trap the Phantom himself had set for Raol.

4 marks
Good realisation of task. Ideas clearly organised with suitable linking. Good range of structures and vocabulary. Some awkwardness of expression. Generally accurate with non-distracting errors, some due to ambition. Register, on the whole, appropriate to the task.

Use of English Part 1
1 D   2 A   3 C   4 B   5 D   6 A   7 B   8 C   9 B   10 D   11 A   12 C

Use of English Part 2
13 whom   14 onto   15 through   16 being   17 viewers   18 their   19 down   20 of   21 how   22 enough   23 prizes   24 be

Use of English Part 3
25 phenomenal   26 legendary   27 Northern   28 spectacular   29 marked   30 symbolize   31 walking   32 earlier   33 congregation   34 awarded

Use of English Part 4
35 the last time   36 as far as we   37 am past caring   38 can't wait for   39 I wish I hadn't said   40 shouldn't have invested   41 is being collected   42 so it wouldn't

Listening Part 1

1 A 2 C 3 B 4 C 5 A 6 C 7 C 8 B

Listening Part 2

9 built 10 worship 11 inner 12 transported 13 glaciers
14 criss-cross 15 antler 16 racetrack 17 outer pits
18 bluestones

Listening Part 3

19 D 20 E 21 F 22 A 23 C

Listening Part 4

24 C 25 A 26 B 27 C 28 B 29 B 30 C

Speaking Part 1

Students' own answers

Speaking Part 2

Candidate A

The first picture shows a small girl and her obviously loyal companion, her dog, a golden retriever. They seem to be on some sort of veranda and it is a bright sunny day. The little girl and her dog are sitting on a white blanket – she is looking at a book and the dog appears to be very interested in what she is doing. The little girl is wearing a long-sleeved top with a short floral skirt, she has long hair held back with a striped band. On the blanket, there are some taps – what appears to be part of a dolls tea set, with a pink tea pot. There is also a basket holding some bright flowers. The dog is very handsome and he is wearing a collar. He sits very patiently watching his young friend to whom he is obviously devoted. Having a dog, or any other animal as a pet, teaches children to have consideration for them and take care of them and also shows them, in the case of a dog particularly, what a good friend a pet can be and how much fun can be had with them.

The second picture shows a group of children who all look very happy in each others' company. I think they are probably around ten to eleven years old. Three of them are on bicycles while one girl has a scooter and another girl is holding a skateboard. It is a sunny day and the children are lightly dressed. Two girls and one boy are in jeans while one boy has shorts and the third girl has cut off trousers. They are all wearing summer tops. One girl is wearing a brightly coloured checked sun top. One boy and one of the girls are very dark and in fact look as though they could be brother and sister. The other children have fair skins and one of the girls is blond. The children with the bikes and skateboard all have safety helmets – the cyclist have theirs hanging on their handlebars and the girl with the skateboard has hers hooked over her arm – no doubt all ready to put on their heads before they set off on another adventure. They seem to be on grass and there are lots of trees around them. Perhaps they all live in the same road and so have become friends or they may have become friends at school, as they all appear to be around the same age. They certainly seem to have some similar interests: being out on their bikes, skateboard and scooter, enjoying the sunshine and fresh air. Hopefully, they will remain friends as they grow older and will learn the importance of staying in touch even though they find new interests and make new friends.

Candidate B

The first picture shows a street artist sketching a portrait of a young woman. It seems to be quite a busy street; it might be a holiday town. There are several people watching the artist and standing where they can see the portrait he is working on. The artist is young and perhaps he has this hobby to make some extra money to enable him to study. The girl he is sketching is sitting very still and looking straight ahead. There is a large rucksack behind her but I think perhaps this belongs to the artist and is used to keep all his equipment in. The girl is wearing dark trousers or jeans, white sandals and a top. Her hair is long and dark and her skin is very pale. Perhaps she is going to give the portrait to her boyfriend or her parents as a present. The artist has long fair hair covered with a back to front baseball cap. He is also wearing jeans and a dark striped long-sleeved top. Behind him on the ground, is a corner of a portrait showing, so there are probably several more and the people watching him work are no doubt looking at these, too. Maybe the girl will one day remember having her portrait done and wonder where the young artist is and whether he became famous or perhaps just mildly successful.

The second picture shows two people – a girl and a young man tending to plants in a green house. They are surrounded by many brightly coloured plants both on the benches in front of them and trailing from baskets above them. It is a very large green house and seems far too large for the average garden – perhaps they go there at weekends and in the free time they have, in order to learn more about their hobby and at the same time perhaps earn some money. The girl is wearing gloves to protect her hands while she is handling the plants and soil. The young man is wearing a checked shirt but I cannot see his hands so I don't know if he is wearing gloves. If this green house belongs to them they are very lucky to be able to follow their hobby in such a way – they might have turned their interest into a business to support themselves – this way they would have the best of both worlds. The girl certainly looks very happy with what she is doing.

Speaking Part 3

Andy Has Steven decided yet what sort of career he wants yet?

Tom Well, not really. There are one or two things, but he hasn't really made up his mind.

Andy I went to the theatre the other evening and I wondered what it might be like to have a career involving the theatre. How about acting?

Tom But don't you need to have talent for that? I mean apart from the training you would get at drama school, you have to be talented and I don't think Steven would get very far on his talent!

Andy No, I don't think he would and although it always sounds very exciting and glamorous, it must be very demanding and leave you very little time for yourself.

Tom Yes, imagine working every night in the theatre or every weekend.

Andy Well, what about something to do with sport? Steven was always keen on sport when he was younger.

Tom Yes, but I don't think that he was ever good enough to consider a career although he was pretty good at running.

Andy Well those are two careers he won't be taking up!! Another friend of mine is a medical student. He is in his third year and absolutely loves it. He says it is very tiring and stressful because you can't help getting involved in other peoples' problems but at the same time he finds a lot of satisfaction in what he does and says it is extremely rewarding to think that you can be of so much help to a patient and be partly responsible for returning that person to good health and possibly even saving a life.

Tom That must be a great job but there's no way Steven could do it. He wouldn't be able to cope with people who are so ill, besides he's really rather squeamish!

Andy I think you have to be a particular sort of person to go into the medical profession. I think it is more 'a way of life' than a job.

Tom Yes, I agree. I think becoming a vet is also something that requires a great deal of dedication and it must involve so much study and learning – after all a doctor only has to study one animal, a vet has to study many – from a mouse to perhaps even an elephant!

Andy But what a great job for a true animal lover if you have the brains and the dedication.

Tom I know he's got the brains, but would he have the dedication? What about a career as a chef? I notice there are many cookery programmes on TV and so many celebrity chefs. Cooking for a living seems to have become very popular – but I suspect many chefs spend their lives hidden away in restaurants and hotel kitchens – they can't all be famous I guess.

Andy What other careers do you think could bring real satisfaction to someone?

Tom Well, how about an architect? Now, there's a job where you could really leave proof of your skill and artistic talent.

Andy That must be such a difficult job! Imagine being asked to design a building. You have to make it fit into its surroundings and not look like an oddity. And you have to make sure that it will stand the test of time!

Tom How about something just as artistic, but on a much smaller scale like pottery? Have you ever seen anyone, what's the expression, *throwing* a pot?

Andy Hmm. It would be quite an interesting thing to do and perhaps eventually you could start up your own pottery business.

Andy Why not? Well, we have been through a few possibilities and we still haven't come up with a job for Steven!

Tom I don't know. He might just follow in the footsteps of his grandfather.

Andy Oh really? What did he do?

Tom He was a landscape gardener. I think Steven would like to be a landscape gardener. He's always said it's like being an artist; starting with a blank canvas and them watching as the 'picture' takes shape.

Andy So, that's settled then. Steve, the artistic landscape gardener!

Speaking Part 4
Students' own answers

CD 1 Track 2

Unit 1 – Page 12 – Exercise 11

Announcer	Unit 1 Listening Part 2
	You will hear an interview with a man from a voluntary organisation about a competition to promote equality and human rights. For questions 1-9, complete the sentences.
Interviewer	I'm joined in the studio today by Simon Jefferies from Birmingham RAP, an independent voluntary organisation working to promote 'race' equality and human rights in collaboration with young people. Good morning, Simon.
Simon	Hi
Interviewer	Is it true that the ethnic communities in Birmingham are increasing so much so that by 2020 people from black and ethnic minority backgrounds will make-up over 50% of the population?
Simon	It certainly is.
Interviewer	And how are the city's young people reacting to this news? What kind of impact do they think this will have on their future?
Simon	Well, to find out exactly what young people had to say about living in a multicultural society, we decided to go out into schools and youth clubs across the city. We wanted to explore their experiences of inter-ethnic relationships and their attitudes towards people from different backgrounds.
Interviewer	And were you surprised by the results?
Simon	Yes. You see, the findings revealed that whilst, on the surface, young people appear to have positive opinions and relationships, when explored further, some young people expressed slightly different views.
Interviewer	Such as?
Simon	One girl complained that Asylum seekers get whatever they want, while people born in the UK have to go on endless waiting lists.
Interviewer	Hmm. I see her point.
Simon	Several others admitted that they had stopped going to some areas, because they were just too afraid. And one boy even talked about Birmingham being his territory and how he felt he had the right to defend himself against troublemakers if he had to!
Interviewer	That's rather worrying.
Simon	Isn't it!
Interviewer	So, after hearing these views, you decided to hold a competition which aims to improve relationships in the city.
Simon	That's right. We hope to get young people to explore their own ideas on how to encourage positive relationships between people from different backgrounds in a competition called *One Birmingham*.
Interviewer	And how precisely do you expect to do this?
Simon	Well, by inviting young people from secondary schools and youth groups across the city to explore their own ideas. They have to try and think of ways to bring people from different backgrounds together while offering the same opportunities to everyone.
Interviewer	And what do they have to do to enter this competition?
Simon	First and foremost, they have to be between fourteen and nineteen years of age. Then they need to form a group and develop and present their ideas using a medium of their choice.
Interviewer	What sort of medium? Can you provide some examples?
Simon	Well... erm... for example, artwork, photography, a newspaper article, or even a short film. They can be as creative as they like using whatever media they feel is most appropriate.
Interviewer	Can any school enter the competition?
Simon	No, the *One Birmingham* competition is only for secondary schools and youth organisations in Birmingham.
Interviewer	I see. And is there a deadline?
Simon	Yes. All entries must be submitted by 31st December.
Interviewer	So, that leaves a fair amount of time to get organised. And what about prizes?
Simon	The winning school or youth organisation will receive £500 to help implement their idea.
Interviewer	That's marvellous. Well. I'm afraid that's all we have time for today. Thank you for joining us and now...

Track 3

Unit 2 – Page 18 – Exercise 8

Announcer	Unit 2 Listening Part 3
	You'll hear five different people talking about food allergies and intolerance.
	For questions 1 to 5, choose from the list A–F the effects this has had on their lives. Use the letters only once. There is one extra letter which you do not need to use.
	Speaker 1
Woman	I have been allergic to peanuts for as long as I can remember; ever since I was a toddler. I can't even get near the dreaded things without my mouth and throat swelling up. As soon as I feel I'm having difficulty breathing, I grab the EPI-Pen I always keep in my handbag and give myself a jab of adrenalin. It works wonders and I'm fine in no time at all. I couldn't live without it! My friends and colleagues at work are all aware of the problem and they keep their peanut butter sandwiches well away from me!
Announcer	Speaker 2
Man	I woke up one morning and as I looked in the mirror I was horrified to see my face and neck covered in a rash. I called the doctor at once and he said it was most likely an allergic reaction to something I had eaten and he booked me in for a skin prick test that very morning. I went down to the surgery and a nurse did the test. She pressed a funny looking device against the skin of my forearm and then we waited and watched to see how my skin reacted. After about ten minutes the skin turned red and started itching like mad and the nurse told me I was allergic to shellfish.
Announcer	Speaker 3
Woman	I was forever complaining about feeling bloated and often had stomach ache. Our local GP advised me to consult a dietician who took a detailed look at the kind of foods I had been eating and advised me to keep a food and symptoms dairy. The idea was that

the diary would help track down and identify the foods I was particularly sensitive to. To be honest, I was a bit sceptical, but then when I went back a month later, he told me he suspected a lactose intolerance. Since then I've removed all foods containing lactose from my diet and my symptoms have vanished altogether.

Announcer Speaker 4

Man I'm allergic to soya and I do my best to avoid it but you never know where it might be lurking as it can crop up in some of the most unlikely foods. It took me quite a long time to get used to checking food labels. It isn't as easy as it might sound as some of the ingredients aren't that obvious.

I mean some food labels for instance list soya as texturised vegetable protein! You can't even play it safe and always buy the same products by the same manufacturer either as they often change their recipes. So you should never let your guard down or you might be in for a nasty surprise!

Announcer Speaker 5

Woman When I was a child I was particularly sensitive to the protein found in cow's milk. I wasn't allowed to eat bread, cereal, biscuits, cake, soup, and even some types of meat and fish I had to steer clear of. Luckily, as I got older, my intolerance improved. I was taken to the doctor on a regular basis and foods were gradually introduced back into my diet until I had grown out of it altogether. I'll never forget the sheer joy I got out of eating a huge piece of cake at my best friend's birthday party, just like all the other kids. But my biggest satisfaction was when I could finally drink a whole glass of milk!

Track 4

Unit 3 – Page 25 – Exercise 12

Announcer Unit 3 Listening Part 4

You'll hear an interview with the chairman of the Olympic Delivery Authority.

For questions 1 to 7, choose the best answer, A, B or C.

Interviewer The hub of the London 2012 Games will no doubt be the Olympic Park in east London, which will house the new sport venues. The Chairman of the Olympic Delivery Authority, is here in the studio today to tell us more about the Olympic Park.

John Hello. It's my pleasure to be here. Well... the Olympic Park will be designed in such a way that the main venues will be easily accessible through a network of footbridges and walkways.

Interviewer I've heard that up to 180,000 spectators a day will enter the Park to enjoy the Games.

John That's correct. A central unifying concourse will carry spectators and competitors over the roads, waterways and rail lines that cross the site. The Park will be designed to ensure visitors always feel part of the Games, whether they are watching the 100 metres final, strolling along the river edge or sitting in front of one of the big screens relaying live Games action throughout the Park.

Interviewer Is it true that a large part of East London, the size of the city of London, is being regenerated for the construction of the Olympic Park?

John Yes, it is. As well as creating world class sports venues it will renew utilities, infrastructure, transport links and homes that will serve future communities long after 2012.

Interviewer Really?

John Yes, after the Games the area will be transformed into the largest urban park created in Europe for more than 150 years.

Interviewer I see, and is construction already well on its way?

John Building work began in May 2008 with the start of construction of the eighty thousand seat Olympic Stadium which is in the south of the park. It is surrounded by water on three sides giving it the feel of an island.

Interviewer And what can you tell us about the Aquatics centre?

John That will include two 50 metre swimming pools as well as a diving pool. After the games the centre will provide the new community with elite swimming and diving facilities that London currently just doesn't have.

Interviewer That's wonderful. Have plans been made for shopping centres at all?

John Of course! Sitting right in the centre of the park is a major new shopping and leisure complex with Stratford International Station alongside. During the games, Olympic Javelin trains will arrive every ten minutes bringing thousands of spectators to the park each day.

Interviewer And what provision has been made for athletes?

John The Olympic Village built next to the Park and to the North of the International Station, will be home to thousands of athletes and officials, with easy access to training and competition venues. Eighty percent of athletes will be able to reach their venues from the Village in fewer than 20 minutes.

Interviewer Will the village provide other facilities besides accommodation?

John Yes, along with accommodation the Village will comprise shops, restaurants, medical, media and leisure facilities. It will also include an 'International Zone' where athletes can meet with friends and family.

Interviewer Is good progress being made on the site?

John Yes, new designs that show what the Olympic Village will look like after the Games, have just been unveiled. The designs show how the housing units may look, as well as courtyard areas, pedestrian walkways and the new open spaces that will be created in the Village. And more than 300 workers are now on the Olympic Village site putting in place its foundations.

Interviewer That's wonderful news! My passion has always been cycling. What can you tell us about that venue?

John A 6000 seat Velodrome and a BMX circuit will be located in the North of the park. This venue will provide lasting world class cycling facilities for the community including a new road cycling circuit and mountain bike course.

Interviewer Fantastic! Well, thanks very much for coming into the studio to talk to us today.

John My pleasure.

Interviewer Now, if you've got any questions or concerns about Construction of the Olympic Park call the Construction hotline on 08000 722...

Audio Transcripts

Track 5

Unit 4 – Page 30 – Exercise 10

Announcer Unit 4 Listening Part 2

You will hear an interview with a musician about the effects the Internet has had on local bands.

For questions 1 to 9, complete the sentences.

Interviewer We're joined once more in the studio today by musician, Steve Pritchard. Hi Steve, nice to have you back.

Steve Nice to be back, Tom.

Interviewer Over the last ten years, the way bands promote their music has undergone a huge change with the expansion of the internet. We're all aware of the consequences this has had on major labels, but what has it really meant for local music?

Steve The one thing that has really effected local music is the birth of the 'online community' since the launch of MySpace.com.

Interviewer But hasn't this 'online community' been around for several years now... you know, what with all the different websites there are nowadays?

Steve Yes, there were other similar sites where bands could upload their details and samples of their music as well as sites where anyone could post details about themselves, including profiles and blogs, with the idea of making friends. These websites have all had varying degrees of success, but none of them have been able to match the success of MySpace.com.

Interviewer So, what's their secret to success, then?

Steve Well, what distinguished MySpace from these other sites, is that it combined the two into one. It was first designed as a place for people to communicate with each other and make friends, and then it developed a music section which could be interlinked to the standard section through the use of 'friends'.

Interviewer Ah ha.

Steve This 'friends list' allows users to set up lists of contacts which include separate users and bands. This way the users can keep track of what their favourite bands are doing, whether they're major label groups or new up and coming bands recording in their garage.

Interviewer But it's not all fun and games, is it? I mean, MySpace does have its problems, doesn't it?

Steve I'm afraid it does. The site often suffers from server problems due to its intense traffic. Plus it's not always easy to sort the wheat from the chaff when browsing, due to the proliferation of unsigned bands.

Interviewer So, what are the advantages for unsigned bands?

Steve Well, to start with, they can build up a fan base through the site without the need for huge publicity budgets. They can even promote their own gigs.

Interviewer So, what it means is that through online communities, bands can promote themselves more easily without the need of a middleman?

Steve That's right! Besides that, is the potential for one on one contact with a band. This is, of course, easier to do in a place like here in Guernsey, where everything is concentrated in a very small area and usually involves people who already know one another. It allows the band to build up a rapport with its

audience who give instant feedback through their page, without having to wait for official publications to print their views.

Interviewer Doesn't the fact that you can see how many 'friends' a band has, help deduce the number of potential buyers of a new release?

Steve Yes, it does and it also makes it easier to work out how many people would be likely to attend the band's gig. The important novelty is that several major record labels have announced plans to start scouting bands online.

Interviewer Really?

Steve Yes, but let's not get too excited! It's unlikely that many bands will be chosen to sign major deals, but the great thing is that online communities offer unsigned bands the ability to promote themselves both within their local music scene as well as to a wider audience even on an international scale. This, together with the breakthrough of web based sales systems and home based music production software, now enables bands to write, record and distribute their own music to anyone willing to listen anywhere in the world.

Interviewer That's marvellous. Well. I'm afraid that's all we have time for today. Thank you for joining us and now...

Track 6

Unit 5 – Page 36 – Exercise 10

Announcer Unit 5 Listening Part 4

You'll hear five different people talking about books they recently bought.

For questions 1 to 5, choose from the list A–F, what each person said about their purchase. Use the letters only once. There is one extra letter which you do not need to use.

Speaker 1

Woman When I first started this book, I was not too sure of how much I would like it. But then as I left it and went to do some other things, I realized that I kept thinking about the story, and could not get it out of my head! It is a great little book that should be read by all mid to high school girls. It is so real to life and it does match up to every type of girl. You can see yourself and remember your own history within each individual girl. I was really disappointed when I got to the end, as I could've carried on reading it forever. Anyway, I've had a glance at the preview of its sequel and I've told James down at the bookshop to put me a copy aside as soon as it comes in. That's bound to be just as good!

Announcer Speaker 2

Woman I bought this book for my 14 year old son who began reading it as soon as I handed it to him. 'Hmm,' I thought, 'this is a good sign.' While I was cooking dinner that evening, I listened to lots of laughter and comments like, 'Wow, this is great!' and, 'Hey! You've just got to hear this!' ... followed by several snippets he just HAD to read aloud to me. The next morning I asked him if he was enjoying the book and to my amazement he told me he'd finished it. So, if you are looking for a good, captivating read for your kid, don't pass up this book. It is a must-have!

Announcer Speaker 3

Man This book was a huge disappointment. One of my biggest complaints about it, is the characterization. Let's start with the narrator, Bella Swann. I mean her name! It basically translates into 'Beautiful Swan'! What kind of name is that for a teenage protagonist? Then there's the fact that we're obviously supposed to believe that she lives her life by putting others ahead of her, but if you look at the Bella of the novel and her disdain for her fellow classmates, it just doesn't ring true. And Edward! The most boring character in existence. He doesn't have one interesting, charming, or funny thing to say. And the themes! If there was ever a book that deserved an award for Worst Messages of All Time to Send to your Teenage Audience, then this is the one.

Announcer Speaker 4

Man I was eager to read the third book in this series after having read the first two. It is an enjoyable read, and a worthy third installment to the series. I thought that Eragon was a very good story, Eldest not quite as good, but Brisingr the best of the three. I got caught up in the story right away. It is the tale of a hero's journey, complete with absence, devastation and return. It is one of the oldest tales there is. We already know the story, but it is the storytelling that makes it good or bad. It's one of those books that's hard to put down. I'm glad my son recommended it to me.

Announcer Speaker 5

Man After seeing this book was second on the New York Times bestseller's list, I just had to read it. The book starts extremely well with a modern and interesting narrative. The flashback scenes are done extremely well and in no time at all the reader is lost within its pages. About half way into the book, the characters become well defined and start to take on more complex roles. Unfortunately that is where the development stops. The second half of the book is a tedious uneventful read. In an attempt to create a dramatic ending, the author has made the characters one dimensional and the storyline drearily predictable. It's certainly not second on my bestseller's list!

Track 7

Unit 6 – Page 43 – Exercise 9

Announcer Unit 6 Listening Part 4

You'll hear an interview with a man who has an extremely unusual job.

For questions 1 to 7, choose the best answer, A, B or C.

Interviewer Our guest today is a man who makes his living being fired out of a cannon. Please welcome to the studio, human cannonball, David Zebor.

David Hello.

Interviewer So, how often do you get fired out of the cannon, then David?

David Twice a day, actually.

Interviewer So, once isn't enough! You have to go through it twice!

David Absolutely!

Interviewer But you do have a safety net, don't you?

David Oh, yes. I wouldn't do it without. I might be looking down at the audience shouting and cheering, but my mind's firmly set on the safety net as I fly through the air at sixty miles an hour!

Interviewer How do you feel beforehand?

David I always feel nervous. I have to concentrate. Everything has to be 110% perfect. If I get the timings wrong, it's not just my job at risk.

Interviewer Was the circus life always a career option?

David Yes. My father and mother were part of a big top acrobatic act based in Eastern Europe - that's how they met, actually. Then they moved to the UK and I was born soon after. I grew up around the performers and started training with the trapeze and high wire when I was eight.

Interviewer So, moving on to the job of human cannonball was therefore an obvious next step.

David That's right.

Interviewer And what do you do in your act?

David Well, I start my act by standing on top of the cannon. Then
I clamber inside the barrel of the cannon and stand on a platform three quarters of the way down. Air is then pumped at high pressure into the space left beneath my feet and, after final checks to make sure I'm ready, my flight begins.

Interviewer What does it feel like?

David I feel free when I'm flying. It's a nice feeling. It's a bit like bungee jumping. Then two seconds later, it's time to land in the net. Job done.

Interviewer You make it sound so easy, but I bet it requires more talent that most people might realise. And the sudden acceleration must put an awful lot of strain on the body.

David It does. You have to fly straight, keep your body rigid and turn at exactly the right moment so that you land on your back.
I also have to make sure I'm not fired headlong into the canopy or the acrobat's wires! That's would be a disaster!

Interviewer I suppose the cannon's position and angle has to be calculated every time the circus moves.

David Ah ha. And a dummy model of me is test fired several times to check everything is okay before I climb inside the cannon.

Interviewer What should anyone tempted to explore a career in human cannonballing find out more about?

David Well, for one thing, the pay isn't great. This is a job done for the enjoyment, not for the money and you have to live on site.

Interviewer I see.

David And while your act may last just a couple of minutes, the circus requires your presence throughout the show as part of the troupe.

Interviewer Do you have to keep your eye on your weight a lot?

David Yep! I spend a couple of hours in the gym every day. I have to keep the strength in my knees and back up.

Interviewer What about being propelled at such high speeds? Did you have to do any special training for that?

David Yes, I went to the Guyana space centre in French Guyana where I completed a course to help prepare my body.

Audio Transcripts

Interviewer	Goodness me! Well, thanks for coming out of the cannon to talk to us today and have a good flight tonight!
David	Thanks. I will!

Track 8

Unit 7 – Page 48 – Exercise 7

Announcer	Unit 7 Listening Part 2 You will hear an interview about the man who invented the cash machine, John Shepherd-Barron. For questions 1 to 9, complete the sentences.
Interviewer	Welcome back to *Inventors and their Inventions*. Have you ever wondered, while queuing up at the cash dispenser, who invented these wonderful machines? Well, to tell us today, is security expert, Tom Bridges.
Tom	Hi. Well, the man to invent the very first cash machine was a Mr John Shepherd-Barron.
Interviewer	Is that so? This invention dates back to 1967, doesn't it?
Tom	That's right. It was installed in a branch of Barclays, in Enfield, north London, 40 years ago this week, actually.
Interviewer	Really? Do you know who the first person to withdraw cash was?
Tom	As a matter of fact I do! It was an actor from a television series that was being broadcast around that time. But I can't for the life of me remember his name!
Interviewer	That's alright. How did Mr Shepherd-Barron come up with this idea?
Tom	Well, you'll never believe me, but actually he was lying in the bath at the time. It struck him that there had to be a way he could get hold of his own money, anywhere in the world or anywhere in the UK, at any time of the day or night. That's when he hit upon the idea of a chocolate bar dispenser and he thought... rather than dispensing chocolate... it could dispense cash!
Interviewer	How extraordinary! So, once he'd come up with the idea, what did he do?
Tom	He went to talk to the chief executive at Barclays bank who thought it was a fantastic idea. He was so convinced that he signed the contract, that had been drawn up, there and then.
Interviewer	And how did the machine first work? I mean plastic cards didn't exist then, did they?
Tom	No, they still hadn't been invented. The machine used cheques that were soaked in carbon 14.
Interviewer	Carbon 14? Isn't that a radioactive substance? I mean, wasn't it a bit dangerous?
Tom	No, not as it might seem. There were no health risks for the users whatsoever. I know for a fact, that Mr Shepherd-Barron actually sat down and worked out that you would have to eat 136,000 cheques for it to have any effect on you.
Interviewer	Goodness me!
Tom	Yes. The machine detected the carbon 14 and then matched the cheque against a Pin number.
Interviewer	How much could you withdraw from the dispenser, then?
Tom	When it first came out, the machine would only pay out a maximum of £10 at a time.

Interviewer	£10! Is that all?
Tom	That was regarded as more than enough for a wild weekend in those days!
Interviewer	Yeah, I suppose so. There were a few hiccups along the way, weren't there?
Tom	Yes, there were a few teething problems. The first machines were vandalised, and one that was installed in Zurich, in Switzerland, began to malfunction mysteriously. It was later discovered that the wires from two intersecting tramlines nearby, were sparking and interfering with the mechanism.
Interviewer	One by-product of inventing the first cash machine was the concept of the Pin number. Mr Shepherd-Barron came up with that idea, as well, didn't he?
Tom	Yes, that came about when he realised he could remember his six-figure army number!
Interviewer	Six figures? But the Pin number is only made up of four.
Tom	I know, well, that was thanks to his wife. When he asked her what she thought of using a six-figure number, she said she could only remember four figures, and that's how four figures became the world standard.
Interviewer	I see! It's a shame but customers using the cash machine at Barclays in Enfield High Street don't seem to be aware of its historical significance, do they?
Tom	I know. A small plaque was placed there on its 25th anniversary, but few people ever notice it.
Interviewer	According to statistics, there are more than 1.6 million cash machines worldwide. Do you think this number will increase?
Tom	I'm not sure. I think its use will certainly be very different in the future. We'll probably stop using cash altogether within the next few years.
Interviewer	Really? Do you think so?
Tom	Well, money costs money to transport. I wouldn't be surprised if we soon start swiping our mobile phones at the till!
Interviewer	You never know! Well it's been fascinating having...

Track 9

Unit 8 – Page 54 – Exercise 10

Announcer	Unit 8 Listening Part 1 You'll hear people talking in eight different situations. For questions 1-8, choose the best answer, A B, or C. One. You hear a young man talking. Why did he decide to take part in the campaign? A He wanted to make some money working on the stalls. B He wanted an opportunity to fight discrimination. C He lives in an intolerant community.
Man	I have always felt very strongly about racial discrimination and when I heard about this campaign I just jumped at the chance. We live in a multicultural society with different ethnic backgrounds which has enriched our community. People should learn to be

more tolerant and understanding towards other cultures and less prejudice. I'm sure that if people were prepared to compromise there would be much less conflict.

I will be manning one of the stands along with a couple of friends. We'll have on show all the different everyday things that have been influenced by the cultures that make up Britain such as food and clothes, not to mention music.

Announcer Two.

You hear part of a lecture about the chilli pepper.

What is the lecturer describing?

A How the chilli pepper reduces inflammation in arthritis.
B The benefits you can get from eating chilli peppers.
C How to prepare tasty dishes with chilli peppers.

Man Surprising as it may sound, the chilli plant can protect us from common winter ailments. If you can tolerate the 'hotness' of the chilli that is. Chilli peppers contain a substance called capsaicin, which gives peppers their characteristic spicy taste. The hotter the chilli pepper, the more capsaicin it contains. Red chillies are very high in Vitamin C and pro Vitamin A. Eating chillies is known to help in alleviating pain in arthritis as it helps to reduce the inflammation. Caution must to be taken while cutting chillies, so as not to get them on the skin and in the eyes. Some chilli lovers now opt for gloves and swimming goggles when they attack and chop chillies!

Announcer Three.

You hear a woman talking about training for the Olympics.

How does she feel?

A She regrets taking part.
B She thinks all the hard work was worthwhile.
C She wishes she'd done better.

Woman It was like nothing I'd ever done before. I spent every living, breathing moment with my trainer. He never let me out of his sight. We'd start training at dawn and wouldn't stop till dusk. Getting a good night's sleep was essential and I was kept on a strict diet the whole time. There were good days and bad days. On several occasions I was really tempted to throw in the towel and sometimes I thought I'd never get through. But I did and although I didn't win a gold medal, I've still got this silver one to show for it! And I couldn't be prouder.

Announcer Four.

You hear a doctor being interviewed on the radio.

What is he concerned about?

A the decibels some mp3 players are unable to reach.
B the noise safety levels imposed upon users.
C the increasing number of people listening to dangerously loud music.

Interviewer What risks do people subject themselves to by listening to loud music through headphones?

Doctor Well... first and foremost, the surge in sales of iPods and other portable music players could mean many more people will develop hearing loss. If the volume through headphones is too high, there is a real risk of permanent damage to hearing. 80 decibels is the level at which hearing is threatened but some MP3 players can reach 105 decibels.

Interviewer EU iPods have a sound limiter to comply with noise safety levels, don't they?

Doctor Yes, however sometimes users hack through this in order to listen to it louder, especially when attempting to drown out unpleasant noise from traffic and on the Tube. The first sign of danger is a ringing or buzzing noise in the ears to warn you that the sound was loud enough to damage your ears, if exposure became frequent.

Announcer Five.

You hear a woman talking about the famous writer, Beatrix Potter.

What difficulties does she mention?

A Publishers were unwilling to accept her work.
B She was unable to replace the black and white sketches.
C She couldn't publish the letter without Noel Moore's consent.

Woman The story of the naughty Peter Rabbit and his adventure in Mr McGregor's garden, was the first of Beatrix Potter's books to be published, in 1902, by Frederick Warne. The book was an expansion of the original letter to Noel Moore, with black and white drawings and was refused by several publishers. Finally, Beatrix had the book printed herself, and gave it to her family and friends. Frederick Warne saw the book and agreed to publish it if Beatrix would replace the black and white images with colour sketches. This was to be the birth of a legend.

Announcer Six.

You hear a man talking on the radio.

What is he?

A a restaurant manager
B a chef
C a waiter

Man My hands are always spotlessly clean and I always do my best to keep my uniform spic and span – wine stains are the worst to get rid of. Most days are really busy and I certainly don't have time to stand over the cooker contemplating the dishes as if they were a work of art like somebody I could mention! Not me! No! I go whizzing through those swing doors as if my life depends on it! I'm terrified that one day I'll trip and end up spilling the food into the lap of some poor unsuspecting customer! The manager would have no greater delight than giving me the sack if I did!

Announcer Seven.

You hear a man talking about an exhibition he recently went to.

Which invention appealed to him the most?

A the glasses
B the bell
C the burglar alarm

Man	This weekend the British Library opened an exhibition of weird and wonderful inventions. Some of them were testaments to mechanical ingenuity while others were not. One of the most ingenious, I thought, was a pair of night-time reading glasses with lights fitted on the rims which were designed in America in the 1930s. A good idea except for the inconvenience of the battery you had to carry around with you. But the one I was most taken with, was a wind-up burglar alarm which dates from the 1890s. The mechanism was wound up, a lever above the bell raised and the device put at the foot of a closed door. If anyone tried to come in, the upright lever would be pushed down and set off the bell.
Announcer	Eight.
Announcer	You hear a woman talking about a holiday experience.
	Why did she miss her flight?
	A She forgot to pick up her tickets.
	B Her alarm didn't go off.
	C She didn't get a good night's sleep.
Woman	I hadn't been on holiday for ages and I was really looking forward to it. I planned everything down to the last detail, getting visas and vaccinations, making sure I didn't forget tickets and traveller's cheques. I even wrote out a 'things to remember when you pack' list. You name it, I did it. The night before I was due to leave, I set the alarm for 5am and drifted off soundly to sleep. I woke up the next morning and glanced at the clock. It was half past five! The alarm hadn't gone off! I jumped out of bed and the next thing I knew, I was speeding down the motorway to the airport. I parked the car and ran to the check-in desk but I was too late. The plane had gone without me!

Track 10

Unit 9 – Page 61 – Exercise 11

Announcer	Unit 9 Listening Part 4
	You'll hear Dr Robert Townsend, an animal psychologist talking about working with animals and their owners. For questions 1–7, choose the best answer, A, B or C.
Dr Townsend	When I come face to face with a growling dog, decidedly intent on sinking his teeth into my arm or leg, I wouldn't say I see danger, I'd be more inclined to say I see a challenge. You might wonder what led me to opt for such an unlikely career and why I've stuck to it for over thirty years. Well, I get a great deal of satisfaction out of making people happy and by dealing with cases like the one I just mentioned, I believe I am helping people get rid of their anxieties. I founded the Animal Behaviour Centre over twenty-six years ago and as the name suggests we specialise in the treatment of behaviour problems in pets. In the past I have worked with birds, horses, elephants and even bears but here the emphasis is on treating dogs.

I have also written a number of books and I am the proud inventor of several devices which assist pet owners, such as a special harness for dogs.

I lead a very busy life with an extremely tight schedule. Let's take yesterday, for example. The first task of the day involved giving an inventor some feedback and advice on a prototype feeding bowl she has just developed and wanted me to try out. She travelled all the way from Londonderry, in Northern Ireland for the consultation and when she was leaving she thanked me and said it had been very useful and that I had inspired her to make some crucial changes. I was pleased to be of help.

Then I saw Max, a one year-old border collie who had been brought in by his worried owners concerned that his unruly behaviour was starting to border on dangerous. Amid constant barking, I questioned Max's owners to find out about his background and then came to the conclusion that Max was simply misunderstood and in need of firm guidance.

To confirm my assessment I then put a special harness on the dog and I took him outside for a walk. I introduced him to various stimuli along the way - from cows and chickens on the farm to other dogs - in an attempt to get a profile of the dog's psyche. After the walk I returned to my office where I observed the dog's reactions to orders and then I gave Max's owners a debriefing session with suggestions on how to control their dog's unruly behaviour.

After seeing Max, I saw two more dogs and then I had to rush over to Wentworth, a town nearby, to visit a distraught client whose German shepherd wouldn't stop chasing its own tail!

For those of you who may be interested in pursuing a career in animal psychology, I suggest you get a veterinary degree or a degree that touches on physiology and psychology. I got a Bachelor of Science in Zoology and Psychology and then a PhD some years afterwards. It's hard to say how much I earn each year, but I charge £200 for consultations and £80 per hour for court appearances involving pets. You'd be surprised at the number of people who are taken to court because their dog bit someone and it's not always the postman!

This job requires compassion, heaps of energy, a logical mind and you also need to know how to carry out tasks which involve a certain amount of counselling.

Some people are simply adored by animals - they give off a certain magnetism which the animals just can't resist. You either possess it or you don't. It isn't vital, but it does make the job a lot easier.

It's a privilege to work with animals and their owners. I must say I'm very fortunate to have a job like this. It takes so little to make a dog happy.

Track 11

Unit 10 – Page 66 – Exercise 11

Announcer   Unit 10 Listening Part 3

You'll hear five different people talking about fashion. For questions 1 to 5, choose from the list A–F what each person thinks about the clothes they wear. Use the letters only once. There is one extra letter which you do not need to use.

Announcer   Speaker One

Woman   I like to follow the fashion trends and so do most of my friends even if we can't afford the brand names! It means we always have something to talk about and it's fun when several of us go clothes shopping together at weekends. At the moment where we live lots of people are wearing ankle boots and patterned tights. We also like to wear trendy little cardigans rather than school blazers. Where jewellery is concerned we like to wear several earrings in each ear. When

I talk to my friend who lives in Leads she tells me everyone is walking around in jungle trousers with string vests, girls actually go around sucking dummies. I think I prefer the fashions in my town!

Announcer   Speaker Two.

Man   I am eighteen years old and I live in Lichfield. When it comes to fashion, I am a follower of the skate look. I suppose it's a bit like wearing a uniform: baggy jeans, a metal belt and a very special make of trainers - no other label will do. I also have a tattoo, which I don't think my mum was very pleased about. Some people ask me why I feel I have to dress a certain way but I wear this type of outfit because I feel comfortable in these clothes and I think it reflects my personality. You may think I look scruffy but I don't! Anyway it takes a long time in the morning to achieve this look!

Announcer   Speaker Three.

Man   I am a man of forty-two and fairly fashionable or at least I like to think so. While working I have to be smartly dressed in a conventional business suit and tie, but I don't think this means

I have to look dull. I always make sure that my shirts and ties complement each other and are in colours that don't make me look like a bank manager! For evenings and weekends, I prefer more casual clothes: well cut jeans or cords and either a sweatshirt or T-shirt. I only ever wear a tracksuit when I go the gym, because I think they look scruffy.

Announcer   Speaker Four

Woman   I think it is important to adapt to fashion changes in order to remain fresh and youthful. This doesn't mean following extreme trends but just updating the style and colours of your wardrobe from time to time. I wear a uniform in my job so it is nice at weekends to choose my outfits.

I like to wear feminine clothes so I have several evening dresses which I wear to formal functions. I choose soft materials and simple styles which can be dressed up if I wish. I wear casual clothes with my family such as trousers and sweaters and I'm also keen on long skirts and gypsy type blouses.

Announcer   Speaker Five

Woman   I think as you get older it is important not to get stuck in a fashion rut. What looked good twenty years ago just looks dated today. I like trouser suits as well as skirts which I usually wear with smarter shoes.

I choose bright colours now in preference to darker shades which are no longer flattering and I have adapted my make up accordingly. I think accessories are very important – scarves, handbags, jewellery can make or break an outfit. I like a fairly large handbag to accommodate what

I need to carry but not the size of a suitcase and I like my shoes to tone with rather than match my bag.

Track 12

Unit 11 – Page 72 – Exercise 11

Announcer   Unit 11 Listening Part 2

You will hear a woman talking about personality types. For questions 1 to 9, complete the sentences.

Woman   We all have different ideas and tastes, for instance, in the way we dress. A young woman might choose to wear a plain dark suit with simple jewellery, while someone of a similar age might dress in bright gaudy colours and have a trendy hair style and outrageous make up. This shows that we have very different ideas about what looks good and that our personality affects our dress sense.

There are many personality types formed by various characteristics in each individual and though some people may display similar traits, their personality will never be exactly like anybody else's.

Although some psychologists believe that there are various personality types, they are of the opinion that different people with the same personality type do not always behave the same way, in fact, they can react quite differently to a situation.

If you want to discover your personality type you can try an online survey or you might want to answer a questionnaire based on the theory of psychological type by the famous psychologist Charles D. Faith. Our personality type is something we are born with. We are given personality traits and characteristics that we are more comfortable and at ease with than others. Some people have quite similar personality types while some others are complete opposites. Take, for instance, the extrovert and the introvert. The extrovert wants to be the centre of attention, taking part in everything, being introduced to many people, maybe even willing to take risks in the things he or she does, as long as there's always something going on he or she will always be happy. The introvert, on the other hand, is quite happy living a quiet life and is not afraid of spending time alone, enjoying his own thoughts and feelings and looking back on pleasant experiences, such as an enjoyable holiday or times spent with family or perhaps a close friend.

Experts in the field of psychology declare that we develop our personality according to our way of life.

For instance our surroundings while we are growing up, our family and school life and eventually our working life. We tend to rely on the personality traits that come more naturally to us but, as we mature, we realise we have to adapt our behaviour to the situations and the people we share our lives with or spend time with. Someone who is rather shy or quiet at some time may have to try and become more confident and therefore better able to cope with different situations and people. A person who is an extrovert and loud, might need to learn how to remain calm when the situation calls for it. This shows that our personality changes and develops over the years.

As some people get older they appear to change in their behaviour and outlook. They may no longer be as concerned with things that worried them when they were younger, perhaps they have learned to relax more. Some people appear to change quite drastically – others not at all.

Perhaps we could try to modify our personality by changing it for the better, if we know how to develop the traits which make us a nicer or more likeable person. For instance, those of us that are always over anxious about things, ready for an appointment an hour too soon, checking and double checking everything, perfectionists in every aspect of our lives, perhaps we could try to relax a bit more and not fuss about every single thing.

Then, there are those people who just couldn't careless about anything: always late, untidy, never do anything until the very last moment, totally selfish - although they would probably say they're just 'laid back' and relaxed. That person would do well to cultivate some of the traits of the anxious, over-organised type and would probably find that life would become easier and definitely less frustrating for family and friends.

If you're intent on trying to change your personality remember that these changes take time, effort and a lot of determination.

Track 13

Unit 12 – Page 78 – Exercise 10

Announcer   Unit 12 Listening Part 2

You will hear an interview with Michael Harris, a representative of the Advertising Society. For questions 1 to 9, complete the sentences.

Interviewer   Advertising affects all of us, surrounded as we are by newspapers, television and radio, not to mention the posters we see on buildings, buses and lorries, when we're out and about. I asked Michael Harris, a representative of the Advertising Society, how long advertising has been around.

Michael Harris   Hello. Well, advertising, actually, goes as far back as Egyptian times, when... erm... when... papyrus was used for advert hoardings, but I suppose advertising really started to develop when handbills, were used in the fifteenth and sixteenth century... erm... after the invention of the printing press.

Interviewer   Fascinating. And what about the advertising we see on television? When did that first evolve?

Michael Harris   Around about the fifties. In fact, the very first one to emerge was in 1955, erm...for toothpaste, if I'm not mistaken...

Interviewer   You don't say! And when were adverts first used in newspapers?

Michael Harris   Well, in England it was during the seventeenth century. Yes, that's when adverts first started to appear in newspapers and...

Interviewer   I see and when did it become the big business it is today?

Michael Harris   Well, it must have been around about the fifties, when sponsors were offered the chance to buy advertisement time.

Interviewer   But it really flourished in the sixties, didn't it?

Michael Harris   That's right. In fact in the sixties, advertising took on a more creative and scientific approach which had two advantages: it kept the viewer entertained while also explaining the mechanics, formula, make up or purpose of the product being advertised.

Interviewer   Can you tell us what it takes to make an advert a success, a true winner?

Michael Harris   Well...I can try. It has to be pleasing to the eye, amusing, straightforward and short and to the point. Personally,
I can find nothing more irritating than a noisy advertisement with actors speaking so fast, you can't even understand what is being advertised. In successful adverts, you'll find that quite a lot of emphasis is placed on the comical aspect, particularly when using small children or animals.

Interviewer   I see. What happens to the films of advertisements when they are no longer broadcast? You know, like the most popular ones in which actors are remembered for many years as 'the coffee girl' or such like.

Michael Harris   Ah yes. I remember the 'coffee girl'. There is, actually, a very large archive of advertising material in the History of Advertising Trust tucked away in the middle of Norfolk, in Raveningham. Adverts from newspapers and billboards, as well as television, are kept there. You can even find several props belonging to some of the most famous ads.

Interviewer   Really? On a sore note, the advertising world is often criticised for the way it targets children, encouraging them to eat junk foods rather than promoting healthier products or constantly drawing their attention to expensive toys or computer games and so on which some parents can't possibly afford. Is this a fair criticism?

Michael Harris   A fair criticism? That's hard to say. There are rules surrounding food and soft drink advertising to children erm... products high in fat, sugar and salt have been banned from being advertised during children's programmes. Then... erm... as far as toys is concerned, I am of the opinion that it's up to the parents, you know, to decide what they can and can't afford and what toy or game their children should be given.

Interviewer   Ah ha and... what about the moral aspect of advertising? Do you think the manufacturers and advertisers make exaggerated claims as to what their products can achieve? I mean, isn't that immoral? What with all those so-called slimming products, the cosmetics and skincare products and the pre-packed meals that are presented as being as fresh as food that is prepared at home...

Michael Harris Hmm. Well, I believe that advertisers must be honest, particularly in relation to food; especially food which claims to help you lose weight. As for cosmetics and skincare products, they are, of course, tested stringently to make sure that they are suitable for the purpose they are sold for. However, whether or not they will suit everyone seems unlikely as skin types vary so much. Therefore,
I think it's up to the customer to know what type she needs and not to expect miracles. On the whole, I think TV and newspaper and magazine advertising is of a high standard and many people are helped, advised and entertained by it.

Interviewer Well, thanks for coming into the studio today.

Michael Harris My pleasure.

Interviewer Next week, we'll be talking to...

Track 14

Unit 13- Page 84 – Exercise 10

Announcer Unit 13 Listening Part 3

You'll hear five different people talking about what, in their opinion, constitutes good entertainment. For questions 1-5, choose from the list A–F what they say about different sorts of entertainment. Use the letters only once. There is one extra letter which you do not need to use.
Speaker One

Woman Personally, I think most of the programmes they show on TV today are rubbish, but I would say that at my age, wouldn't I? I don't listen to the radio that much anymore but when I did, I liked programmes where the public took part, such as Any Questions. On television I like programmes about antiques or the old junk people find in their attics. It's interesting to learn about their history and how much they're worth. I like some soaps, but I'd rather sit and watch one of the old detective series like Columbo or a bit of court room drama such as Perry Mason, who I'm particularly fond of. No one dares disturb my Monday afternoon when he's on!

Announcer Speaker Two.

Man I suppose sport would have to be at the top of my list of favourite TV entertainment. I don't play much sport, but
I certainly make up for it with all the hours I spend jumping up and down in front of the screen! I adore drama but I'm not at all impressed with what they show on TV, so I go to see a play whenever I can – this way I have the chance of seeing what I really like and getting a few more autographs to add to my autograph book . I also like the odd pop concert now and again, which is something
I share with my wife. In fact we've got tickets for one this coming weekend.

Announcer Speaker Three.

Woman You'd never catch me watching soaps or any of that nonsense. No way! The only programmes I ever watch are on fashion and beauty care. I love watching 'make-over' programmes – the results can be truly

amazing. Another form of entertainment I like is live music. I quite often go to clubs with friends when my favourite local singers or bands are on and we have a great time singing along and dancing. I don't really think there is much on TV for my age group really, there's a whole lot more for little children and teenagers or older people but not much for the likes of me.

Announcer Speaker Four

Woman I don't really watch that much TV because I'm usually far too busy trying to get all my homework done or I'm out and about with my friends. I like anything to do with modern music and I quite often watch the X Factor. I think it is really exciting waiting to see who is going to win. If only I could go on it! I'd jump at the chance! I'd love to go to a pop concert but they are far too expensive for kids my age especially if we're talking about the really big stars.

Announcer Speaker Five

Man I love TV, especially the X factor, Big Brother and Dr. Who.
I like all the programmes where the public are involved especially 'I'm a celebrity – get me out of here.' That's my favourite one of all. It's great to see how good, or not, famous people are, at handling real life situations. I watch a fair bit of sport, too. I've become pretty good at Athletics and I like following all the events on TV especially now that I'm going to be competing in races!

Track 15

Unit 14 – Page 91 – Exercise 13

Announcer Unit 14 Listening Part 4

You'll hear an interview with Director of Admissions, John Hampdon, about university applications. For questions 1 to 7, choose the best answer, A, B or C.

Interviewer ... and now let's move on. Today in the studio, is Director of Admissions, Mr John Hampdon. Good evening Mr Hampdon and welcome back to the show.

John Hampdon Good evening.

Interviewer What do you think of the Government's target to have half of all young people in higher education?

John Hampdon It is obviously desirable to have as many of our young people as possible in higher education. We must not waste their talent and I think it is vital that they be given fair access to the most competitive selective universities.

Interviewer How easy is it for a student to go about applying to university?

John Hampdon The Government works with universities to promote wider participation and encourages universities to work with schools in an effort to get students to apply for university places regardless of their background or social status. The Government does not tell individual universities how to run their admissions policy because their strength depends on their autonomy and we want to assist not interfere.

Interviewer	Are universities given targets for the number or proportion of students they should take from low income backgrounds?
John Hampdon	That's right. Universities are given targets or benchmarks, for the proportion of students they should take from low income or non-traditional backgrounds.
Interviewer	Is this target linked to funding?
John Hampdon	No, I'm afraid it isn't, but universities do receive extra money according to the number of students taken from areas where usually not many young people would be attending university. This extra money is used to cover the cost of doing outreach work in schools which enables recruitment of students. The extra money also helps to support them in their first year because they are more likely to drop out.
Interviewer	What if a student feels he has the potential but not the right grades or subjects to be able to get into university?
John Hampdon	Sometimes if students had had better tuition they would probably have got better grades or if they had chosen different or more suitable subjects, for them, they would be in a much better position to earn a place at university.
Interviewer	So, what help is there available for these students?
John Hampdon	Cambridge University may start offering foundation courses to pupils whose A level grades are not good enough for admission to the colleges. The course might be run at the university or in local colleges. The foundation course is just one of a number of ideas being considered by the University to make it possible for more students from various backgrounds to gain access to the colleges.
Interviewer	Has there been an increase in the number of applications to University in the past few years?
John Hampdon	Well, for example, Cambridge University has had 15,000 applicants this year, while the yearly average for the past four years was 13,500...so there's been a 12% increase. Changes have been made to the application process and entrance requirements including removing the rule that every applicant must have a language at GCSE level.
Interviewer	Do you think there has been an increase in applications from low income families, too?
John Hampdon	Well, a report out earlier this year, stated that people from lower social and economic backgrounds make up about one half of the population of England. It also reported that they represent less than thirty percent of young full time entrants to higher education. However, the report also tells us that participation in higher education by people from low income groups had increased more than that of better off groups over the last decade. This year fifty-nine percent of admissions were from state schools and colleges, which is very encouraging because it tells us that we are leaving behind the belief that a low income background and any ideas about not fitting in need not deter brighter young people from exploiting their full potential as they go on with higher education.
Interviewer	Well... that's about all we have time for today.

Track 16

Unit 15 – Page 96 – Exercise 11

Announcer	Unit 15 Listening Part 2.
	You will hear a doctor speaking about the importance of getting a good night's sleep. For questions 1 to 9, complete the sentences.
Woman	We spend a third of our lives asleep. Some famous people – Napoleon, Florence Nightingale and Margaret Thatcher claimed to have managed on four hours a night and this is possible because even after only four hours, the brain has gained many of the important benefits of sleep, maintaining normal levels of cognitive skills such as speech, memory, innovative and flexible thinking. In other words, sleep plays a significant role in brain development.

People often complain of having difficulty sleeping and the reason could quite simply be their sleeping conditions: a bedroom which is too cold or too warm, eating unsuitable foods or eating too close to bedtime. It may be because the bedroom contains a television or a computer which cause the brain to be active rather than restful or relaxed. Some people may find they have a sleep disorder, most of which can usually be treated effectively. Sleep deprivation not only has a major impact on cognitive functioning but also on emotional and physical health. There is a disorder called sleep apnoea which results in excessive daytime sleepiness – this has been linked to stress and high blood pressure. Research has also suggested that because chemicals and hormones, that play a part in controlling appetite and weight gain, are released during sleep, then perhaps the risk of obesity may be increased in people who are seriously sleep deprived.

There is no set amount of time that everyone needs to sleep since it varies from person to person. Research has shown that the average period of sleep is between seven and a half and eight hours. Some people manage on five hours, others need to sleep up to eleven hours. Although lack of sleep might appear sometimes to just be a nuisance because of the boredom of lying awake at night and the unpleasantness of being tired during the day, it can be far more serious and sometimes the consequences are grave. For instance lack of sleep is said to have contributed to several international disasters such as Exxon Valdez, Chernobyl, Three Mile Island and the Challenger Shuttle explosion. It is hardly surprising that people who are sleep deprived have difficulty in responding to rapidly changing situations and making rational judgements and decisions when the part of the brain that controls language, memory planning and sense of time is severely affected. A good way to try to understand this is to think of times when maybe you have been without sleep for a whole night. It may be because you have worked all night without sleeping during the previous day or maybe you have been to a party or other social event. Just one sleepless night and you will find yourself becoming irritable, forgetful and bad-tempered, your attention span will shorten quite dramatically and your concentration becomes more difficult. Think how much more serious these symptoms would be if you were deprived of sleep for very long periods and you were taking part in difficult and complicated work where maybe other people's lives were at stake. Thankfully for most of us this will never be an issue.

For those of us who suffer from sleepless nights but do not have a serious sleeping disorder there are things we can do to try to ensure that we do have peaceful and restful nights. For instance regular exercise is a good way to improve your sleep but not too close to bedtime as exercise produces stimulants that stop the brain from relaxing quickly. Simple breathing exercises before bed, using lavender oil or other herbs is sometimes beneficial. Making sure your bedroom is calm and sleep inducing without television and computers and is of an agreeable temperature can also help. Caffeine, which is a stimulant that can stay in your system for many hours should be avoided. This also applies to coffee, chocolate, cold drinks and non-herbal teas. The same goes for too much alcohol which can make you restless, it can also lead to snoring which restricts airflow into the lungs and will disturb your sleep by reducing oxygen in your blood. If your tummy starts rumbling just before going to bed avoid spicy or fatty foods which could cause discomfort with heartburn, choose instead something that triggers the hormone serotonin which makes you sleepy. Carbohydrates such as bread or cereal are perfect for this. If after all this, you still have problems, forget about sleep, maybe even leave the bedroom and do something like a jigsaw or may be read a book-nothing too exciting though!

If none of this helps you could consider massage, aromatherapy or even acupuncture and, of course, if lack of sleep is causing serious problems and interfering with your daily life and work then you must seek the advice of a doctor who will be able to give you further help and ascertain if maybe you have a serious sleep disorder.

2 **Track 1**

Unit 16 – Page 102 – Exercise 10

Announcer	Unit 16 Listening Part 1.

You'll hear people talking in eight different situations. For questions 1-8, choose the best answer, A B, or C.

One.
You overhear a woman talking to a friend.
What does she say about the clothes she wears?
A She doesn't care what she looks like as long as she's fashionable.
B She dresses for the occasion.
C She doesn't think she looks scruffy when she's casually dressed.

Woman	I don't think I am a fashion fanatic, but I do know what I like and that's trendy or fashionable clothes. I would never wear something just because it's *in*

regardless of whether it suits me. I prefer casual clothes and by casual I don't mean scruffy. If I'm going somewhere special I usually make an effort and dress up in something nice. They say 'clothes maketh the man' but I'm not sure if that's really true. They certainly do make a difference when chosen with care and they are flattering to the wearer as well as being fashionable.

Announcer	Two.

You hear a man talking about domestic animals.

What does he say about dogs?

A They provide an opportunity for the elderly to exercise.
B They are good company for only children.
C They can be trained to be useful to society.

Man	Domestic animals can play an important role in people's lives. A cat or dog can be an indispensable family member, especially when someone lives on their own. They can sometimes stop that person from feeling quite so lonely and get them out of the house especially a dog that needs to be taken for walks. Dogs also have an important place in society when it comes to helping people such as guide dogs for the blind, therapy dogs for children who have difficulty relating with others and rescue dogs that save people from dangerous or difficult situations.
Announcer	Three.

You overhear a woman talking on a radio program.

What form of entertainment can most people afford?

A amateur plays
B pop concerts
C debates on the radio

Woman	We all have our own ideas as to what classes as good entertainment and most people nowadays prefer being entertained with music. They spend quite a lot of money on tickets for pop concerts, which can sometimes be a bit pricy, or they go and watch a local band in a club or pub. Other people would rather spend their evening at the theatre, watching a musical or a play. Local amateur groups often put on performances of a high standard with very reasonable prices for everyone. Radio also offers good quality entertainment. I'm particularly fond of debates which the listener can take part in at the price of a phone call, but beware of a nasty surprise when you get your bill at the end of the month!
Announcer	Four.

You hear a man talking about advertising.

What is he doing?

A complaining about something
B making a suggestion
C giving advice

Man	We see advertising everywhere we go, traveling by tube or bus, walking along the road, passing through airports – it is everywhere, tempting us to shop, to book a holiday, to buy a new car and so on. When we watch television or go to the cinema, there it is again! We just can't get away from it! It is big business and

has made a lot of money both for the people who sell advertising space and for the people who create the adverts. Have you ever bought something just because you saw it advertised somewhere? I suppose we all have at sometime. After all, that's just what they want us to do! The more we spend, the more they make!

Announcer Five.

You hear part of a talk on the radio about schooling.

What is the man's conclusion?

A Skilled pupils should be given the opportunity to attend special schools.
B Grammar and comprehensive schools should be regarded more highly.
C Schools should be chosen according to individual needs.

Man Most of our lives are taken up with educating or being educated. There are many different ways to learn and improve one's education: evening classes, correspondence courses, distance learning, self-study and so on and so forth. There are many differences of opinion concerning the best methods of education for our children. Some people prefer the comprehensive method while others still regard the grammar school system as the best. It is difficult to know which is the most suitable for so many children with differing skills and abilities and while some do well with one system others might do better with another. All I can say is we must try to do our best for each and every one of our children.

Announcer Six.

You hear an elderly woman talking on the phone.

What is she trying to do?

A convince her son about something
B persuade her son to do something
C warn her son about something

Woman I know you think your music is great but it isn't as nearly as good as the music I used to listen to in the 50s and 60s. I mean, who do you have to compare with Elvis, Bill Haley or Buddy Holly? You see, you can't even come up with one single name! I know that nowadays, lots of people prefer listening to other types of music like Country and Western, Jazz, or Blues, but let's face it no one will ever forget Sinatra or Ella Fitzgerald. Huh! It's pointless talking to you. You'll never agree with me that you just haven't got a clue when it comes to music!

Announcer Seven.

You hear part of a radio program about feelings.

Why are shy people so reluctant to take up something new?

A because they find it difficult to talk to other people
B because they are afraid of making a fool of themselves
C because they might hurt themselves

Man What do we mean by feelings? We talk about hurting people's feelings if we are unkind or tactless. Our feelings really relate to our personalities, whether we are very forceful or perhaps shy or very modest. Very strong people sometimes appear not to have many feelings but someone who is quieter and perhaps rather shy can be very easily hurt. Life can be difficult for someone who is extremely shy. For instance, they are hesitant about joining in with other people or trying something new because they are afraid if they don't do well they will look and feel foolish. Hopefully, with time, their confidence will grow and life will be more fun.

Announcer Eight.

You hear a woman talking about having difficulty sleeping at night.

What was she once obliged to do as a last resort?

A sit up all night doing a puzzle
B drink a couple of glasses of wine
C wander around the house

Woman I often find it difficult to get a good night's sleep when I'm worried about something and I usually wake up feeling tired and irritable. I've tried lots of different remedies when this happens, like taking a relaxing bath, not drinking coffee or too much alcohol before bedtime or reading in bed to try and make me sleepy. If none of these work, I usually end up getting out of bed and going downstairs to make myself a warm drink. Once, I even resorted to doing a jigsaw. This helped me feel more relaxed and took my mind off all the thoughts that keep nagging at me and then I wandered back upstairs and climbed wearily into bed just in time to hear the alarm clock go off!

Track 2

Unit 17 – Page 109 – Exercise 11

Announcer Unit 17 Listening Part 4

You'll hear an interview with a financial expert about the economic crisis in Britain and the USA. For questions 1 to 7, choose the best answer, A, B or C.

Interviewer The topic we'll be discussing today is the credit crash in Britain and America. We have with us financial expert, Mr Donald Jameson.

Donald Jameson Hello.

Interviewer Mr Jameson, can you tell us how this happened and who if anyone is responsible?

Donald Jameson I suppose you could say after ten years of a lending and spending boom, based on cheap credit, this is the inevitable outcome. As for who is responsible...., well, at a time like this people are always inclined to blame anyone but themselves. When there are signs of economic weakness and maybe business investment is declining, steps have to be taken to avoid the possibility of the economy going into recession. In order to do this we sometimes have to stimulate consumer spending but if the levels are pushed too high they cannot be maintained. This pushes up house prices and increases household debt. This side of it is the responsibility of the bankers.

Interviewer Do you think any responsibility lies with anyone else?

Donald Jameson	When cheap credit is available obviously people take advantage of it. They use it for many things, house furnishings, new cars, even clothes and holidays, they may find themselves in a vicious circle which is difficult to get out of because of their increasing debts due to everything being bought on credit. Eventually the cost of credit has to be increased because the total amount of consumer debt runs into million and millions of pounds.
Interviewer	Tell us how it affects the bank and the ordinary members of the public.
Donald Jameson	Well, for instance, in America, afraid of their exposure to losses from US sub prime mortgages, the banks stopped lending to each other. They also no longer lent to companies and ordinary people - this was the beginning of the so called credit crunch.
Interviewer	How are we coping with the problem here in Britain?
Donald Jameson	Here the interest payments on mortgages, loans and credit cards have increased hugely. If you are at all risky, you are going to find it very hard to get credit because the banks do not want anyone who is going to default. If you have had problems in the past with credit or if you need to borrow a lot of money, it will be your income that will determine your spending. It will not be easy to get credit for the things you want. Millions of credit card and loan applications have been turned down.
Interviewer	How do you think people who are deeply in debt are managing to pay their bills and is there anything being done to help them?
Donald Jameson	There is the National Debt Line who are getting calls from clients who have always relied on credit cards and now have to find other ways of dealing with their debts. There are people who have had to declare themselves bankrupt. One such couple have debts of a quarter of a million pounds and their home is being repossessed by the bank. Now they know that if you want to buy something you actually have to have the money to do it because they can no longer rely on credit cards and other credit loans. Another couple who have £50,000 worth of credit card loans and loan debts have decided that rather than file for bankruptcy, they are going to try and pay back what they owe. They have signed up to a debt management plan along with 600,00 others. After all their bills are paid each month including their creditors, they will be left with very little money and they will find it very hard to make ends meet. It will be a while before they can think of spending on non-essentials but at least they will have been able to stay in their home and if they are prepared to stick to their plan to get out of debt then they have a chance eventually to continue their life as before, but without such reckless use of credit facilities. I hope other people in similar situations will find a way of coping and solving their financial problems.
Interviewer	Let's hope so. Well, thank you for coming into the studio today...

Track 3
Unit 18 – Page 114 – Exercise 10

Announcer	Unit 18 Listening Part 3
	You'll hear five different people talking about Liverpool being elected the European Capital of Culture. For questions 1 to 5, choose from the list A-F, whether or not they approve of this decision. Use the letters only once. There is one extra letter which you do not need to use. Speaker 1
Woman	How can we feel proud of the new shopping development by *Grosvenor Estates* when it involved the compulsory purchase of small businesses which were wiped out to make way for a brand new shopping development which, let's face it, with such high unemployment, many people will not be able to afford. While all these new stores were opening, other businesses were having to close down. I just can't see the point of it. Most of the new buildings are ugly and have ruined what was once a fine cityscape. So we have lost out all round and we weren't even given the chance to have our say in the matter.
Announcer	Speaker 2
Man	The general atmosphere of genuine pride in the city really stands out and I like the way the city centre by *Grosvenor Estates* has been regenerated. Its new facilities are fabulous and so is the modern design of its buildings – really pleasing to the eye. It must have cost a pretty penny, that's all I can say! Liverpool has always attracted many overseas visitors. It is known almost anywhere in the world through its reputation as a major portal gateway, its football teams, and last but not least the Beatles. Another highlight for me was the Klimt exhibition at the Tate, a truly remarkable exhibition of the painter's work.
Announcer	Speaker 3
Woman	The QE2 will be visiting for the last time tomorrow enabled by the development of a liner berth which will result in the arrival of many more foreign visitors. They will find lots to see and do including some fine pubs to try out. There have been few improvements in our city up until now but Liverpool is going from strength to strength. I was, however, disappointed in the Klimt exhibition as I had hoped to see more of the painter's famous works but unfortunately most of them were missing and many of the paintings on display were those of his contemporaries. But at least the effort had been made to put it on and hopefully we can look forward to seeing more exhibitions in the future.
Announcer	Speaker 4
Man	There are people on Merseyside who question the value of this event. The event brought in a lot of money but how has this been spent and more importantly has it been well spent? Much re-development has taken place around the city centre but this reminds some of us of the architectural disasters built during the post-war period and we hope that in twenty years or so they won't be seen as the eyesores of their period. A new concert venue has been constructed beside Albert Dock but what if in

future years it is not put to use and is left to stand empty? Won't that have been a huge waste of money?

Announcer Speaker 5

Woman After being away for twenty years, I have moved back to Merseyside with my husband. I was born in Liverpool and
I had been looking forward to going back for quite some time. I was amazed at all the changes that have taken place. Who would have thought that Liverpool could have been voted the European Capital of Culture? We have been to quite a few of the cultural events and I must say the Tall Ships was a highlight for me. It is great that museums and art galleries have been given so much publicity as well. Business is booming and retail opportunities are plentiful – the future looks bright for the people of Liverpool.

Track 4

Unit 19 – Page 120 – Exercise 11

Announcer Unit 19 Listening Part 2

You will hear an expert talking about the phenomena of the Tsunami. For questions 1 to 9, complete the sentences.

Woman Tsunamis are a natural hazard that can cause great destruction and loss of life not only to shores near their source, but sometimes to shores across an entire ocean basin. A tsunami is a series of large waves generated by an impulsive disturbance, for example, an earthquake, landside, volcanic eruption or explosion, that causes disturbance to the sea floor, resulting in a large volume of water being suddenly displaced and then forming tsunami waves.
Tsunamis are sometimes referred to as tidal waves but this is considered incorrect by oceanographers since no tides are actually involved in their creation, although the word tsunami is derived from the Japanese words meaning harbour wave.
Tsunamis have been reported since ancient times and have been extensively documented, which means that we can use this information to further study their characteristics and thereby, help us in developing effective warning programmes. Tsunamis are sometimes referred to as seismic sea waves as they are usually caused by a sudden rise or fall of a part of the earth's crust. They can sometimes be caused by submarine landslides, submarine volcanic eruptions and meteorites but are more likely to be caused by earthquakes. This happens when an earthquake occurs underneath or near the ocean and creates movement in the floor of the ocean. This seismic disturbance can vertically displace the water column which creates fluctuations in the level of the ocean.
Tsunami waves are formed when the mass of displaced water attempts to find its equilibrium. The tsunami waves then move outwards, away from their source and travel unnoticed on the sea's surface at speeds of almost six hundred miles an hour, which means they can cross an entire ocean sometimes in a day or even less. The depth of the ocean basin determines the speed of the tsunami and on reaching shallow water the front of the wave will slow down.

After this the waves pile up to create one gigantic wave that can rise up to thirty feet before reaching the shore.
The effect of the tsunami is devastating with wavelengths that can be in excess of 60 miles carrying rocks weighing as much as 20 tonnes up to 180 metres inland. The enormous energy of the tsunami can demolish houses, lift heavy vehicles and move large and weighty boulders, bringing the threat of injury and death to anyone living near the ocean. Tsunamis can occur in all oceans of the world and have been recorded in all mayor oceans. They are most common around the edge of the Pacific because of the many large earthquakes along the margins of the Pacific Ocean. According to the National Geophysical Data Centre, the first ever recorded tsunami occurred off the coast of Syria in 2000BC. Since 1900 most tsunamis have been generated in Japan, Peru, Chile, New Guinea and the Solomon Islands.
History is full of examples of tsunamis that have caused huge destruction to many countries. Significant examples are tsunamis that occurred in the 18th and 19th centuries in Portugal, China, Indonesia and Japan. Tens of thousands of Portuguese people were killed in 1755 by a tsunami which followed the Lisbon earthquake. Soon after, the tsunami of 1782 in the South China Sea, caused the deaths of over 40,000 people. Over a century later, the Greek Krakatau Volcanic eruption in 1883 ravaged coastlines along the Sundra Straits destroying numerous villages and killing 36,500 people.
In the last half of the 20th century there have been a number of destructive pacific wide tsunamis occurring in 1946, 1957, 1960 and 1964. In the last decade alone there have been at least ten tsunamis, three of which were in Indonesia.
One of the most devastating tsunamis to take place occurred recently in 2004, when the biggest earthquake for over 40 years took place in the Indian Ocean. This probably ranks as the most destructive tsunami on record, spreading across four and a half thousand kms wide, over a period of 7 hours and resulting in the deaths of 280,000 people - the greatest loss of life in Tsunami history.
The U.S. coast and Geodetic Survey established the tsunami warning system as a result of the loss of life and damaged caused in the Pacific. The Pacific Tsunami Warning Centre became operational in 1948 and now links to over 30 seismological stations throughout the pacific basin. It provides data on earthquakes in the Pacific and issues a tsunami watch to all receiving stations.
There was no warning system in the Indian Ocean prior to the 2004 tsunami, arrangements are now being made to implement a hi-tech network of ocean monitoring technology and a community response drill which will take a warning to every beach.
Tsunamis cannot be predicted but numerical models and historical records can help determine where they are likely to be generated, so preparation can be made for these natural hazards.

Track 5

Unit 20 – Page 127 – Exercise 13

Announcer   Unit 20 Listening Part 4

You'll hear an expert on mythology talking about Paganism. For questions 1 to 7, choose the best answer, A, B or C.

Woman   Paganism has been, and still is, often represented and described as something bad when, in fact, it is an umbrella term which covers many beliefs and religions. Paganism describes a number of contemporary religions based on a reverence for nature, while drawing on the traditional religions of indigenous peoples throughout the world. There are a few common themes which run through these belief systems and align them under the Pagan umbrella. Pagans have a deep respect for nature and see contact with nature as a way of coming closer to deity in all its aspects.

Tribes came from lands such as Normandy, Denmark, Saxony to settle here in Britain and modern paganism draws heavily on the indigenous beliefs of the lands the tribes left as well as the beliefs of this country.

Paganism has evolved and to many pagans their beliefs are not just a religion but a way of life. They seek to live in sympathy with nature in the modern world and see themselves as part of nature, not above it. At the same time, they believe in taking responsibility for their actions – they advocate self-responsibility.
Due to misrepresentation and persecution over the years, it is important and necessary to define what pagans are not as well as what they are. They do not practise black magic, they are not evil and their practices do not involve harming people or animals.

There are many paths within paganism, some of which are Druidry, Heathenry, Wicca and Shamanism. A representative of the Druid Network defines druidry as the native spiritual tradition of the islands of Britain. We have discovered a little information about druidry from the writings left by the Romans during the time of the Roman conquests. Its ethics are based on honour and respect.

The original Heathens were pre-Christian people who, more than a thousand years ago, lived in Northern Europe in the lands around what is now called the North Sea. This included the people of Anglo-Saxon England, Scandinavia, Germany and Frisia. Through holy rites and their day to day actions, Heathens aim to build healthy relationships with gods and goddesses, ancestors, spirits of the land and others in their communities. Great respect is given to ancestors in general, whether they be a person's literal forebears or people who have inspired them in some way. Heathen gods are best known from Norse Mythology but they were honoured by many peoples outside of Scandinavia. Some of our English days of the week are named after the Heathen Gods: Tuesday is named after Tiw, Wednesday after Woden, Thursday after Thunor, and Friday after the goddess, Frige.
Wicca is an earth based, Nature focused spirituality, drawing on the beliefs and practises of pantheism, Gnosticism, ceremonial magic, witchcraft and the pagan religions of the old worlds. It is the only religion to be given to the world by Great Britain. It is an eclectic religion with the original founders of Wicca drawing upon many sources to promote their religion.

Most Wiccans work in a group called a Coven, which can contain from two to thirteen people. Wicca believe in a Goddess and God and celebrate the union between them, they perform their ceremonies in a circle and work closely with the four elements.

Shamanism originally meant a spirit walker or healer from the tribes of Siberia. Today it means someone who walks between the worlds. The main characteristic of Shamanism is its focus on an ecstatic trance state in which the soul is believed to leave the body and ascend to the sky or heavens or descend into the earth or underworld.

Track 6

Practice Test – Page 160 – Part 1

Announcer   FCE Buster Practice Book – Practice Test

Now open your test paper and look at part one.

You will hear people talking in eight different situations. For questions 1–8, choose the best answer (A, B or C).

One

You overhear a woman talking to her son on the phone. What would she like him to do?

A stop getting into debt
B buy better quality clothes
C get a better paid job

Woman   If don't watch out, you're going to wind up in trouble and don't expect me to get you out of it like I did last time. I know you needed a new suit for your interview, but was it really necessary to spend over a thousand pounds on it, knowing full well the cheque would bounce? I was so embarrassed when the bank manager phoned this morning! What on earth were you thinking of? You don't expect someone to employ you just because you've got a brand name on your back, do you?

Announcer   Two

You hear a man talking about city life. What is he complaining about?

A that he finds it difficult to breath when he goes out
B that he has to wear a mask when he rides to and from the office
C that he can't afford to live in the countryside

Man	Lots of people are moving away from the crowded city centres to the countryside and who could blame them? Life in the city has become almost unbearable due to the chaos caused by traffic not to mention the smog. There has also been quite a remarkable increase in respiratory diseases due to people breathing in exhaust fumes while walking or cycling to work and so they've had to opt for the healthier way of life in the countryside. But what about the rest of us who don't earn enough to just hand in our notice and take off? I suppose we'll just have to resort to wearing protective masks when we're out and about!
Announcer	Three

You overhear a man and a woman talking. What is the woman upset about most?

A that nobody raised the alarm
B that her husband could be so forgetful
C that she had to wait outside in her night wear

Man	Did you manage to save anything at all from the flames?
Woman	No, if only we had been warned, we could have got some of our belongings out. But we just stood their in our night clothes and watched while it burned to the ground.
Man	How awful for you!
Woman	You can say that again, but disaster really struck when I found out we weren't insured!
Man	What!
Woman	That's right. My husband didn't renew our insurance policy! Apparently, it slipped his mind, and so we've lost everything!
Announcer	Four

You hear a teacher reciting the myth of Jason and the Golden Fleece. How was the Golden Fleece stolen?

A Hercules and Orpheus gave the dragon a potion to send it to sleep.
B The Argonauts got it out of the wood and took it back to Greece in the Arno.
C Jason managed to steal the fleece while the dragon was sleeping.

Woman	The Golden Fleece was the skin of a golden ram which hung in a sacred grove guarded by a dragon. The hero Jason was summoned to win the fleece and he called upon the aid of other Greek heroes. These fifty heroes, including Orpheus and Hercules, were called the Argonauts after the ship they sailed in, the Argo. Upon reaching the land of the fleece, Jason was helped by the king's daughter, Medea, a mighty sorceress. She drugged the dragon, so that she and Jason could escape with the Golden Fleece. The heroes fled in the Argo and sailed along the coast until they got back to Greece.
Announcer	Five

You hear part of a talk on the radio. What is the man talking about?

A a short trip
B an expert on Shakespeare
C a play

Man	Last Friday, we went on a weekend break to the ancient city of Stratford-upon-Avon. A guide took us on a tour of the city and told us all about the old buildings, historic sites and showed us around some of the houses belonging to the Shakespeare family. In the evening, they had organized a trip to the theatre to see one of Shakespeare's plays which was being put on by the local theatrical group. They were brilliant! My wife and I loved it and will certainly be returning in the not too distant future.
Announcer	Six

You hear a woman talking about a diet. What does she say about the diet?

A It made her feel weak.
B It left an awful taste in her mouth.
C She couldn't stick to it.

Man	I'd been trying to lose weight for ages, when I saw this diet in one of those health magazines and I thought I'd give it a try. All I could eat for the first week was minestrone. Minestrone for lunch and minestrone for dinner and by Saturday lunchtime I just couldn't face another dish of the awful stuff. It didn't make me feel sick or dizzy or anything like that, it just didn't taste particularly appetizing. You can't blame me for throwing in the towel and opting for a nice juicy steak instead. But guess what! When I stood on the scales the next morning I'd lost over 2 kilos!
Announcer	Seven

You overhear a man talking about his new job. What does he do?

A a doctor
B a psychologist
C a salesman

Woman	How do you like your new job then, Steven?
Man	It's much more rewarding than the last place I worked in. People come to me for advice and I try and help them solve their problems. They might be suffering from backache or they might just want a nice comfy recliner to stretch out on and forget about all their troubles. There's a huge range to choose from and we can get them delivered in no time at all.
Woman	I'll know where to come if my back starts playing up then.
Man	You bet!
Announcer	Eight

You overhear a woman talking to a friend. What is she doing?

A complaining about something
B giving him advice
C warning him

Woman	I wouldn't go there if I were you. It was just about the worst place I've ever stayed at. When we got there, the room wasn't ready and they made us wait in the reception for ages. Then, when they finally did let us have the key, it wasn't the room we'd asked for. We'd booked a sea-view room and this one looked out over the park! The service in the restaurant was appalling, too and I told them so. I suggested the manager got a

better cook unless he wanted all his customers going down with food poisoning!

Announcer That's the end of part 1.

Now turn to part 2.

Track 7

Practice Test – Page 162 – Part 2

Announcer You will hear an expert talking about the mystery surrounding the origins of Stonehenge.
For questions 9-18, complete the sentences.

You now have 45 seconds to look at Part 2.

PAUSE 45 SECONDS

Man For thousands of years archaeologists have been trying to solve the puzzle of the origin of Stonehenge and discover a reason why this huge circle of stones was built five thousand years ago to align perfectly on the summer and winter solstice.
For centuries experts have wondered if it was built as a place of worship or if it could have been part of a huge astronomical calendar. Some experts believe it is possible that the stones were put in place to serve some form of ritual function but despite numerous theories no one really knows why Stonehenge was originally built.
A geology team declared that the stones that form the inner ring came from the Preseli Mountains in Wales and had been carried two hundred and forty miles over land and sea. A geomorphologist living in Pembrokeshire contradicted the assumption that the stones had been dug out of a quarry and transported by Bronze Age man to Stonehenge saying that it 'stretched credibility'. It has been suggested in the Oxford Journal of Archaeology that the bluestones were ripped from the ground and moved by glaciers during the ice age. The debate will go on until someone is able to prove beyond doubt what happened one way or the other.
The origins of Stonehenge have baffled archaeologists since its discovery in seventeen twenty-three. There are ancient avenues which criss-cross the land surrounding the stones but no one knows what they mean. The most famous of these avenues is the *Cursus*. This is an extraordinary feature of the landscape stretching for two miles but the reasons why it was built and what it was built for, have not yet been discovered.
During a recent excavation on the site, there was a remarkable find. A fragment of an antler which was used as a pick was found while working was being done on an old burial barrow at the end of the Cursus. The archaeologists working on the dig hope to find material which will enable them to possibly date when the burial borrow was built and how it links to the Cursus. There have been many theories over the years. One, that it could have been a racetrack for Roman chariots until it was discovered to be much older than that.
A new excavation puts the arrival of the stones at three thousand BC – which is nearly five hundred years

earlier than originally thought and suggests that perhaps it was mainly used as a burial site. This conflicts with research that had dated the construction of Stonehenge to two thousand three hundred BC and had proposed it was a healing centre. This date was arrived at by carbon dating and was the major find from an excavation inside the henge. It has also been declared that the two thousand three hundred BC date relates to the time when the stones were moved from the outer pits to the centre of the site.
An earlier theory was that the holes had held bluestones due to a discovery in nineteen twenty in three of the pits of crushed and compacted chalk. The stones were very closely associated with the remains of the dead. Cremation burials were carried out from inside the holes holding the stones and also the areas around them. The archaeologists believe that it is possible that very early in the history of Stonehenge there were fifty-six Welsh bluestones forming one ring which would have measured eighty-seven metres across.
Although Stonehenge has existed for thousands of years, it still holds a fascination not only for archaeologists but also members of the public and the site is visited by up to a million people every year – at the same time Archaeologists and other enthusiasts continue their work in the hope that one day they may find the true reasons for the building of Stonehenge.

PAUSE 10 SECONDS

Announcer That's the end of part 2.

Now turn to part 3.

Track 8

Practice Test – Page 163 – Part 3

Announcer You will hear five different people talking about various holiday experiences. For questions 19–23, choose from the list (A–F), what each person says about the holidays. Use the letters only once. There is one extra letter which you do not need to use.

You now have 30 seconds to look at part 3.

PAUSE 30 SECONDS

Announcer Speaker 1

PAUSE 2 SECONDS

Man When we got to the airport we were offered a leaflet giving information about scams involving fake Spanish holiday clubs. It was warning tourists to be wary of touts handing out scratch cards which tell them they have won a prize. Apparently, these cards were being used to lure poor, unsuspecting holiday makers to a high cost sales pitch. Tourists who had attended sales presentations, had ended up spending thousands of pounds in membership fees by signing up for fake holiday clubs. Most of them found they had simply bought access to an internet booking service offering a service which they could have got for free at a travel agent. The leaflet said that, on average, the victims lost about three thousand pounds each with absolutely no hope of getting their money back!

PAUSE 3 SECONDS

Announcer   Speaker 2

PAUSE 2 SECONDS

Man   Do you remember the good old times when holidays were booked as a package, covering flights, transfers and accommodation and if there were any problems you could usually rely on the travel agent to sort them out? Well, my wife and I decided to try the old-fashioned way and we booked an all-inclusive holiday with 'Holiday World' for our 25th wedding anniversary. Unfortunately, I had a bad fall while on holiday and was advised by the doctor to get in touch with my travel insurance. That's when I discovered from the hotel manager that we had not been booked at the hotel with 'Holiday World' but with 'Comos' – he explained that different parts of our holiday had been booked with different companies. So, we tried to claim through our agent's insurers for the medical costs but because we weren't actually on a package holiday, we weren't able to claim compensation for the accident. Have you ever heard such nonsense?!

PAUSE 3 SECONDS

Announcer   Speaker 3

PAUSE 2 SECONDS

Woman   Two friends of mine booked a package holiday to Sharm-el-Sheikh in Egypt with Corner Street Travel at a cost of £1,438. They'd seen it advertised on TV, so one of them rang up and paid for the whole package, including travel insurance, immediately. A letter confirming full payment arrived, stating they would fly with TVA Airways, but two weeks before the holiday, the airline went into liquidation and they were asked to pay a further £1,000 for new flights. The company they had booked with, had paid separately for flight transfers and accommodation which meant my friends had to rebook their flights and pay the new fare.
They could have claimed a full refund because the airline was covered by insurance, but the travel agency didn't even bother to let them know.

PAUSE 3 SECONDS

Announcer   Speaker 4

PAUSE 2 SECONDS

Man   There's nothing worse than going on holiday and not being able to get home because the airline has gone into liquidation. A friend of mine is being badly affected. She is due to marry in Florida and has

booked all the flights and transfers through a local travel agency. Forty of her guests were due to fly out on 26th September with XL Airlines and all the flights have been cancelled. Poor thing! She was so enthusiastic when she booked. She even paid £3000 in cash because she didn't want to pay the 3% charge on her credit card and now she might have to get a bridging loan so that she can pay for a new set of flights at a later date. She is worried she might not be able to get out there for her own wedding!

PAUSE 3 SECONDS

Announcer   Speaker 5

PAUSE 2 SECONDS

Woman   We had an awful journey to reach our holiday destination in Turkey. Heavy traffic on the motorway in England followed by delays at the airports, not to mention a three and a half hour bus ride to reach the hotel! After sixteen hours travelling, we were both exhausted, so we had a quick snack and retired to bed. The next morning, I awoke to find my sister very excited after waking in the early hours to watch the dawn break and listen to a donkey braying, birds singing and the mosque calling people to prayer. My sister thought this was a fun start to our holiday, whereas I just snuggled further down under the covers and went back to sleep.

PAUSE 10 SECONDS

Announcer   That's the end of part 3.

Now turn to part 4.

Track 9

Practice Test – Page 164 – Part 4

Announcer   You will hear an interview with a musician about teaching children to play a musical instrument. For questions 24-30, choose the best answer (A, B or C).

You have 1 minute to look at part 4.

PAUSE 1 MINUTE

Interviewer   In the studio today is musician, James Holland, who's come to tell us about the pleasure and satisfaction that can be gained from the love and practice of music.

Man   I could not imagine a life without music, not being able to play an instrument or having access to music whether through radio, television, CDs or concerts. The best thing about music is that anyone can take it up. It is easily accessible and very rewarding, it is also an amazing combination of physical coordination and intellectual and expressive activity.

Interviewer   How would someone with an interest in music go about finding a suitable instrument and learning to play?

Man	Well, the first and obvious thing is to decide on the instrument. Most people, whether musical or not, have their favourites. Then, learning to play your chosen instrument, this can be done perhaps with private lessons or depending on your choice of instrument, maybe in a class or with a group of likeminded would-be musicians.
Interviewer	What about children? When do you take their wish to learn an instrument and study music seriously?
Man	You will soon discover how enthusiastic your child is, by the way they decide on an instrument and whether they practise without always being told to do so. They may find a new way of playing around with their instrument. In other words, they are not just 'practising', but learning to make music with it.
Interviewer	How would you go about helping a child choose an instrument and what age do you think they should start?
Man	It needn't be too much of a problem, most children will begin with a piano, recorder, violin or cello, they need to feel comfortable with it. Some instruments are more suitable for younger children: the recorder, for instance, is easy to handle and some stringed instruments are available in smaller versions. Brass and woodwind should be left until they have the strength to blow and they have their second teeth. To find out which type of music your child really likes, you can take them to concerts to listen to live music and find out about different instruments. You shouldn't make the mistake of starting them too young or too soon because lessons can be hard to cope with under the age of eight.
Interviewer	What about children with a disability?
Man	Music can be great therapy, it can be a way of exploring the world or simply a pleasurable experience in its own right whether the child is listening to or creating music. Most children respond beautifully to music. Attending music classes is stimulating and it gives the child the chance to socialize with children who don't treat him any differently. One case which comes to mind is David, an autistic boy who ignored his brother for several years. Music therapy has made a positive impact on their lives and their interaction has increased remarkably.
Interviewer	And where can parents find this sort of help if they have a disabled child?
Man	If parents are looking for a music therapist, they should contact A.P.M.T, the Association of Professional Music Therapists, as only the therapists who have completed a recognized course are allowed to be state registered. There is also a centre in London called Norway Robins, which provides music therapy, training courses and a research department. It was founded on the belief that we can all respond to music even when ill or disabled. The ability to express ourselves through music and sound is an innate capacity which does not depend on musical skills or verbal language. The children have lots of fun and a great social life as a result of the fact that they play musical instruments. They are learning a universal language beyond words and you don't have to be academic to be musical. So children with differing abilities can play together, this plays an important part in that it can bring together able-bodied and disabled children to enjoy the same musical pastimes.

PAUSE 10 SECONDS

Announcer	Now you'll hear part 4 again.

PAUSE 5 SECONDS

Announcer	That's the end of part 4.

FCE Buster Practice Book

Editorial Project Development: Sarah Howell
Eli Editorial Dept: Grazia Ancillani, Simona Franzoni
Art Director: Marco Mercatali
Picture Researcher: Giorgia D'Angelo
Production Manager: Francesco Capitano
Layout: Federico Borsella
Cover Graphic Design: Paola Lorenzetti

© 2009 ELI S.r.l.
P.O. Box 6
62019 Recanati
Italy
Tel. +39 071 750701
Fax. +39 071 977851
info@elionline.com
www.elionline.com

The Authors, the Publisher and the editorial team would like to thank the writers of Kid, Teen and Sure magazines, © ELI s.r.l. and Laura Bonci for her contribution to the *Multi-part Verbs* section.

Printed by Tecnostampa 09.83.200.0

ISBN 978-88-536-1273-1	Self-Study Edition with Answer Key + 2 Audio CDs
ISBN 978-88-536-1272-4	Student's Book without Answer Key + 2 Audio CDs
ISBN 978-88-536-0454-5	Practice Book with Answer Key + 2 Audio CDs
ISBN 978-88-536-0351-7	Practice Book without Answer Key + 2 Audio CDs
ISBN 978-88-536-1274-8	Teacher's Book + 1 Audio CD

Acknowledgements

Illustrations: Roberto Battestini

Photo acknowledgements
Marka: Cover Photo; Shutterstock pp: 8, 10, 16, 18, 22, 24, 26, 30, 31, 34, 36, 38, 40, 42 (photos 2-8), 45, 50 (buttom), 53, 55, 56, 57, 59, 60, 61, 62, 63, 65, 66, 67, 68 70, 71, 72, 73, 74, 75, 80, 84, 86, 87, 88, 90, 92, 96, 97, 98, 99, 102, 103, 104, 105, 106, 107, 108, 109, 110, 112, 113, 114, 116, 117, 120, 121, 123, 125, 126, 127; Gettyimages pp: 15, 42, 48;
©arcspace.com:
p. 35; Robert Brook: p. 50; The Royal Mint (top): p. 108; Andrew Braithwaite: p. 123; Public Domain: 20, 21.

Texts and sources acknowledgements
p. 8: 'The Great ID Card Debate', *Teen*, Year XXIX No. 4, © ELI Magazines; p. 14: 'Well-crafted Mealtimes', by Tana Ramsay, © Guardian.co.uk, 12 October 2008 (adapted); p. 20: 'The Joy of Six: Great Olympic Moments', by Andy Bull, © Guardian.co.uk, 31 July 2008 (adapted); p. 23: 'Famous last words – Allyson Felix', *Teen*, XXVII No. 6, © ELI Magazines; p. 26: 'Breaking the email compulsion', by Suw Charman, © The Guardian, 28 August 2008 (adapted); p. 29: 'Digital killed the radio star?', *Teen*, Year XXX No. 2, © ELI Magazines; p. 32: 'Why I write: Anne Fine', by Sarah Kinson, © Guardian.co.uk, 05 December 2007 (adapted); 'Why I write: Louis de Bernieres', by Sarah Kinson, © Guardian.co.uk, 20 March 2007 (adapted); p. 33: 'Why I write: Philip Pullman', by Sarah Kinson, © Guardian.co.uk, 16 February 2007 (adapted); 'Why I write: Adam Thorpe', by Sarah Kinson, © Guardian.co.uk, 08 October 2007 (adapted); p. 35: 'The Living Libraries of the Future', *Teen*, Year XXVIII No. 6, © ELI Magazines; p. 38: 'The perfect... CV', by Catherine Quinn, © Guardian.co.uk, 06 November 2008 (adapted); p. 44: 'Tim Berners-Lee, Inventor of the Internet, *Teen*, Year XXIX No 5, © ELI Magazines; p. 50: 'The Return of the Boat Train to Paris', by Andrew Martin, © Guardian.co.uk, 15 September 2008, (adapted); p. 53: 'Travel Bug', *Teen*, Year XXIX No. 5, © ELI Magazines; p. 56: extract from the novel from the novel *Life of Pi*, by Yann Martel, © Conongate Books Ltd 2002; p. 65: 'Jeans, Jeans, Jeans, Teen, Year XXIX No 1, © ELI Magazines (adapted); p. 68: 'The Buzz – Change your life with a life coach', *Teen* Year XXVII No. 6, © ELI Magazines; p. 71: 'Gossip', *Teen*, Year XXIX No. 4, © ELI Magazines (adapted); p. 74: *Kid* are new 'shopaholics' and Buy Nothing Day, Kids, Year XXVI, No. 3, © ELI Magazines; p. 80: 'Unreal... The Reality TV Phenomenon', *Teen*, Year XXIX No. 6, © ELI Magazines (adapted); p. 86: 'I just want the best for my kids', by Arabella Weir, © The Guardian, 03 September 2008 (adapted); p. 92, 95: 'How did you sleep last night?', by John Crace, © The Guardian, 30 December 2006 (adapted); p. 98: 'Silence, please!', *Teen*, Year XXIX, No. 3, © ELI Magazines (adapted); p. 104: extract from the short story 'The Rocking Horse Winner', by D. H. Lawrence; p. 110: 'Berlin', *Teen*, Year XXX, No. 1, © ELI Magazines; p. 113: 'Dubai', *Teen*, Year XXX, No. 3, © ELI Magazines (adapted); p.116 : 'Waste not, want not', by Tanis Taylor, © The Guardian, 30 October 2008 (adapted); p. 119: 'Towards a Greener Future', *Teen*, Year XXIX, No. 4, © ELI Magazines (adapted); p. 122: 'Prehistoric Britain', *Teen*, Year XXX, No. 3, © ELI Magazines; p. 125: 'Myths and Legends of Australia', *Sure*, Year XVIII, No. 6; 'Uluru – Australia's Spiritual Icon', *Teen*, Year XXIX. No. 4, © ELI Magazines (adapted); p.144: extract from the novel *Emma*, by Jane Austen.

All websites referred to in FCE Buster Practice Book are in public domain and whilst every effort has been made to check that the websites were current at the time of going to press ELI disclaims responsibility for their content and/or possible changes.

While every effort has been made to trace all the copyright holders, if any have been inadvertently overlooked the publisher will be pleased to make the necessary arrangements at the first opportunity.